A VOYAGE

UP

THE MEDITERRANEAN

IN HIS MAJESTY'S SHIP THE SWIFTSURE,

ONE OF THE SQUADRON UNDER THE COMMAND OF

REAR-ADMIRAL SIR HORATIO NELSON, K. B.

NOW VISCOUNT AND BARON NELSON OF THE NILE,
AND DUKE OF BRONTE IN SICILY.

WITH A

DESCRIPTION OF THE BATTLE OF THE NILE

ON THE FIRST OF AUGUST 1798,

AND A

DETAIL OF EVENTS THAT OCCURRED SUBSEQUENT TO THE BATTLE
IN VARIOUS PARTS OF THE MEDITERRANEAN

By the Rev. COOPER WILLYAMS, *A. M.*
LATE OF EMMANUEL COLLEGE, CAMBRIDGE;
VICAR OF EXNING, SUFFOLK; CHAPLAIN OF HIS MAJESTY'S SHIP THE SWIFTSURE;
AND
DOMESTIC CHAPLAIN TO THE EARL OF ST. VINCENT.

The Naval & Military Press Ltd

Published by the
The Naval & Military Press
in association with the Royal Armouries

© 2008

Unit 10 Ridgewood Industrial Park,
Uckfield, East Sussex, TN22 5QE
Tel: +44 (0) 1825 749494
Fax: +44 (0) 1825 765701

MILITARY HISTORY AT YOUR FINGERTIPS
www.naval-military-press.com

ONLINE GENEALOGY RESEARCH
www.military-genealogy.com

ONLINE MILITARY CARTOGRAPHY
www.militarymaproom.com

ROYAL ARMOURIES

The Library & Archives Department at the Royal Armouries Museum, Leeds, specialises in the history and development of armour and weapons from earliest times to the present day. Material relating to the development of artillery and modern fortifications is held at the Royal Armouries Museum, Fort Nelson.

For further information contact:
Royal Armouries Museum, Library, Armouries Drive,
Leeds, West Yorkshire LS10 1LT
Royal Armouries, Library, Fort Nelson, Down End Road, Fareham PO17 6AN

Or visit the Museum's website at
www.armouries.org.uk

In reprinting in facsimile from the original, any imperfections are inevitably reproduced and the quality may fall short of modern type and cartographic standards.

TO
The Right Honourable
John Earl of Saint Vincent,
VISCOUNT SAINT VINCENT and BARON JERVIS
of Meaford, in the County of Stafford,
Knight of the Most Honble Order of the Bath,
First Lord Commissioner of the Admiralty,
ADMIRAL OF THE WHITE SQUADRON
of His Majesty's Fleet,
and Lieutenant General of Marines,
This Work Is with the greatest respect Dedicated & Inscribed
By HIS LORDSHIP'S
Most Obed.^t & grateful H.^ble Servant,
COOPER WILLYAMS.

Girtin Sculp.^t
56 Drury Lane

PREFACE.

The candid and favourable reception which an indulgent public gave to the author's "Account of the Campaign in the West Indies in 1794," has inspired him with courage to lay before them a narrative of some important subsequent events of the war in a very different part of the world, which his active destiny has afforded him an opportunity of recording as an eye-witness. In this work, as well as in the former, it is on the result of peculiar and accidental opportunity that he relies for his passport. He is conscious his habits and pursuits have little qualified him for the claims of literary merit.

Placed as he was in the midst of a battle as splendid and extraordinary as the page of history has ever recorded, an attendant of the chase which preceded it, and of many interesting occurrences and scenes which the shores of the Mediterranean exhibited for nearly two years after its termination, he daily minuted with his pen and pencil the observations and images which obtruded themselves upon him. The authenticity of such memorials, and the views of places and people, which the present as well as the past has rendered subjects of such warm curiosity and interest, may, as his friends flatter him, give a value to his simple diary, and the sketches, even if unskilful, of a self-taught artist. All know how soon the numberless minutiæ now vivid in the memories of the actors would yield to the pressure of more recent occupations, and fade away without a record: but these pages will furnish remembrances of their activity and glory, on which they may look back with pleasure; and where their posterity may hereafter be proud to point out their names.

After what has been said, it will not be expected that the accounts of places here described should be loaded with the endless learning connected with them, on which many would find no difficulty to pour out the contents of libraries, and extend the work to bulky volumes. There seem indeed neither bounds nor use in such repetitions. But if there were, it was not the present author's purpose to expatiate beyond the occurrences which fell within his own experience; for the scanty aid which the very few books of a naval life supplied, would alone have precluded him from the attempt. Yet he has since endeavoured occasionally to vary and enliven his narrative by a few references to ancient events: this liberty, however, has been very sparingly exercised.

Too many books of travels and voyages are ornamented by fictitious views, as well as embellished relations. The reader may be assured that the drawings from which the plates of this volume were copied are genuine, and that they were taken on the spot by the same hand, and at the same time, which wrote the journal. This agreement of time and place will, he trusts, ensure the accuracy and peculiarity of his work.[a]

---

[a] The reader, who is curious, may find in Sandys's Travels, which, though their language is rather obsolete, have not lost their reputation, at least as much of the ancient history of the places described in this volume, as he may wish to know. These travels have been a copious source of pillage to his successors, through whose attenuated pages his profound and comprehensive information has been superficially spread. They were first published in 1615 under the title of "A Relation of a Journey begun A. D. 1610. Four Books containing a description of the Turkish Empire, of Egypt, of the Holy Land, of the remote parts of Italy, and Islands adjoining." George Sandys, a younger son of Edwin archbishop of York, died 1643. The author hopes he may be excused for this humble tribute to the memory of a traveller, a poet, and an amiable man, from whose brother he confesses to feel some gratification in tracing his descent.

In tracing the actions here recorded, of which neither the glory nor the beneficial effects can be questioned, some pangs of regret must undoubtedly arise at the waste, not only of treasure, but of human lives. Yet what is there enviable in an obscure and selfish existence here, compared with an honourable and patriotic death?

If ever the beautiful sentiment of Horace, the

"Dulce et decorum est pro patria mori,"

if ever those pathetic lines of a poet of our own country,

"How sleep the brave, who sink to rest,
By all their country's wishes bless'd;"[b]

were applicable, they are well applied to those who fell so nobly in the tremendous contest. "The calculation of profit in all such wars," says Burke with inimitable elevation, "is false. The blood of man should never be shed but to redeem the blood of man. It is well shed for our family, for our friends, for our God, for our country, for our kind. The rest is vanity; the rest is crime."

After such passages as these, it becomes the present

[b] Collins.

author to drop the pen. It may however be necessary to say a few words regarding some prints of the battle of the Nile which have been already published, and to state the reason of his omitting to give drawings of the most eventful part of his description, the naval action. But he was aware that a seaman only, or one at least who had made marine drawings his study, could ably pourtray that grand machine which so eminently places this nation, both in war and commerce, above all the powers of the globe.

He thinks it needless to say more, than that several who are so gifted, having published drawings of that event, it became unnecessary for him to do it. The three large engravings of different periods of the action are most ably pourtrayed by Captain Weir, who commanded the marines on board the Audacious; and who with an accurate knowledge of the subject, was himself stationed where he could form the best judgment of it; and who is also well qualified as a draughtsman for the task. These plates certainly stand pre-eminent both for correctness and picturesque effect. Four smaller engravings, with an explanation of them, were published by G. Riley soon after the news of the victory reached England.

The first of Captain Weir's plates, representing the French fleet at anchor in the bay of Aboukir, and the British fleet bearing down to engage them, strikes the author of this work as giving the best idea possible of that event; and he is the better enabled to judge of the merits of this plate, as the Swiftsure with the Alexander were the two last ships that entered the bay, which gave those on board them an opportunity of viewing and accurately observing the first part of this awful scene.

The plan of the action given in this work is copied from what Captain R. W. Miller of the Theseus made on the following morning; and as all who knew that excellent officer are well acquainted with his abilities and judgment, it may be relied on as correct in every respect. The size of the plate would not allow room to place the castle of Aboukir at the proper distance from the island. It is therefore introduced merely to shew its relative bearing from the island. The time of the occurrences during the action he can also state to be equally well founded, for they were corrected from the minutes made by Mr. Gamble, purser of the Swiftsure, who was employed in the honourable post of signal-officer during the combat, and marked down the events as they occurred. To that gentleman he is also indebted for the communication of several circumstances that otherwise he could not have related with accuracy.

At length, then, the author commits himself with diffidence and anxiety to a discerning though indulgent public: yet whatever be their decision, he will submit without a murmur. In the retirement of a domestic life he will at least look back with pleasure on the busy, varied, and important scenes in distant parts of the globe to which he has been a witness, and he will always feel gratified by the reflection of having been even an humble memorialist of a splendour and heroism so glorious to his country and his friends.

LIST OF PLATES,

WITH DIRECTIONS TO THE BINDER.

1 DEDICATION, with the Earl of St. Vincent's Arms engraved, next after the title page.
2 General Chart of the Mediterranean to face page 1
3 View of the Rock and Town of Scylla on the Coast of Calabria 12
4 Landing Place at Syracuse 25
5 Temple of Minerva at Syracuse 26
6 Latomiæ, or Caverns, near Syracuse 29
7 Entrance into Dionysius' Ear, one of the Caverns called Latomiæ 30
8 Inside of a Cavern, one of the Prisons of Dionysius, near Syracuse 31
9 Piazza, or Grand Place, in the City of Syracuse 32
10 Subterraneous Gardens belonging to the Capuchin Monastery near Syracuse 35
11 Curious Cemetery of the Capuchin Monastery near Syracuse 37
12 Plan of the Battle of the Nile on the 1st of August 1798 60
13 Tower on the Island of Marabou at the Entrance of the Western Harbour of Alexandria 96
14 Moors returning from a Pilgrimage to Mecca; on board the Swiftsure off Alexandria 96
15 Castle of Aboukir; taken from the Burial Ground on the Island 100
16 Arsenal and Guardhouse at Rhodes; formerly a Monastery when the Island was in the Hands of the Knights of St. John of Jerusalem 109
17 Arabs on board the Swiftsure 120
18 Turkish Gun-boats, conducted by Captain Hallowell, battering the Castle of Aboukir 123
19 Attack on the French Camp near the Lake Maadie 126
20 Ancient Egyptian Relicks found on the Island of Aboukir, or Nelson's Island 134
21 A Mamaluk delivering a Message from Mourad Bey 136
22 The Pharos or Castle at the Entrance of the Eastern or New Port of Alexandria .. 142
23 A Street in Caiffe, a Town at the Foot of Mount Carmel 151
24 View of the Bay of Acre from the Summit of Mount Carmel 152
25 View of the Town of Caiffe and Mount Carmel 155
26 Peasants Plowing, and Mode of Acriculture in Syria 160
27 The Court-yard of Hassan Bey's Palace at Rhodes 171
28 Mount Pelegrino, and the Light-house, in the Bay of Palermo, Sicily 174
29 The Castle and Town of Ischia 185
30 View on the road near Lacco, in the Island of Ischia 186
31 Palazzo di Aqua Viva, or the Palace of the Duke of Aqua Viva, near Lacco in the Island of Ischia 190
32 The Benedictine Monastery of Vallombrosa on the Appenines 229
33 Cubillario, an Inn on the Appenines, on the Road from Florence to Bologna 231
34 View on the Grand Canal, with the Ponto Rialto, Venice 236
35 View of Monte Baldo on Lago di Garda 244
36 Flying-bridge on the River Po, in Lombardy 246
37 Grand Parade at Mahon, in the Island of Minorca 258
38 Inhabitants of Minorca, with the Manner of making Butter 265
39 The Bay of Fournelles, in the Island of Minorca 271
40 Entrance to the Spanish Church at Gibraltar 284
41 Interior of a Gallery, or Fortified Excavation in the Rock of Gibraltar 286
42 Inside view of the Entrance to Poco roca Cave, Gibraltar 288
43 Interior of St. Michael's Cave, Gibraltar 291

CONTENTS.

CHAPTER I.

"Through various hazards and events we move."
DRYDEN, Æn. b. i.

SECRECY and dispatch the best means of insuring success in war. Rear-Admiral Sir Horatio Nelson, K. B. appointed to command the squadron destined to defeat the projects of General Bonapartè in the Mediterranean. He arrives in the Vanguard off Cadiz. Having received further instructions from the Earl of St. Vincent, he proceeds to Gibraltar; from thence he sails with the Orion and Alexander for Toulon, to watch the motions of the enemy. The Earl of St. Vincent dispatches a strong reinforcement from his fleet, on the arrival of Sir Roger Curtis. The Earl's liberal conduct on this occasion. The squadron under command of Commodore Troubridge pass the Straits of Gibraltar, and form a junction with Rear-Admiral Nelson off Toulon. Account of the accident that had befallen the Vanguard in a gale of wind. The Admiral sails in pursuit of the French fleet, and enters the Bay of Naples .... p. 1

CHAPTER II.

"Far on the right, her dogs foul Scylla hides:
Charybdis roaring on the left presides;
And in her greedy whirlpool sucks the tides:
Then spouts them from below; with fury driven
The waves mount up, and wash the face of heaven."
DRYDEN's Trans. Æn. b. iii.

Scylla described. Poetical description of an earthquake by Cowper. The British fleet passes the Straits of Messina. Picturesque appearance

xii   CONTENTS.

of the shores on each side. Charybdis and Mount Ætna described. Intelligence gained that the French having captured Malta, through the treachery of some of the Knights and Grand Master, had sailed from thence to the eastward. The British fleet arrives off Alexandria. The Admiral dispatches Captain Hardy, in the Mutine brig, to the governor, and receives no account of the French fleet; his disappointment thereon. He shapes his course back towards Sicily, and makes the Bay of Syracuse, which he enters with his fleet .... p. 11

CHAPTER III.

> "Right o'er against Plemmyrium's wat'ry strand
> There lies an isle, once call'd th' Ortygian land:
> Alpheus, as old fame reports, has found
> From Greece a secret passage under ground:
> By love to beauteous Arethusa led,
> And mingling here, they roll in the same sacred bed."
> DRYDEN's Trans. Æn. b. iii.

Description of the Bay of Syracuse. Watering party meets with difficulty. Captain Troubridge obtains a supply of fresh provisions for the fleet. Description of the landing place, and of the city of Syracuse; of the temple of Minerva; and of the fountain of Arethusa. The Latomiæ, or caverns near the city. Dionysius' ear. Roman theatre. Further description of Syracuse. The piazza, and convents. Mode of raising water. Church of St. John near the city, with the catacombs. The monastery of the capuchins, and the subterranean gardens described; the curious cemetery under the convent .... p. 23

CONTENTS.

xiii

CHAPTER IV.

> " Thrice happy they beneath their northern skies,
> Who that worst fear, the fear of death despise;
> Hence they no cares for this frail being feel,
> But rush undaunted on the pointed steel,
> Provoke approaching fate, and bravely scorn
> To spare that life which must so soon return."
>
> LUCAN Trans. by ROWE, b. i.

Admiral Nelson uneasy at gaining no account of the enemy, at length determines to revisit the ſhores of Egypt. Account of the hostile fleets having crossed each other in the night of the 22d of June. The fleet sails from the Bay of Syracuse on the 24th of July and proceeds along the coast of the Morea. The Culloden enters the port of Coron, and receives intelligence of the motions of the enemy; captures a French wine-vessel. The fleet passes the island of Candia. The captains of the fleet repair on board the Vanguard to receive instructions from the admiral. The Alexander and Swiftsure ordered a-head to reconnoitre, and on the 1st of August arrive off Alexandria, and perceive the French colours flying there: disappointment at perceiving no signs of the French fleet; prepare to attack some French gallies anchored off the harbour's mouth; are recalled by the admiral. Signal to prepare for battle. The French fleet descried at anchor in the Bay of Aboukir. The admiral makes the signal to prepare to anchor, &c. The Culloden strikes on a reef of rocks. No accurate chart of the bay in the fleet. The admiral determines to attack the enemy without delay. The fleet bear down to engage the French fleet at anchor. The Goliath leads into action. The rest of the fleet follow. Description of the action .... p. 39

xiv   CONTENTS.

CHAPTER V.

> " How to the sea his tribute Nilus pays
>   By his seven mouths, renown'd in stories old,
>   And by an hundred more ignoble ways:
>   They pass'd the town built by the Grecian bold,
>   Of him call'd Alexandria till our days:
>   And Pharos tower and isle removed of yore
>   Far from the land, now joined to the shore."
>   FAIRFAX's Trans. of TASSO, b. xv.

Reflections arising from the various circumstances of the pursuit and conquest of the French fleet. The impiety of the French. Bonaparte's scheme of attacking the British possessions in the East Indies thwarted by the victory of the Nile. Pious order of the admiral to the fleet in consequence of the victory. The admiral thanks the officers and seamen of the fleet for their good conduct in the action. The fleet had been trained under the Earl of St. Vincent, whose excellent management and discipline had prepared it for the severest service. The Leander sails from the bay; in her Captain Berry carries the dispatches containing an account of the victory obtained off the Nile. The Leander is captured by the Genereux. Captain Thompson's gallant conduct, and his honourable acquittal by a court-martial. The fleet prepares to sail from the Bay of Aboukir with the prizes. Captains Troubridge and Hallowell sent with a flag of truce to Aboukir. The French prisoners landed under an engagement not to serve again till regularly exchanged; but are instantly formed into a regiment called the Nautic battalion. The island taken possession of, and the batteries destroyed. A courier with dispatches from Bonapartè taken. The Swiftsure captures La Fortune corvette; anecdote of a French surgeon. The Swiftsure ordered to chace three sail, which prove to be the Emerald and Alcmene frigates, and La Bonne Citoyen sloop of war. The Honourable Captain Capel, bearing duplicates of the dispatches before given to Captain Berry, sails in the Mutine for Naples. Contents of the admiral's official letter concerning the action. Return of the killed and wounded in the British fleet.

CONTENTS.

Lieutenant Duval sent with an account of the action to the government in the East Indies. Poussielgue's account of the action. Part of the fleet under command of Sir James Saumarez sails from the bay with several of the prizes. Some of the captured French ships burned. Statement of the inequality of the two fleets. The Swiftsure sails on a cruize off Alexandria. The Seahorse frigate joins. Account of an action which had taken place between the Seahorse and Sensible. Admiral Nelson burns the ships that endeavour to escape from Alexandria. The Zealous joins from Aboukir. Admiral Nelson sails for Naples. The Torride captured by the boats of the Goliath. The Alcmene takes La Legere; intrepid conduct of two seamen who recovered the dispatches from the waves. The Lion, with a Portuguese squadron, arrives. The latter return to Gibraltar. The Goliath sails for Naples. A French cutter attempting to enter the harbour of Alexandria is driven on shore by the Emerald and Swiftsure. General Carmin and others murdered by the Bedouins. The enemy erecting batteries near the tower of Marabou are fired on by the Swiftsure and Emerald. A boat with French officers and others, endeavouring to escape from Alexandria, captured and sent back. A young Russian baron detained .... p. 61

CHAPTER VI.

> " 'Tis pleasant when the seas are rough to stand,
> And view another's danger, safe at land;
> Not 'cause he's troubled, but 'tis sweet to see
> Those cares and fears from which ourselves are free."
> CREECH's Trans. of LUCRET. b. ii.

Captain Hallowell employs his ship's company in weighing up anchors and procuring iron and timber from the wrecks in Aboukir Bay. Hadji Hassan, an Arab, comes off to the ship. The island of Aboukir described. The Swiftsure ordered to Rhodes for a supply of provisions, is driven by a gale of wind into the Gulf of Symea and nearly lost. The city of Rhodes described, and occurrences there. Hassan Bey, governor of Rhodes. Ancient history of Rhodes. A Turkish dinner described. The Swiftsure sails from Rhodes and rejoins the fleet off Alexandria p. 99

CHAPTER VII.

"How Egypt mad with superstition grown,
Makes gods of monsters, but too well is known;
One sect devotion to Nile's serpent pays,
Others to ibis, which on serpents preys."
DRYDEN's Trans. of JUVENAL, b. v.

Vessels endeavouring to escape from Alexandria are burned. The cause of this. Hadji Hassan returns on board with an Arab who undertakes to convey a message from the British commander to Mourad Bey. Russian and Turkish men of war and gun-boats arrive. A messenger from the Grand Signior arrives with the pelice and aigrette for Admiral Nelson. Captain Hallowell anchors in Aboukir Bay with the Turkish gun-boats, and employs them in annoying the French. Some Arabs come off from Rosetta. Hadji Hassan dismissed from the Swiftsure for giving false intelligence. Information received of an action between the Mamaluks and French, in which the former were successful. Egyptian chiefs come off with favourable intelligence. The Turkish ship Haptap in danger from a squall of wind. Massoud Abdulla arrives with letters from Mourad Bey. The Torride gun-brig goes to the Nile for water. The author sails in her. Manner of procuring the water. A supper on board a Turkish frigate. Turkish gun-boats carreened. Docks and wells dug. Ancient Egyptian relicks found. A Mamaluk arrives from Mourad Bey. Hassan Bey sails from Aboukir with the Turkish gun-boats. The officers and ship's company of the Swiftsure put to a short allowance of provisions. The Swiftsure sails from the bay, and is relieved by the Seahorse frigate . . . . p. 119

CONTENTS.

CHAPTER VIII.

> "Fast by the breezy shore the city stands,
> Amid unbounded plains of barren sands;
> Which high in air the furious whirlwinds sweep,
> Like mountain billows of the stormy deep,
> That scarce th' affrighted traveller, spent with toil,
> Escapes the tempest of th' unstable soil."
>
> HOOLE's Trans. of TASSO, b. xvii.

The Swiftsure joins the squadron off Marabou. Account of an illumination at Alexandria. Description of the pharos, and of the situation of Alexandria. Heavy gales common at this season. Impolicy of the Turks. The Fortune joins from Acre. The French send flags of truce to the British squadron. Conversation with the French officers on the subject of fire-balls, and an experiment tried with them. Conjecture as to the cause of the fire on board l'Orient. Anecdotes of the French in Egypt. Of the military ardour and discipline of the Mamaluks. The Swiftsure sails to the Bay of Acre. A description of Caiffe. The author ascends Mount Carmel. Description of the surrounding country. Wild boars and Syrian goats described. Monastery of Carmelite monks. Turkish women. Presents of rice from Dgezzar Pacha; his character. A short account of Acre. The author intends to visit Jerusalem; the cause that prevented him. A visit to the monastery on Mount Carmel. The Swiftsure departs from Syria and rejoins the squadron off Alexandria. Commodore Troubridge arrives with a squadron from Sicily. Gallant conduct of the Lion .... p. 141

CHAPTER IX.

> " Or oak, or brass with triple fold,
> That hardy mortal's daring breast enroll'd;
> Who first, to the wild ocean's rage,
> Launch'd the frail bark."
>
> Francis's Trans. Hor. b. i. ode 3.

Names of the ships, &c. that arrived off Alexandria under Commodore Troubridge. Alexandria bombarded; several vessels come out from thence; among them a Turkish man of war. Mr. Beauchamp discovered on board, and brought as a prisoner to the Swiftsure, which sails from the coast of Egypt with the Turkish man of war. They arrive at Limesol in the island of Cyprus. A heavy gale of wind. The Turkish man of war in danger. The Swiftsure driven from her anchorage. Description of Limesol, and it's environs. The Swiftsure sails from thence, and meets the Tigre commanded by Sir Sidney Smith. Arrives at Rhodes. Occurrences there. Mr. Beauchamp left with Hassan Bey. The Swiftsure sails from Rhodes, and encounters a gale of wind near Candia. Arrives in the Bay of Syracuse. The Culloden and other ships arrive, and soon after sail for Palermo. The Swiftsure departs from Syracuse; is in great danger on the coast near Catania. Passes the Straits of Messina; and enters the Bay of Palermo. Description of that bay, and of the city. The author accompanies Lord Nelson and other officers to a monastery of capuchins near the city. Description of a cemetery. A ball on board the Swiftsure. Further description of Palermo. Account of the capture of Naples by the French .... p. 163

CHAPTER X.

> " The great Misenus, of celestial kind,
> Sprung from the mighty monarch of the wind;
> Whose trump, with noble clangors fired from far
> Th' embattled host, and blew the flames of war.—
> ....
> The pious hero rais'd a lofty tomb;
> The tow'ring top his well known ensigns bore,
> His arms, his once loud trump, and tapering oar:
> Beneath the mountain rose the mighty frame,
> That bears from age to age Misenus name."
>
> WARTON'S Trans. Æn. b. vi.

A British squadron, commanded by Commodore Troubridge, sails from Palermo to the Bay of Naples, and anchors near Point Miseno. The islands of Procida and Ischia surrender. The inhabitants of those islands in great distress for want of corn. The Swiftsure sails on a cruize in the bay. The Seahorse burns some vessels near Sorrento. Corn arrives at Ischia and Procida, from Palermo, in small quantities. Cardinal Ruffo collects an army in Calabria, and marches for Naples. Violent proceedings of the French General Macdonald. The author accompanies Mr. Rushout to Ischia; description of the castle, town, and surrounding country. The Swiftsure and the Minotaur sail with troops to Castel-a-mare, which is taken possession of, but the French retake it. Account of a similar attempt by the Zealous on Salerno. Short account of the island of Capri. The author returns to Ischia, and takes up his residence at the palace of the Duke of Aqua Viva. Description of the palace. The view from it. Captain Hallowell sends a present of wine, &c; the boat on its return to the fleet is overset, and the coxswain drowned. Manner of taking quails in Ischia, also the tunny fishery described. Volcanic nature of the island of Ischia exemplified .... p. 181

CONTENTS.

CHAPTER XI.

"But fortune, ever changing dame,
Indulges her malicious joy;
Constant she plays her haughty game,
Proud of her office to destroy."
FRANCIS's Trans. HOR. b. iii. ode 29.

The squadron returns to Palermo. An account arrives of the French fleet having entered the Mediterranean. Lord Nelson embarks on board the Vanguard, and the fleet cruizes near the island of Maretimo; returns to the Bay of Palermo. Extraordinary conduct of the court of Naples towards a gentleman in the suite of Mr. Wyndham, the British ambassador at Florence. An account arrives of Sir Sidney Smith's gallant conduct at Acre. The death of Captain Miller of the Theseus; his character. Description of the environs of Palermo, Monte Reale, and the benedictine convent of St. Martino. An entertainment given by the King of the two Sicilies in honour of the birthday of his Majesty the King of Great Britain. Description of an ancient Moorish castle near Palermo. Oxen. Rear-Admiral Duckworth arrives from Lord Keith's fleet. Troops embarked on board Lord Nelson's fleet for Naples, but relanded in consequence of news brought by the Bellerophon and Powerful. Intelligence received that Cardinal Ruffo had invested Naples with his Calabrian army. The fleet under Lord Nelson sails for Naples. The Neapolitan insurgents capitulate to the Cardinal, but are brought into the fleet. The marines of the fleet landed. Commodore Troubridge invests the castle of St. Elmo. Occurrences during the siege and capture of that place. Capua besieged and taken. Captain Hood commands at Naples. Atrocious acts of the lazaroni and royalists at Naples. The King of the two Sicilies arrives. Admiral Carraccioli executed. The town of Pompei and Mount Vesuvius described. Lord Nelson sails from the Bay of Naples. The Swiftsure departs from thence .... p. 195

CONTENTS.

CHAPTER XII.

"............ Vallombrosa ....
That to an ancient abbey gave the name,
Wealthy and fair, in hallowed rituals bless'd,
And courteous to receive the stranger guest."
Hoole's Trans. of Ariosto, b. xxii.

" Thick as autumnal leaves that strow the brooks
In Vallombrosa, where th' Etrurian shades
High over-arch'd embow'r;".............
Milton's Paradise Lost, b. ii.

Lord Nelson dispatches the Swiftsure to Civita Vecchia. The Seahorse frigate is driven on the rocks near Leghorn. The Swiftsure proceeds thither to her assistance; from thence to Civita Vecchia. Occurrences there. The author lands at Leghorn, and proceeds to Pisa. Description of that place, and of the baths of Pisa. From thence to Lucca, and Florence. Description of those places. Vallombrosa. Journey across the Appenines to Bologna; from thence to Tedo and Ferrara. Fate of the benedictine monks. The Po. Padua. Palace on the banks of the Brenta. Venice. Padua described. Vicenza; politeness of the inhabitants. Verona described. Fortress of Peschiera. Desenzano on the banks of Lago di guarda. Description of the lake. Mode of crossing the Po. Mantua described. Journey from thence through Carpi and Modena to Bologna. The author recrosses the Appenines. Remarkable volcano at Pietra Mala. The author returns to Florence. Further account of that city. The King of Sardinia arrives at Leghorn. The author proceeds thither and embarks on board the Santa Teresa for Minorca.. p. 217

CHAPTER XIII.

> "At length they came, where press'd in narrow bounds,
> Between the capes the boiling deep resounds.
> 'Tis feign'd that first Alcides forc'd a way,
> And gave this passage to th' indignant sea;
> And here perchance a lengthen'd tract of land,
> With one continu'd mound the flood restrain'd;
> But now the furious main with rushing tides,
> From tow'ring Calpe Abyla divides;
> A streight 'twixt Lybia now and Spain appears:
> Such is the force of time, and change of years!"
> HOOLE's Trans. TASSO, b. xv.

Voyage to Minorca. Excellence of Mahon harbour. The town of Mahon described. Ingenious method of constructing arches in Minorca. Fort St. Philip. Roads in Minorca. The country described. The hospital and arsenal. General Stuart's regiment. Large breed of asses and mules on the island. Costumè of the inhabitants of Minorca. Account of occurrences at the capture of Minorca by General Sir Charles Stuart and Commodore Duckworth. Round towers. Fournelles Bay. Mount Toro. Retrospective history of Minorca. Amusements at Mahon. Lord Nelson and Commodore Troubridge arrive. Lord Nelson returns to Palermo. Rear-Admiral Duckworth, in the Leviathan, arrives at Mahon. The Port Mahon brig launched. The Peterell sloop arrives. Death of Lieutenant Brenton; his character. Rear-Admiral Duckworth sails from Mahon. The author takes his passage in the Leviathan, which anchors in Rosia Bay, Gibraltar, and soon after sails on a cruize off Cadiz. The Swiftsure joins, and the author accompanies Captain Hallowell on board. The squadron anchors in the Tagus. Short description of Lisbon. The squadron sails on a cruize, and encounters heavy gales of wind. The Powerful and Vanguard receive much damage. Separate from the squadron and sail for England. A Spanish brig captured. La Belle Desiada, another Spanish brig, taken. The Bellerophon parts company. The Leviathan loses her main-top-gallant-mast in a gale of wind off Cape Finisterre. The Flora frigate with orders from Lord Keith arrives. The Bellerophon rejoins the squadron. The Swiftsure loses her fore-top-mast and main-top-gallant-mast in a squall. A seaman falls overboard and is drowned. The squadron anchors in the Tagus. An opera at Lisbon described. The Weymouth wrecked near Belem castle. Rear-Admiral Duckworth provides a passage for the officers and men of the Cambrian Rangers, who were wrecked in the Weymouth. Arrives at Gibraltar. The Swiftsure taken into dock. The author resides on shore. The rock described. The town of Gibraltar. The convent, and Spanish church. General O'Hara the governor. The galleries and caves; with other places of the rock described. Gallant action of the Speedy brig. The squadron under command of Rear-Admiral Duckworth resumes its station off Cadiz. Part of a Spanish fleet of merchantmen and frigates captured. The squadron and prizes anchor in Rosia Bay. Dangerous situation of the Swiftsure. Admiral Duckworth sails with the squadron. Anchors in Lagos Bay. Returns to Gibraltar. Admiral Duckworth departs to the West Indies. Rear-Admiral Sir Richard Bickerton takes the command of the squadron, and hoists his flag on board the Swiftsure. Sails on a cruize. The Kent and Dragon arrive from England; and soon after, the Hector. Insolent conduct of the crew of La Mouche privateer. The author embarks on board the Kent for Gibraltar, and takes his passage in the Anson for England. APPENDIX .... p. 257

ERRATA.

page. line.
- 4   7 for Albaran, read Alboran.
- 6 20 for *having* immediately, read *and* immediately.
- 7   4 for 70 guns, read 74 guns.
- 7 14 for Wescote, read Westcot*t*.
- 9   1 dele the *first line*.
- 3   2 for has, read *and* has.
- 3 21 for *as* by their social, read *and* by.
- 36 19 for ced*ar*, read ced*rate*.
- 37 15 for *with* none, read *had* none.
- 44   2 for we had, read we *have since* had.
- 44   6 dele *that*.
- 49 20 for Che*lard*, read Chey*là*.
- 54 14 dele the *comma* after Vanguard.
- 77   3 for fortun*a* read fortun*e*.
- 96   5 dele *us*.
- 100   1 for Mam*elukes*, read Mam*aluks*.
- 106   2 dele *on it*.
- 126   1 for *Toridè*, read *Torride*.
- 126   2 for Autride, read Autridge.
- 135 24 for the enterprise, read the *spirit of* enterprise.
- 180 3 and 4 for *This cause*, read *The cause of this*.
- 192 in the note g for Orbitillo, read Orbitello,
- 245 10 for you *did not*, read you *do not*.
- 257   5 in the Italian motto, for Passo*vir* a for*g*a a l'oce*a*no, read Passo*vvi* a forza l'oce*à*no.
- 271   6 for compelled *them*, read compelled *the enemy*.
- 308 24 for by *Rear-Admiral Nelson achieved*, read *achieved by Rear-Admiral Nelson*.

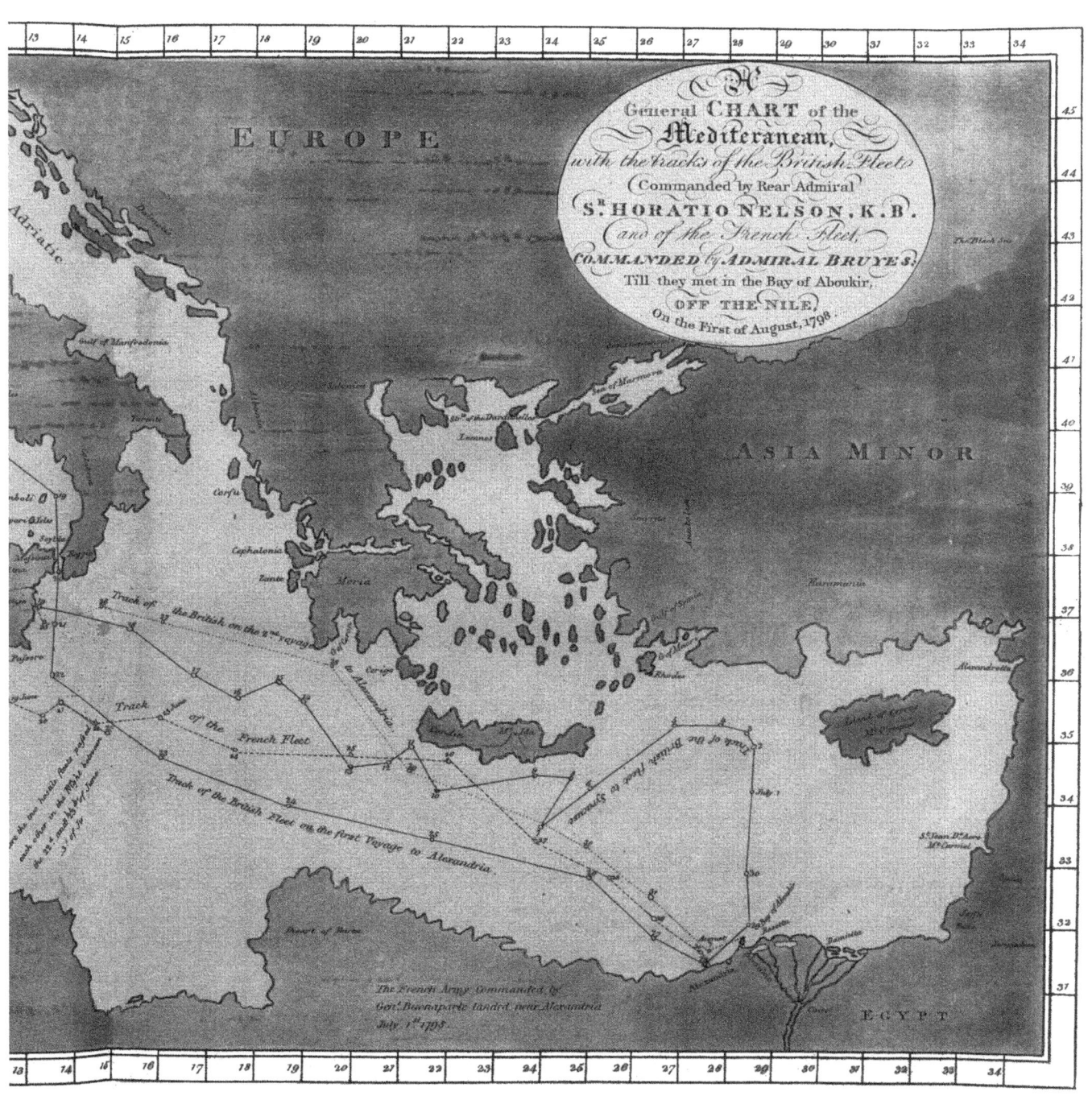

A VOYAGE

UP

THE MEDITERRANEAN.

CHAPTER I.

PER VARIOS CASUS, PER TOT DISCRIMINA RERUM.

It is, I believe, a general and allowed principle, that to infure fuccefs in war, the meafures of government fhould be carried into execution with fecrecy and difpatch. That fuch has been the cafe in almoft all the military adventures of the French, muft be allowed. Though fome fhare in the fuccefs they have fo often experienced, may be attributed to the fuperiority of their numbers, yet I will venture to affert, that much more has been gained by the celerity of their movements, and the fecrecy with which they have commenced their attacks, than with an equal number would have been obtained by thofe more regular governments whofe hands have been confined by counfels, that muſt clog the machine, though they are altogether indiſpenſable to the wellbeing of the ſtate.

The Expedition which the following pages will relate, is, however, free from the objection above alluded to, as it was planned with ſecrecy, and executed with a promptneſs highly creditable to all concerned. It had been known by the Britiſh government, that the French were preparing a powerful armament whoſe principal rendezvous was at Toulon, and the ſeaports in the Mediterranean; and from the number of tranſports and troops that were getting ready, it appeared that they meditated a deſcent on ſome of our allies in thoſe ſeas. Rear Admiral Sir Horatio Nelſon was appointed to command a ſquadron whoſe object was to defeat the projects of General Buonaparte's intended operations, whatever they might be; and about the latter end of April 1798, having his flag on board the Vanguard of 74 guns, he joined the fleet off Cadiz, under the command of Admiral the Earl of St. Vincent; and having received further orders from him, ſoon after arrived at Gibraltar, where he took in ſome ſtores and other neceſſaries; and ſailed from thence on the 9th of May, taking with him the Orion of 74 guns, commanded by Sir James Saumarez; and the Alexander, Captain Alexander Ball; with the Emerald and Terpſichore frigates, and Bonne Citoyen ſloop of war; and proceeded towards Toulon to watch the motions of the enemy. In the mean time, the Earl of St. Vincent being apprized by government that a reinforcement would be ſent to enable him to strengthen Rear Admiral Nelson's squadron, had made such arrangements in his fleet as might prevent all loss of time. On the 24th of May, the Hector, being on the look-out to the northward, made the signal for a fleet being in sight, and soon after, that it was a fleet of men of war, consisting of the Prince of 98 guns, Leviathan, Centaur, Montague, Powerful, Edgar, and Marlborough, of 74 guns; the Lion, of 64 guns, and the Success frigate and Incendiary fireship; the whole under the command of Rear Admiral Sir Roger Curtis. No sooner was the signal seen, than the order for the advanced squadron, then anchored off the mouth of the harbour of Cadiz, to get under weigh, and for the division under Sir Roger Curtis to take their station, was instantly executed.

It is here to be observed, that the number of ships that joined Lord St. Vincent from England, to replace those he had dispatched with Admiral Nelson, was eight sail of the line, one frigate, and a fireship. The fleet sent with Admiral Nelson, exclusive of his own ship, consisted of thirteen sail of the line, two frigates, and two brigs. Lord St. Vincent, aware of the possibility of the French being in superior force than was at home imagined, weakened his own fleet to give the greater power to Admiral Nelson's; a conduct to be more admired, as it is not often practised. Captain Troubridge in the Culloden, sailed from the honourable post[a] which he had maintained off

---

[a] That of Commander of the in-shore squadron forming the blockade of Cadiz.

Cadiz, in the evening of the 24th [b] of May 1798, having under his command the Bellerophon, Zealous, Defence, Majestic, Minotaur, Goliath, Swiftsure, and Theseus. On the 27th we passed the Straits of Gibraltar, and were joined by the Audacious of 74 guns, and the Leander of 50 guns, who had been some days there taking in water and other necessaries. On the 28th we passed the little uninhabited island of Albaran: it is quite flat; and with only low shrubs and grass, which must be burnt up in summer, maintained, I was informed, a great many hares and other game. It seems about three miles long, and is on the coast of Fez, in lat. 36. At night we lay to. The next morning proceeded with a fair and pleasant breeze to the eastward: on the 30th the signal for seeing strange ships was made by one of the squadron; and the Commodore made that to prepare for battle, which was accordingly put in execution by the rest of the ships, by knocking down the bulkheads and keeping the quarters clear for the great guns; every article of useless lumber being carried below, or thrown overboard. The Mutine brig was also directed to proceed to the northward of Majorca, in hopes of meeting the Admiral. The following day the Bellerophon and Swiftsure gave chace to a strange vessel; the latter being called in, she was spoke by the former, and

[b] The same day the Author was appointed to be Chaplain of the Swiftsure, and was received by his Commander, Captain Hallowell, with an hospitality and kindness for which he begs here to make his public acknowledgments. To the Earl of St. Vincent, in addition to many other obligations, that of giving him, by this appointment, a firm and honourable friend in Captain Hallowell, excites his lively gratitude.

proved to be a merchantman from Sardinia: from her no intelligence was obtained. On the third of June we met with squalls of wind and rain, which, however, did not long annoy us. On the sixth, being near the rendezvous, Commodore Troubridge made the signal for the Captains of the Swiftsure and Zealous to repair on board the Culloden; and on the next morning, the 7th of June, we saw the high hills behind Toulon, and two sail off that port; towards which we made all sail, and had the happiness to find one of them to be the Vanguard, bearing the flag of Rear Admiral Sir Horatio Nelson. Our pleasure was however a good deal damped by perceiving that she must have met with a severe disaster in the loss of her foremast, having replaced it with a jury-foremast.

It appears, that on the 22d of May, being in the gulph of Lyons, a violent squall of wind assailed the Admiral and his squadron, carried away all his topmasts, and soon after his foremast shared the same fate: the other ships were more fortunate; though in the same gale of wind, they received no damage. During this gale the frigates disappeared, nor did they again join the fleet till some days after the action in Aboukir Bay. This was a moment of infinite difficulty and danger, which however the spirit and resolution of the Admiral were fully equal to combat. The French fleet was known to be only a few leagues distant, having lately sailed from the Bay of Toulon. Admiral Nelson, with his little squadron, bore up for the Island of Sardinia, and reached with difficulty the road of St. Pietro, where the governor endeavoured in vain to obstruct his coming to an anchor. British seamen in distress are not easily intimidated. After remaining four days in this road without receiving the smallest assistance from the natives, the Vanguard again put to sea with top-gallant yards across, having set up a jury-foremast and replaced her topmasts. The inhospitality of the Sardinians must have originated in the fear their government was under of the vengeance of the French republic, whose tyranny at that moment palsied with terror all the Italian states; but what have they gained by their servility? After receiving repeated insults, many of them have undergone a total change in their constitution, have been drained of all their valuable property by repeated requisitions and forced loans, and at last annexed to the dominions of their insulting false friends, or made over by way of exchange to some other power.

The Leander was the same evening ordered to look out for the Orion and Alexander, and we continued lying to off Toulon. In the evening of the 9th, the Orion, and at three o'clock the following morning, the Alexander, Leander, and Mutine, joined the fleet, having immediately made sail after the French fleet which, under the command of General Buonaparte, had sailed from Toulon on the 20th of May, with 15 sail of the line, besides frigates and gun vessels, and 200 sail of transports, having 40,000 troops on board. Whither they were gone, and what their object might be, was as yet totally unknown to us. Our first point of research was Naples, knowing that there had existed strong symptoms on the part of the new republic of attacking that weak and impolitic monarchy. Our fleet now consisted of the following ships.

The Vanguard of 70 guns,	{ Capt. Berry, bearing Sir H. Nelson's flag.	
Orion	74	Capt. Sir J. Saumarez,
Culloden	74	.... Thomas Troubridge,
Bellerophon	74	.... H. Desterre Darby,
Minotaur	74	.... Thomas Louis,
Defence	74	.... J. Peyton,
Alexander	74	.... Alexander J. Ball,
Zealous	74	.... Samuel Hood,
Audacious	74	.... Davidge Gould,
Goliath	74	.... Thomas Foley,
Majestic	74	.... G. B. Westcote,
Leander	50	.... T. B. Thompson,
Swiftsure	74	.... Ben. Hallowell,
Theseus	74	.... R. Willet Miller,
And Mutine Brig	16	.... Thomas M. Hardy.

Previous to the junction of the fleet, the Orion and Alexander fell in with 15 sail of Spanish merchantmen, two of which they captured, but were called off by the Admiral, who did not wish to risk a failure of his more important object for the sake of prizes. By these means the Spaniards had the good fortune to escape. On the 12th we were off Cape Corse, the northern promontory of Corsica, and in the evening saw Capraia, and lay to, off the Isle of Elba; and the Mutine was dispatched for intelligence to Civita Vecchia. The winds were light and variable, the climate soft and pleasant; the next day, however, the sky was overcast, and we were assailed by torrents of rain, accompanied by most vivid lightnings, and heavy peals of thunder. During this grand display of nature in her robes of terror, we were entertained by one of those curious phenomena which used to create so much alarm to the superstitious ancients, a water spout; it frequently varied its form, and was often of a bended shape, like an S: at length it burst, and the space where it fell was whitened with foam. In the evening the weather cleared up, and we passed the small and flat island of Planosa, on the north point of which we discovered a few buildings, but at this time no appearance of inhabitants. Several of these islands are used as a summer residence for the poorer farmers from the neighbouring places, who bring their families and cattle with them: the latter always find plenty of feed, and the former employ themselves in fishing. There are also hares and other game in the islands. But, alas! such is the insecurity of these seas, that it sometimes happens that a single Algerine corsair will make a descent upon the helpless and pusillanimous inhabitants, carry off all their cattle, and not uncommonly make slaves of the proprietors themselves. This day a fishing-boat was descried by the fleet; the Alexander stood towards her, and found she had been left by her crew stood towards her, and found she had been left by her crew, and scuttled. From subsequent information I have reason to believe she had been met by the French fleet, her men taken out to reinforce their crews, and so left: for this we find was their mode of action with whatever they fell in with; *neutrals* or *enemies* were alike to them.

On the 14th, having a fresh breeze from the N.N.W. we passed the island Gianuti, on the coast of Tuscany, near which the Leander spoke a Moorish vessel that gave information of the French being at Syracuse in Sicily: the Mutine joined, without having obtained any intelligence. On the 15th instant, with a light breeze, we passed the islands of Palmaria and Ponza, the former rocky and uninhabited, the latter well cultivated, and rendered pleasing to the view by a village, several detached houses, and a white watch-tower on an eminence: to the southward we saw the little island called Le Botte, which at a distance has frequently been mistaken for a sail. On the 16th, we passed the island Ventotiene, on which is a large handsome white building, and on a small island near, a walled-in place like barracks; we had no opportunity of knowing what it was. In the evening we arrived off the island of Ischia, which forms the north-west boundary of the Bay of Naples. The next morning the fleet made sail into the Bay; Captain Troubridge and Captain Hardy were dispatched to Sir William Hamilton, the British Ambassador, from whom they received all the intelligence that had reached him, and learned that the French fleet had not entered that port, but were gone to the southward, having coasted the island of Sardinia. It since appeared, they had sent in to Cagliari, and were informed by our Consul (an Italian[c]) of the crippled state of Admiral Nelson's ship, but that he expected a reinforcement of thirteen sail of the line. This account the Admiral purposely left with him, knowing that he would report it to the French the first opportunity, should they visit that port.

[c] Many of the Consuls employed by our government, are foreigners; whether it is beneficial to our commerce that it should be so, is not for me to decide.

CHAPTER II.

> " Dextrum Scylla latus, lævum implacata Charybdis
> " Obsidet, atque imo barathri ter gurgite vastos
> " Sorbet in abruptum fluctus, rursusque sub auras
> " Eriget alternos, et sidera verberat unda."   ÆN. 3. v. 420.

The Admiral having now fome clue to go by, failed from the Bay of Naples in full hopes of falling in with the French fleet, the conqueft of which he could not but anticipate, well knowing the unanimous fentiments that pervaded the fleet he commanded, the tried bravery of many of his captains, and the fpirit of all. Light airs prevailed, a mortifying circumftance at fuch a moment, and we found ourfelves very little to the fouthward of the Bay of Naples on the 18th. On the 19th we ftill hung on the coaft of the Upper Calabria, from whence we had a view of the Burning Mountain on the ifland Stromboli; in the evening we paffed within a few leagues of it, and had a fine view of the picturefque appearance of a volcano by night. The next day we faw the other Lipari iflands, and had a diftant view of Sicily, with Mount Ætna, whofe fummit, though conftantly emitting flame and fmoke, is covered with perennial fnows. We now made for the far-famed Straits of Meffina, and had the honour of being the firft European fleet of men of war, in modern times, paffing the dangers of Scylla and Charibdis. Whatever dangers might formerly have given occafion to the celebrated fictions of the ancient poets, we found none, but with a full fail entered the Straits, paffing clofe by the caftle, or what is generally called the Faro of Meffina, a fquare red tower like a church fteeple, near which are fome indifferent buildings, the habitations of fifhermen: there is always a fmall garrifon in the caftle.

As we paffed within a few miles of the rock of Scylla, I took the opportunity of making a drawing of it, which is here given. The town bearing the fame name, is built on the neck of land that connects it with the main, and has a beautiful effect from the fea view; an old caftle crowns the rock. Near this place a Calabrian prince, and 2473 of his people, were fwept into the deep by a tremendous wave, occafioned by the dreadful earthquakes that defolated Calabria and the oppofite fhores of Sicily in the year 1783; of which Sir William Hamilton fent a very accurate account to the Royal Society; but the nervous poetic defcription of this calamity from the pen of the late Mr. Cowper, is so truly defcriptive, that I fhall here beg leave to tranfcribe it, as I am sure every feeling mind muft receive entertainment from it.

> Alas for Sicily! rude fragments now
> Lie fcatter'd where the fhapely column ftood.
> Her palaces are duft. In all her ftreets
> The voice of finging and the fprightly chord

Scylla, on the Coast of Calabria.

London: Pub by I. White Fleet Street, 1801.

Are silent. Revelry, and dance, and show,
Suffer a syncope and solemn pause,
While God performs upon the trembling stage
Of his own works his dreadful part alone.
How does the earth receive him? With what signs
Of gratulation and delight, her king?
Pours she not all her choicest fruits abroad,
Her sweetest flow'rs, her aromatic gums,
Disclosing Paradise where'er he treads?
She quakes at his approach. Her hollow womb
Conceiving thunders, through a thousand deeps
And fiery caverns, roars beneath his feet.
The hills move lightly, and the mountains smoke,
For he has touch'd them. From th' extremest point
Of elevation down into th' abyss,
His wrath is busy and his frown is felt.
The rocks fall headlong and the vallies rise.
.... The Sylvan scene
Migrates uplifted, and with all its soil
Alighting in far distant fields, finds out
A new possessor, and survives the change.
Ocean has caught the frenzy, and upwrought
To an enormous and o'erbearing height,
Not by a mighty wind, but by that voice
Which winds and waves obey, invades the shore
Resistless. Never such a sudden flood,
Upridg'd so high, and sent on such a charge,
Possess'd an inland scene. Where now the throng
That press'd the beach, and, hasty to depart,
Look'd to the sea for safety? They are gone!
Gone with the refluent wave into the deep,
A Prince with half his people!.............

As our squadron entered the Straits of Messina several boats, with many of the principal people of that city and the neighbourhood, came off to us, who expressed their joy and satisfaction at seeing a British fleet, when they discovered the object of our pursuit, being apprehensive that the next visit of the French marauders, after the capture of Malta, was destined for their coast. From the British Consul we learned that the islands of Malta and Goza had fallen into the hands of the French, by the treachery of the Grand Master and some of the Knights of Malta; who, forgetful of the solemn oaths, by which their order was bound to support the independence of it, had contrived, by various means, to prevent any opposition being made by the garrison: many of the batteries were totally unprovided with any means of defence, some of the cartridges were filled with sand, and the shot too large for the guns; yet this conquest, as Buonaparte pompously stiles it, is boasted of by the French, as one of their brilliant exploits. Here I cannot help observing, that the perfidious conduct of our enemy has recoiled upon his own head. Malta, possessing perhaps the finest harbour for its size, and certainly the strongest fortifications in the world, has now fallen into our possession, which otherwise never could have happened; as the well known justice and honour of our government would have forbidden any attack upon an unoffending state, however weak and unprotected it might have been. But since the fortune of war has fairly brought this island under our dominion, I cannot avoid expressing an ardent wish and hope, in which I am sure of being joined by all who are acquainted with the value and importance of it, that whatever may be the claims and demands of our opponents when the terms of peace come under consideration, we may still retain this place. As long as we are possessed of the trident of the seas, and by that means enabled to throw in supplies of provisions and ammunition, it cannot be taken from us: and since it affords at all times a commodious harbour for our shipping, and commands the entrance of the Archipelago, its importance to our commerce in these seas, is incalculable.

The passage of our fleet through the Straits of Messina must have afforded a grand spectacle to the multitudes who beheld it from the shore; who hailed our arrival with acclamations of joy and gratitude, which conveyed to our minds the highest gratification. To us the surrounding scenery was truly grand; the channel, narrow[d] at the entrance, widened as we proceeded, and opened a display of picturesque beauty that beggars all description. The rapidity with which we were carried by the current and the wind, prevented any long inspection of particular places; at the same time it rendered the change of objects more pleasing and diversified. On the left, the high mountains of Calabria, so lately shaken to their foundation by earthquakes, presented objects of infinite variety; the town of Regio forms a

[d] The entrance of the Straits between the Coda de Volpe on the Calabrian shore, and the point or promontory of Pelorus in Sicily, is scarcely more than a mile over. At Messina the channel is four miles broad, and from thence it rapidly widens till it opens again into the Mediterranean.

very beautiful feature in the landscape; it is situated at the base of the mountains, on the banks of a river which appeared to have owed its origin to one of those concussions of nature that have often changed the face of the country.

On the right, the city of Messina, with its handsome buildings, adorned with spires and steeples, presented a fine foreground to that side of the picture. Behind the town, on an eminence, is seen the castle, which, though it commands the harbour and town, is itself overlooked by high lands; from which it would soon be reduced by an invading army, that might easily gain those heights.

The far-famed Charybdis is situated near the entrance of the harbour; and by ancient historians and poets we are told, that ships, sucked into the vortex of the whirlpool, were in imminent danger from the violent commotion of the waters, by which the helm lost its power, and the seamen's exertions were rendered vain, so that with the most favourable wind they could not gain the port. The noise occasioned by the tumult of the waves, gave rise to the fictions of poets, who likened it to a voracious monster roaring for its prey; and by them the passage of these Straits has been described as the most dangerous adventure that mariners could undertake. In those days we find, that ships were obliged to go as near as possible to the Calabrian shore, in order to avoid the whirlpool; and then they ran a hazard of being carried on the rock Scylla, and dashed to pieces against its rugged sides. From this circumstance arose the proverb, 'incidit in Scyllam, cupiens vitare Charybdim,' applied to those who, in their endeavour to avoid one danger, fall into another. But we found none of these difficulties. Perhaps the constant friction of the waters has worn away the rocks and shoals that obstructed the passage, and given more ample room to the current, which, however, is now extremely rapid.

As we sailed down the Straits our eyes were regaled with a view of flourishing corn-fields, vineyards, orchards, and plantations. Cultivation, though in some places neglected, in others was carried high up the side of the mountains, on the summits of which appeared towns or villages, with here and there detached houses, churches, and convents. Towering over all, we beheld the majestic heights of Mount Ætna, whose summit, whitened with perpetual snows, was seen frequently above the clouds emitting volumes of smoke that sometimes ascended to a vast height; at others, came rolling down its sides.

> 'Portus ab accessu ventorum immotus, et ingens
> Ipse; sed horrificis juxta tonat Ætna ruinis,
> Interdumque atram prorumpit ad æthera nubem,
> Turbine fumantem piceo et candente favilla;
> Adtollitque globos flammarum, et sidera lambit:
> Interdum scopulos, avulsaque viscera montis

Erigit eructans, liquefactaque faxa fub auras
Cum gemitu glomerat, fundoque exæftuat imo.'[e]

ÆN. III. 570.

Having quitted this delightful fcenery, we at length emerged into the main, and were fteering with a prefs of fail for Malta with a frefh breeze from the north-weft, in full hope of finding the French fleet at Goza, where report faid they were anchored. On the 22d of June, at daylight in the morning, the Mutine fpoke a Genoefe brig from Malta, and received information from her, that the French had failed from thence on the 18th inftant with a frefh gale from the north-weft.

The Admiral now determined to fail for Alexandria; though uncertain what courfe the enemy had taken, he judged that to to be their probable deftination, and accordingly made the fignal to bear up and fteer fouth-eaft with all poffible fail.

Every mind now anxioufly looked forward to the glorious conflict; but what would have been our feelings if we could then have forefeen that the French fleet was to pafs us in the

---

[e] The port capacious, and fecure from wind,
Is to the foot of thund'ring Ætna join'd.
By turns a pitchy cloud fhe rolls on high;
By turns hot embers from her entrails fly;
And flakes of mounting flames, that lick the fky.
Oft from her bowels maffy rocks are thrown,
And fhiver'd by the force, come piecemeal down.
Oft liquid lakes of burning fulphur flow,
Fed from the fiery fprings that boil below.' DRYDEN.

following night? Such, however, was the cafe, as we afterwards learned from confulting and comparing the journals of French officers made prifoners in and after the action. It appears almoft incredible that a fleet confifting of near four hundred fail of various defcriptions, fhould crofs an adverfe fleet of fourteen fail of the line, even in the darkeft night, without fome of them being difcovered, yet fo it was. We failed on in expectation that they had got the ftart of us by feveral days, and they fhaped their courfe acrofs our track, making a more northern tour by the ifland of Candia, wrapped in perfect fecurity, and unconfcious that any adverfe fleet of force fufficient to alarm them was at that moment in thofe feas.[f]

We could form no certain opinion whither the enemy had fhaped his courfe up the Adriatic, towards Conftantinople, or to Alexandria; but one of thefe deftinations, we were well affured, muft be the object of his enterprize. In our paffage to the coaft of Egypt, we faw only three veffels, which we fpoke; two of them were from Alexandria, but could give us no account of the French fleet; and one from the Archipelago was equally unable to afford us the wifhed-for intelligence. On the 28th of June, fix days after we bore up, we came in fight of the city of Alexandria, and, to our great difappointment, faw nothing of the French fleet. Only one Turkifh line-of-battle fhip, with

[f] See the chart of the Mediterranean, in which I have given an accurate delineation of the track of the Britifh and French fleets till they met off the Nile on the 1ft of Auguft.

some merchantmen of different nations, were in the two harbours.

When we arrived off the Pharos, or castle which guards the entrance of the eastern harbour, the Admiral dispatched the Mutine towards the port for intelligence. Captain Hardy, after some delay, was permitted to land, and was conducted under a guard to the Governor, who expressed his surprise at seeing a British squadron, and seemed to feel some uneasiness at the visit; but on being informed of the object of our pursuit, his alarm was increased, though he declared his determination to resist the attempt of either power to land. The Admiral now experienced the greatest degree of disappointment at finding the enemy had eluded his pursuit, nor could he at the instant form any determinate resolution what course he should take, as their destination was totally enveloped in mystery. His anxious mind would not, however, permit him to rest long in the same station, and he resolved to shape his course back again, taking a northern direction, in hopes of hearing some tidings of the enemy.

On the 29th we stood to the N. E. with a fresh breeze from N. N. W. The Swiftsure was ordered, by signal, to chace a strange sail, which she came up with in the afternoon, and found her to be a French merchantman of 144 tons burthen, in ballast, bound from Alexandria to Smyrna. After taking out the prisoners, four of whom, including the captain, were Frenchmen, the rest of the crew Greeks and Italians, she was burnt by order of the Admiral, who was unwilling to be delayed by taking her with him. The wind in this part of the Mediterranean during the summer months generally blows from the westward, consequently we now had to beat back, against a strong breeze, which we did with all the sail we could carry. On the 4th of July we made the coast of Natolia, near Cape Cheledonia; the same day the Mutine parted company. On the 5th, the Admiral made the signal to close round him, many of the ships being greatly to leeward; for although the Vanguard had lost her foremast, which she had supplied with a jurymast, yet she sailed by far the best of the fleet. On the 7th, the Orion having parted company in the night, the fleet wore and stood to the northward, and towards the evening of the same day she rejoined us. On the 9th, being off the southern coast of the island of Candia, we had a view of Mount Ida, situated near the centre of the island. The weather had been excessively hot ever since we made the coast of Egypt, and now, though we were two degrees to the northward, the thermometer was as high as eighty-four.

On the 10th and 11th we were yet off the south-west side of Candia, and saw the little island of Goza; the wind being still against us we made but slow progress to the westward, and continued beating to windward till the 16th, when it became more favourable: our latitude observed this day was $35^d\ 45^m$ N. Long. $20^d\ 5^m$ E. of Greenwich. On the 18th, at six p. m.

we defcried Mount Ætna, and by eight faw Cape Paffero[g]. On the 19th of July the fleet ftood towards Syracufe, and the Admiral determined to enter the bay, being in great want of water, the Vanguard having had no opportunity of taking in a fupply of that neceffary article from the beginning of May, when fhe failed from Gibraltar; feveral other fhips of the fleet were nearly in the fame fituation. The entrance of the harbour is very narrow and difficult of accefs, nor was any perfon of the fleet acquainted with it; but by the fkill and attention of the captains and officers each fhip got fafe into the bay and anchored by three p. m. and without delay proceeded to take in water, though at firft fome difficulties prefented themfelves from the inconvenient fituation of the watering places; however, by the laborious exertion of the officers and men employed on that fervice, under the immediate direction of Captain Troubridge, the whole was completed in five days, and an ample fupply of frefh beef and vegetables procured; articles of the higheft importance to the health of feamen after a long voyage.

[g] Cape Paffero formerly bore the name of Pachinus, and is thus celebrated by Virgil.

' Hinc altas cautes, projectaque faxa Pachyni
    Radimus.' Æn. iii. 699.

' Then doubling Cape Pachynus, we furvey
    The rocky fhore extended to the fea.' DRYDEN.

CHAPTER III.

> " Sicanio prætenta sinu jacet insula contra
> " Plemmyrium undosum; nomen dixere priores
> " Ortygiam. Alpheum fama est huc Elidis amnem
> " Occultas egisse vias subter mare: qui nunc
> " Ore, Arethusa, tuo siculis confunditur undis." Æn. iii. 692.

While the ships were taking in water and live stock I took the opportunity of viewing the curiosities of Syracuse and its environs. But before I begin my account of what I saw on shore, I must say a few words of the Bay of Syracuse, in which the British fleet was anchored.

The form of this excellent harbour is nearly circular; the entrance, as I before observed, is very narrow, that without a tolerably fair wind it would be dangerous, if not impossible, for a large ship to beat in or out. But when once entered, it is so spacious that it would contain with ease an immense fleet; and, by being completely land-locked, ships may rest in perfect security during the heaviest gale, from whatever quarter it might blow.

Two small rivers disembogue themselves into this bay; that to which the boats of the Swiftsure proceeded on our arrival was so choked with mud and weeds at the entrance that it was with confiderable difficulty any of the boats could approach the shore, many of the larger kind grounded at some distance, and, to my mishap, that in which I was: we were in consequence obliged to wade to land with the water and mud up to our middles. The people now discovered another and worse difficulty in their way: the fields on each side of the mouth of this river (I understand in ancient days it was called Anapus) produced a great abundance of hemp, which is steeped in the river as soon as cut, and there left to soak; this operation renders the water pernicious to the health, as well as horribly unpleasant to the smell and taste. The mode adopted to obviate this difficulty, was rolling the empty casks through the fields to where the waters were uncontaminated; this was found to be beyond a bridge about a quarter of a mile up the river, and here they were soon filled and floated down to the boats. Another, and more convenient watering place, was soon discovered; it was situated near the town, and supplied by means of water courses from an aqueduct some distance up the country. Here, by the able management and exertions of Captain Troubridge, the needful supplies were soon obtained. While he saw that the parties employed in filling the water-casks did their duty, he also negociated with the people of the country for bullocks, sheep, and other stock, which were soon brought down in great profusion, and an ample store of fresh provisions supplied to all the ships of the fleet at a reasonable price.

Landing-place at Syracuse.

London: Pub. by I. White Fleet Street 1801.

In the afternoon, the landing place at the gate of the city was a scene of much gaiety and show; the boats from the fleet pulling in towards the shore, the crowds that lined the strand, the long range of carriages in which the principal nobility of the place came to view the British fleet, the gaudy liveries of their servants, with the variety of dresses which every where presented themselves in the appearance of the several orders of the people, formed so pleasing an assemblage, that I was induced to make a drawing on the spot, which is annexed. On the left hand of the foreground is a bastion of the fortification on the walls; and a little further on is seen the great gateway, from whence extends a length of wall which terminates in the fort commanding the entrance of the harbour.

The town which now exists, is built on what was formerly called the island of Ortygia. At the time when Syracuse was reckoned one of the first cities of the world, it was only the citadel or castle of Dionysius; but then contained many buildings of eminence. Now it exhibits a melancholy contrast to its former grandeur, the streets being in general meanly built, and so narrow that two carriages cannot pass each other with safety; and the eye is offended at every turn, with the most deplorable objects of poverty, filth, and misery. Among the most eminent buildings that adorned this quarter of the ancient city, was the Temple of Diana, of which I saw no remains; but of which, according to De-Non, a small vestige is to be found in an obscure house in a by-street called Resalibra.

The Temple of Minerva owes its preservation to Agio, the tenth bishop of Syracuse, who converted it into a cathedral, and so preserved it from that destruction which many of the other temples of antiquity have experienced. Although the Corinthian front which now adorns the entrance does not coincide with the massive Doric pillars of the ancient building, yet the whole edifice has a noble appearance. The plate annexed presents a side view of the Temple and the majestic marble columns supporting the roof. These columns are fluted from top to bottom, and gradually increase in size towards the base. Originally they were open, and discovered a second row of columns of the same order; but the space between them has been built up to form the walls of the cathedral.

On entering the building our ears were saluted with the harmony of church-music; the rich melody of the organ filling the vaulted roof with its tones, and aided by the voices of the choir, formed an assemblage of solemn sounds that, at the moment, raised our minds in rapture towards that Being whose praises were then chaunting.

No man, I believe, feels the impressions of devotion more strongly than the seaman just landed from the perils of his dangerous occupation; his mind naturally raises itself in grateful acknowledgment towards that Power by whose protecting arm he has been preserved.

Temple of Minerva, Syracuse.
London, Pub. by L.White, Fleet Street, 1801.

When the service was ended, some of the clergy, in a friendly manner, offered to shew us the curiosities contained in their cathedral.

In an apartment behind the high altar, we found a good painting of the Crucifixion, by Urbino: in this room also is kept an agate cup of great antiquity, and very beautiful workmanship, supposed to be coeval with the Temple itself; but some of the monks, with more zeal than knowledge, had inlaid parts of it with legends of their saints. They produced also for our inspection two massive gold rings that were many years since dug up among the ruins of the ancient city.

The fable of the river god Alpheus and the nymph Arethusa, is well known to all classical scholars. Every man of taste must remember, with particular delight, the tale as it is told by Ovid. The whole would be too long to copy here, but I cannot forbear extracting a few of the concluding lines, in which the nymph with such exquisite liveliness describes her own sudden conversion to a stream.

> ' Occupat obsessos sudor mihi frigidus artus;
> Cæruleæque cadunt toto de corpore guttæ.
> Quaque pedem movi, manet lacus, èque capillis
> Ros cadit: & citius, quam nunc tibi facta renarro,
> In latices mutor. Sed enim cognoscit amatas
> Amnis aquas, positoque viri, quod sumpserat, ore,
> Vertitur in proprias, ut se mihi misceat, undas.

Delia rupit humum: cœcifque ego merfa cavernis
Advehor Ortygiam.'[i]   OVID MET. lib. v. ver. 632.

Led by curiofity to fee the place thus celebrated, we paid a vifit to what bears the name of the Fountain of Arethufa; but, alas! found nothing to juftify the eulogiums paid to it by various writers of antiquity: repeated earthquakes, after changing its fituation, have deftroyed its former beauty; the fea has at times found its way through the riven rocks; the facred fifh are no longer inhabitants of its pellucid waters. It now exhibits only the appearance of a dirty pool iffuing from a hollow rock; the waters at fome periods dry up; at others, are tainted by fulphureous effluvia. It is now ufed by the wafherwomen of the city, who, at this time, were employed in their occupation. Standing up to their waifts in the water, they were beating the linen with flat boards upon the broken rocks which had tumbled into the pool. Neither the delicacy of the ladies, the beauty

---

[i] Cold dews at once my weary limbs appal,
And azure drops from all my body fall;
And where my foot was plac'd, a lake is fpread,
And moiftures trickle from my trembling head;
And quicker than these words, my perfon flows
Chang'd to a ftream. The amorous river knows
The lovely current; inftant lays afide
His human figure; and begins to glide
Again in wat'ry waves, with mine to mix his tide.
Diana, ftill my virgin charms to keep,
Cleaves the hard earth; and fafe in caverns deep
To far Ortygia's fhore my darkfome way I weep.

# Caverns near Syracuse

of the fountain, nor the elegance of the employment carried on there, recalled to our minds thofe pleafing images we had formed of it, and we quitted the place with difguft.

We next proceeded towards the land-gates, which are placed in the ftrongeft part of the fortifications. After paffing through two handfome gateways, and over feveral broad and deep foffes filled with water, we came to a large area that led us to the laft gate, which is built in the outward walls of the fortification. Croffing the drawbridge, we entered on the fcite of that part of ancient Syracufe called Achradina, of which not a veftige remains. Proceeding through feveral highly cultivated gardens, well ftored with vegetables, delightfully fhaded by tall poplars, and watered by clear ftreams from the neighbouring hills, we arrived at the celebrated Latomiæ, or caverns in which Dionyfius is faid to have confined his prifoners, and to have enjoyed their groans, by means of a chamber that communicated with one of them. How far this ftory is to be relied on, I fhall not pretend to fay, but muft refer the reader to thofe hiftorians who have made it their ftudy, and whofe leifure and opportunity have enabled them to inveftigate the matter. My bufinefs is to give the beft defcription I can of the place as it now is. The cavern known by the name of Dionyfius's ear, is fuppofed to have been the fcene of that cruelty; and its fhape certainly gives colour to the ftory, being formed to convey found to a particular place. It is hewn out of the folid rock, into the form of a Gothic arch, eighteen feet wide by fifty-eight high, and curved from the entrance to the end; throughout the upper part runs a groove which communicates with a small chamber over the entrance, which must originally have been walled up to prevent the sound escaping. In this chamber the tyrant, according to tradition, used to place himself to hear the discourse of his prisoners who were chained to the walls of the cavern: and to give a colour to this idea, rings are discovered formed in the rock, to which possibly the hands and feet of the prisoners were fastened with thongs. On the right, half-way the length of the cavern, is a large square chamber, also hewn out of the rock, but for what purpose it was formed, except to enlarge the place allotted for prisoners, we could not guess; yet, as it must in some measure have destroyed the conveyance of sound, the original purpose for which this cavern was formed, it may have been a work of later date. The further end of the cavern terminates abruptly, like the gable end of a house; but near the top are seen several holes in the wall, as if a chamber had been there, and up to it, in regular gradations, smaller holes, apparently for iron cramps to support steps.

The dryness of this curious cavern, the effect of the echo, and the solemn appearance of the place, must render it a delightful retreat during the summer months, when the heat of the climate is insufferable; but it does not appear that the Syracusans have taste enough to enjoy so romantic a spot. Near this cavern is another of a different form, being square, flat at

Entrance into Dionysius' Ear.

London: Pub by I. White, Fleet Street, 1801

Inside of a Cavern near Syracuse.

London: Pub.d by I. White Fleet Street 1807.

the upper part, and fubdivided into feveral fpacious chambers by rude pillars formed of the rock, out of which the cavern was excavated; a work that muft have coft infinite labour, and employed armies to accomplifh. In the fpacious area before the entrance of the caverns, is an high white infulated rock; on the top are the ruins of a building, perhaps a guard-houfe; and near are feen the remains of an ancient aqueduct. The rocks furrounding the area are fo fmooth, and fo artfully project toward the fummit, that to climb them would be impoffible. Near the top appear the remains of an earthen-ware channel to convey water from the aqueduct to the caverns below. There is alfo another cavern in the fame direction with the laft-mentioned, but blackened with the fmoke of furnaces ufed to extract the falt of nitre: it is of a fimilar form, but of lefs dimenfions.

Near thefe caverns we difcovered the remains of a bath, of an oblong form; the water within it perfectly clear, and of an icy coldnefs; from the top are fufpended large maffes of petrified ftalactites, which daily increafe by water dripping from above. The approach to this place is hid among plants that have for ages been fuffered to grow in wild luxuriance, and in feftoons of various kinds overhang the entrance, forming a moft romantic retreat.

We next vifited the remains of a Roman theatre hewn chiefly out of the rock: which, of courfe, has fuffered little from the injuries of time, but all that was built on this foundation is deftroyed. The fituation is perfectly beautiful; the fpectators having a full view of the Bay, with the island of Ortygia, and the rich plains through which the Anapus winds, it even now presents a most picturesque appearance. The white steps are nearly hid by bushes and flowery shrubs of various kinds, and the waters escaping from a reservoir above, come tumbling down the rocks in broken torrents.

Being somewhat tired with our walk, we postponed making further researches till the next day, when we again, at an early hour, landed at the usual place. Before we proceeded to explore the venerable remains of past ages, we determined to inspect the more modern edifices that adorn the present city. The first place that we proceeded to was an open area, or piazza, in which are the principal buildings of the city: the annexed plate will give the reader a tolerably correct idea of it. On the right is the Bishop's palace adjoining the cathedral, which I have before observed was built on the ruins of the Temple of Minerva. This view shews the elevation of the modern façade erected on the scite of the old portico. History informs us, that on the summit of the ancient portico was suspended a shining buckler which could be seen at a vast distance. No sooner did the Syracusan mariner lose sight of this talisman, than he threw offerings of honey, flowers, and ashes into the sea to render Neptune and Minerva propitious to his voyage, and ensure his safe return. The modern front is perfectly incongruous with the rest of the building; it is of the Corinthian order, and highly ornamented with Colossal statues. The ascent to it

Cooper Williams del.

I.C. Stadler sculp.

Grand place, at Ayraxxe

London: Pub. by I. White, Fleet Street, 1801.

is by a noble flight of steps, on each side of which is a statue of the two principal apostles, St. Peter and St. Paul, has a fine effect.

Beyond the cathedral is a handsome square building appropriated to the administration of justice, opposite to which is the palace of the Baron de Bosci, a nobleman of large property and consequence in this place.

We next paid our respects to some convents near the piazza. The first was dedicated to St. Lucia; where, over the high altar in the chapel, is a good painting, by Caravagi, of the martyrdom of the patroness. St. Lucia is represented as drawn by oxen to the place of execution; but, by a miracle, she is rendered immoveable notwithstanding the utmost exertion of the animals, who appear to strain every nerve in vain. However the miracle seems to have no object, as a Saracen soldier comes behind her and cuts off her head.

The convent of Monte Virginis is appropriated to females of noble family only. As Englishmen, we could not but lament that so many lovely women should, by superstition, be thus secluded from the world, which otherwise they might have contributed by their presence to adorn, as by their social virtues to have added to the general stock of domestic happiness.

We now once more emerged into the country, and proceeded to a farm-house, where the mode of raising water attracted our attention. A number of earthen pots, connected by bands of rushes, revolved round a wheel (in the manner of a jack-chain)

F

which was put in motion by an ox. As the pots fall into the well below, they fill, and come up to the turn of the wheel, where they empty themfelves into a trough connected with a large refervoir; from whence the neighbouring gardens are refrefhed with conftant ftreams during the heats of fummer, and by this contrivance are bleffed with a perpetual fertility.

From hence we vifited the church of St John, efteemed the oldeft chriftian church in Sicily. The pillars are of the heavieft Gothic, and the walls covered with miferable daubings. But our principal objects of refearch were the catacombs, or burying places, of the ancient Syracufans. We were conducted by an old Capuchin friar into thefe celebrated tombs, and were obliged at the entrance to creep in on our hands and knees, but we foon found it fufficiently lofty. The ftreets and alleys into which thefe vaults are cut, crofs each other in every direction, and had our guide extinguifhed his torch, we muft have remained in this difmal abode till relieved by the hand of death, as it would be very difficult for a ftranger to find his way out, even with a light; without it, impoffible. At certain diftances we came to large round chambers, whofe dome-like roof admitted a fmall portion of light and air from an aperture in the upper part. The walls of thefe rooms were covered with a fort of ftucco, and round them were placed in uniform directions a number of ftone coffins like thofe we faw on each fide of the alleys. Thefe were excavated from the folid rock, and of various dimenfions; fome appearing fcarcely large enough

Garden and Monastery of the Capuchins near Syracuse.

for a new-born infant. We were informed that skeletons had been found in some of them with a piece of money in their jaws; perhaps to pay the ferryman of the Styx for their passage to the regions of Pluto.

The horrid idea of being, by any accident, left to starve in this labyrinth of death[k], made us glad to quit it, filled with astonishment at its vast capacity. For though we walked through a great many streets and alleys, on each side of which are arched tombs excavated from the rock, yet we also passed by the ends of many other passages which we did not penetrate, and could form no idea of the extent of, nor of the number of bodies the whole might be capable of containing.

We next proceeded to a monastery of Capuchins, situated on an eminence near the sea. It is a neat and airy building, placed on a barren rock, without an appearance of any vegetation near it. But no sooner had we paid our respects to the reverend fathers, than we were conducted by them into subterraneous gardens, where verdure and vegetation flourished

---

[k] I have since been informed, that some time ago a gentleman and lady having gone to see the catacombs at Rome, soon after they had entered the gloomy caverns, the roof fell in and closed up the entrance. What agonizing sensations must they have endured on returning to the place through which they had hoped again to behold the light of day, to find it closed against them for ever! Some people who saw them enter, and were aware of the accident, gave the alarm; but those employed to clear away the rubbish, fearful of being involved in the like misfortune, were so tardy in their operations, that by the time they had penetrated through the mass, the unfortunate strangers, with their guide, were discovered lifeless. It appeared that the latter had attempted to work a passage with his hands, but must soon have been convinced that his efforts were unavailing.

in the higheſt degree. The ſcene appeared like enchantment; nor could we at firſt deviſe the cauſe of it, till, on examination, we diſcovered that we were in the ſame ſort of excavations as thoſe of the Latomiæ we had before viſited. By labour and cultivation the ground, rendered rich and productive, is become a luxuriant orchard of orange, lemon, and olive trees. But Mr. Swinburne's deſcription of this place being far better than any I can hope to give, I ſhall take the liberty of uſing it. 'I deſcended by a ſlope into theſe extraordinary bowers, where my view was confined on all ſides by ſhaggy walls of great height, either purpoſely hewn into ſhape, or rudely figured by the corroſive ſea air. Huge maſſes have been broken off and rolled on the platform, where they contribute to the compoſition of a moſt wild, yet ſolemn picture. The area is covered with a thick grove of trees, loaded with rich ſcented bloſſoms and beautiful fruit; I was delighted with their variety of kinds, vigour of growth, and brilliancy of foliage; the ſlim branches of the pale olive were interwoven with the buſhy heads of orange, lemon, bergamot, and cedar trees; while the tender colour of the full blown almond formed a fine contraſt with the fiery buds of the pomegranate, juſt burſting into blow. The gardeners have ſkilfully increaſed the variety of their fruits by grafting and budding, and have procured a great diverſity in their taſte and colour. There are ſeveral ſepulchres in theſe quarries, and ſome projections of the ſtone have been ſcooped into rings, by which I conjecture, that after the place

Curious Cemetry under the Capuchini Monastery, near Syracuse.

London: Pub. by I. White, Fleet Street, 1807.

ceased to be used as a quarry, it was converted into a prison.'

The undercroft or cemetery of this monastery contains as curious a scene as any we had yet witnessed. We entered it by a flight of steps through a trap-door in the nave of the chapel, and found it as light as the place we had just left, having windows in the vaulted roof. But our attention was immediately called off from other matters to an assemblage of venerable personages arranged along the wall, in niches formed for the purpose: they were all dressed in the habit of St. Francis, and, at first sight, had the appearance of life; but, on close examination, their skin appeared dry, shrivelled, and as hard as wood; some of them had been dead for near two centuries; many of them were decorated with long flowing beards, others with none; whether fallen off by time, or the fashion of the age they lived in, I cannot say: the monks of the present day being distinguished by a profusion of that ornament. Besides the bodies of the monks, we saw those of the nobility and gentry who could afford the expence of this mode of sepulture; for the worthy monks do not permit the intrusion of unhallowed laity into their society without receiving, besides the entrance fee, a handsome yearly compensation for it, which is paid in various ways. Some contribute annually a wax candle of many pounds weight; and should any omission of the payment occur, the unfortunate ancestor of the defaulter is turned out of his place to make room for another. These strangers are generally habited in their beſt ſuits, and are laid in boxes with lids faſtened by locks, which were opened for our inſpection: ſome of them had bag-wigs, ruffles, and laced coats, and preſented a very frightful ſatire on human vanity. No ladies are admitted of this ſilent party. The ornaments of this ſolemn repoſitory are entirely appropriate; round the cornices, and over the altar, which has a crucifix on it, are ſculls and croſs bones, and over the entrance to the chapel this motto, ' Commune mori, mors nulli parcit honori.'

On our return to Syracuſe, we paſſed over the rough foundations of part of the ancient city, ſome of which we could perceive extend ſome yards into the ſea. It was at this place Archimedes had his reſidence, from whence he annoyed the Roman fleet by the ingenuity of his inventions.[1]

---

[1] In Heylyn's Coſmography I find the following ſhort account of celebrated and learned men, who in former times adorned the iſland of Sicily, which, I think, will be acceptable to the reader, and ſhall therefore preſent it in his own words: ' This iſland is famous for the worthy ſcholars ſhe once produced; 1ſt, Æſchylus, the firſt tragedian of fame; who being bald through age, once walked into the fields, where, by chance, an eagle taking his bald pate for a white rock, let a ſhell-fiſh fall on it of that bigneſs that it beat out his brains. 2d, Diodorus Siculus, that famous hiſtorian. 3d, Empedocles, the firſt inventor of rhetoric; and his fellow Gorgias. 4th, Euclid, the textuary geometrician, who taught in Megaris. 5th, Archimedes, a moſt worthy mathematician, the firſt author of the ſphere; of which inſtrument he made one of that art and bigneſs, that one ſtanding within, might eaſily perceive the ſeveral motions of every celeſtial orb. He made alſo divers military engines, which, in the ſiege of Syracuſe, ſorely vexed the Romans, and was at laſt ſlain in his ſtudy by a common ſoldier, in the ſack of the town, to the great grief of the general, Marcellus. 6th, Epicharmus, the firſt inventor of comedies; and 7th, Theocritus, the firſt author of paſtoral eclogues.'

CHAPTER IV.

Felices .... quos ille timorum
Maximus, haud urget leti metus; inde ruendi
In ferrum mens prona viris, animæque capaces
Mortis: & ignavum redituræ parcere vitæ.   LUCAN, lib. i. v. 459.

During the time our fleet was in the Bay of Syracuse, Admiral Nelson was impatiently expecting some intelligence of the route of the enemy. From neutral vessels that occasionally entered the port he could gain no certain information: but a vague report reached him, that the enemy were not in the Adriatic, had not been seen in the Archipelago, and were certainly not gone to the westward. From hence he judged that Egypt must be their destination: and though it appeared extraordinary that in our voyage to Alexandria and back to Syracuse, we had neither seen or heard of them; yet, in his own mind, he was confident that Egypt was their object, and he once more determined to proceed thither.

That we did pass by the French fleet in our former voyage to Alexandria, has been ascertained to have happened between the 22d and 23d of June.[m] To account for this circumstance

---

[m] See the chart.

I shall observe, that the French steered their course for Candia, making an angular passage to Alexandria: we, on the contrary, made a direct push for that place; and though it happened at what is generally understood to be the narrow part of these seas, yet the distance of thirty-five leagues between Candia and the shores of Africa, affords ample room for two of the largest fleets to pass each other without observation. But when it is considered that by the inferiority of our numbers we were constrained to sail in a compact body, that we had no frigates to look out, and that the hazy atmosphere in this climate precluded a distant view, the surprise will vanish.

That this circumstance should occur, will to a seaman appear not an extraordinary matter.

The cause why, on our return *from* Alexandria, we missed them will be easily understood by referring to the chart, in which I have marked down the tracks of the hostile fleets. It will there be seen that we made a circuitous route northward at the time the French fleet bore down to Alexandria in a direct line from Candia. We have since been informed that on the evening of the 30th of June, the French appeared off the coast of Egypt, and early in the morning of the same day our fleet was seen from the towers of Alexandria. If we had remained only a few hours longer on the coast we must have fallen in with them previous to their landing. But Providence ordered it otherwise. And from subsequent events we have every reason to believe that our success has been more complete, and the final deſtruction of their vaſt armament been rendered more deciſive than if our own ſanguine wiſhes had taken effect. But as this is mere matter of ſpeculation and conjecture, we ought to reſt ſatisfied with the event, and agree with the poet, that '·whatever is, is right.'

On the 24th of July ſeveral ſhips of the fleet left the Bay of Syracuſe; and the next day the reſt of the ſquadron ſailed from thence, having completed their water, and obtained a plentiful ſupply of live ſtock and vegetables, all which was performed in five days.

To render his ſecond voyage to the ſhores of Egypt more certain, and that no opportunity of gaining intelligence might be loſt, the Admiral determined to coaſt along the extremity of the Archipelago, among the Grecian iſlands. He accordingly made ſail for the Morea; and on the 28th, being off Cape Gallo, diſpatched the Culloden to Coron. Captain Troubridge communicated with the Turkiſh Governor, and ſo far gained his good opinion that he was allowed to take poſſeſſion of a French wine-veſſel at anchor in that port, and we ſoon had the pleaſure of ſeeing him come out with his prize. He alſo brought us the certain intelligence, that the French fleet had been ſeen ſteering from Candia to the ſouth-eaſt about a month before.

Captain Troubridge had the ſatisfaction to obſerve, during his ſhort viſit to the Governor, that a general hatred and deteſtation was entertained of the French; their conduct towards

G

the unfortunate inhabitants of the places, of which they had taken poffeffion in their predatory warfare, having raifed the utmoft horror and dread in thofe who expected a vifit from them.

We now fteered to the fouth-eaft, our hearts elate with the expectation of having our toils rewarded by a fight of the enemy.

For let not thofe who, unaccuftomed to danger, form the moft terrific ideas of it, imagine that the hazard of the fight is the predominant apprehenfion in the minds of men about to be engaged. I believe I may with great truth affert, that courage, on thefe occafions, fpreads like wildfire through all ranks. Our commanders in this glorious expedition afforded fuch great examples, that his muft have been indeed a daftardly fpirit that did not participate in the generous impulfe!

On the 29th a frefh breeze and high fea bore us rapidly from the coaft of Candia; and on the 31ft the captains of the fleet were on board the Vanguard to take the Admiral's laft inftructions: and how well they profited by them will foon appear! In the evening of the fame day the Alexander and Swiftfure were ordered a-head to reconnoitre. About ten o'clock the next morning, being the 1ft of Auguft, the towers of Alexandria, the Pharos, and the far-famed pillar of Pompey, cheered our fight; and with fatisfaction we obferved the altered appearance of the port from what it was when laft we vifited it; then unpeopled, and folitary, now crowded with veffels, and the French flag difplayed on the walls. As we drew nearer, however, we were much mortified to find that the men of war, we expected to meet with, were not there: we counted fix fhips of war, of various fizes; the reft confifted of tranfports and merchant veffels in which the French troops had embarked at Toulon. Captain Ball, by fignal, informed the Admiral of the number and fituation of the enemy, and then hailed the Swiftfure, directing Captain Hallowell to bear down towards a large armed brig and galley at anchor off the mouth of the old harbour, and either bring them off, or drive them afhore. But we were foon recalled by fignal from the Admiral, who was in the offing; and we ftood towards the body of the fleet, which was fteering eaftward under a prefs of fail. That we were thus called off was a moft fortunate event: we have fince difcovered that the galley and the brig had anchored behind a reef of rocks extending from the entrance of the old harbour. But for this feafonable recall, we muft in a few minutes have ftruck on it; and if not loft, fhould have been rendered ufelefs at a time when moft wanted.

At a quarter paft three p. m. the Admiral made the fignal ' to prepare for battle,' and we (in the Alexander and Swiftfure) had not bore up more than an hour, before we alfo defcried the French fleet at anchor, in a line of battle, in the Bay of Aboukir. Towards them we ftood with the enthufiaftic ardour of men bent on conqueft, and who knew there could be no alternative between that and death. By ftanding fo far in towards Alexandria, we were left far aftern. This was at firft regarded as a moft unfortunate event, but we had reafon to think otherwife. At four p. m. the Admiral made the fignal to prepare to anchor with fprings on the cable, and that it was his intention to engage the van and centre of the enemy. At five the Alexander made a fignal to the Swiftfure, that of ftanding into danger; and immediately tacked. Captain Hallowell luffed up to avoid the danger, and we had the mortification to perceive that the Culloden was aground on a reef of hidden rocks. Thefe rocks extend a confiderable way from the ifland which forms the north-weft point of the Bay of Aboukir. In his eager defire to gain a forward ftation in the glorious conteft, the gallant[n] commander had with crowded fail borne down towards the enemy. No one in the fleet had the leaft knowledge of the bay; nor was any known chart of it exifting, except an ill drawn plan found on board the veffel captured on the 29th June, which had been prefented to the Admiral, but from that nothing certain could be made out. Captain

---

[n] Captain Troubridge has paffed almoft the whole of his time in active fervice, and has had occafion repeatedly to diftinguifh himfelf for that zeal and intrepidity which has so juftly raifed the naval character.

On that ever memorable day, when a fleet of only fifteen Britifh fail of the line attacked and conquered twenty-feven fail of Spanifh men of war of the largeft fize, bearing away four of their fhips as trophies of the victory gained by Sir John Jervis off Cape St. Vincent, Captain Troubridge, in the Culloden, had the diftinguifhed honour to lead the van into battle. Now, when his ardent mind had pictured to himfelf frefh laurels to be won in defence and fupport of the honour of his country, to find all his profpects blafted! Not only unable to gain a forward ftation, he was totally rendered incapable of lending any aid to his gallant countrymen, and obliged to remain an inactive fpectator of a conteft in which he had hoped to have borne a diftinguifhed part! His feelings were fuch as only a brave man, by imagining himfelf expofed to a fimilar difafter, can form any idea of.

Troubridge had kept conftantly founding as he proceeded, and, juft before he ftruck, had found ten fathoms of water: before the lead could again be hove, the Culloden was faft aground on the rocks. Warned by his difafter, feveral other fhips, ftanding into the fame danger, were preferved from a fimilar fate. The evening was now clofing in, the bay quite unknown, and the enemy ready to receive us, drawn up in a clofe line from north-eaft to fouth-weft, forming an obtufe angle at the centre.°

Here true heroifm was difplayed in the prompt decifion of Admiral Nelfon. When his fquadron was well collected round him,[p] he determined without lofs of time to attack the foe, formidable as their appearance was; fuperior their number, weight of metal, and fize; night coming on; and an unknown navigation. Surely too much cannot be faid of fuch magnanimity! His honour, character, and life, were to be put to the decifion of the enterprife; for it was well known that conqueft or death was his determined object.

His refolution was inftantly formed, and his intentions made known to the fleet by the fignal ' for the headmoft fhip to bear down and engage, as fhe reached the van of the enemy; the next fhip to pafs by and engage the fecond fhip of the line; and fo on.' With alacrity was this fignal obeyed: the

---

o See the plan of the action.

p Except the Alexander and Swiftfure, who were under a prefs of fail making the beft of their way to join.

sure presage of victory sat on the brow of every Briton, and a general ardour pervaded all ranks. The commanders, with that courage which distinguishes men inured to danger, saw the hazard of the contest and prepared to meet it: their ships were trained to every exercise of arms; all means of preservation from fire, leaks, and other casualties, were arranged in order; a bower cable was got out of the after part of each ship and bent forwards, that she might anchor by the stern; the dreadful engines of destruction ready primed and doubly loaded; the men at their quarters waiting in silent expectation the orders of their superiors; the officers respectfully looking towards their captains, and waiting with firmness the awful moment. The enemy's line presented a most formidable appearance: it was anchored in close order, and apparently near the shore; flanked with gun-boats, mortar vessels, and four large frigates; with a battery of guns and mortars, on an island near which we must pass. This posture gave the most decided advantage to the French, whose well known perfection and skill in the use of artillery, has so often secured to them splendid victories on shore: to that they were now to look for success; for each ship being at anchor, became a fixed battery.

The British Admiral, who saw all the advantages the enemy possessed, but saw them with a seaman's eye, knew that they must have room to swing the length of their cables; and, consequently, that there would be space enough for our ships to anchor between them and the shore.

The Goliath,[q] commanded by Captain Foley, had the diftinguifhed honour to lead the fleet into battle. The water was fmooth, and a pleafant fine breeze foon brought him within reach of the guns of the enemy. By a quarter paft fix p. m. the French commenced the engagement; in two minutes he returned their fire, and then doubled their line and anchored alongfide of the fecond fhip in the van.

Captain Hood,[r] in the Zealous, followed clofe and took his ftation on the bows of the Guerrier with great judgment; and in twelve minutes the Guerrier was totally difmafted. The

---

[q] Captain Foley has again fought under Lord Nelfon, who hoifted his flag on board his fhip, the Elephant, in the late daring attack and victory off Copenhagen. At the capture of the ifland of Corfica, Captain Foley commanded the St. George of 98 guns, the flag fhip of Rear-Amiral Gell. In Lord St. Vincent's victory over the Spaniards, he alfo bore a diftinguifhed part, as he commanded the Britannia of 100 guns, which fhip bore the flag of Vice-Admiral Sir Charles Thompfon.

[r] Captain Hood had been hailed by the Admiral to know if he thought there was fufficient depth of water for our fhips between the enemy and the fhore; Captain Hood faid he did not know, but, with the Admiral's permiffion, he would lead in and try. The Goliath, however, being the fafteft failer, and having the ftart, firft gained the poft of honour.

The following anecdote is fo highly characteriftic, that I muft beg leave to mention it. At the time of the evacuation of Toulon, Captain Hood commanded the Juno frigate on that ftation: previous to that event, he had failed on a cruize. When he returned to port, unconfcious of what had happened in his abfence, he failed into the harbour and anchored without being aware of his dilemma. The evening was hazy, with heavy rains; no colours were difplayed on the batteries, or if they were, they were not vifible, or were Englifh. A boat came alongfide; feveral Frenchmen of the new municipality came on board: they were afked for news, and perceiving the miftake that ftill reigned, they converfed with him as if they belonged to the Britifh government. By good fortune the tricolour cockade in the hat of one of them caught his eye, and he faw the treacherous tendency of their vifit. On this, with great prefence of mind, having fet before them fome refrefhments, he went on deck and communicated to the officers and crew the fituation of the fhip; gave orders to flip the cable, and make all poffible exertion to fail out of the harbour. This he effected in defiance of a heavy cannonade from the fort and batteries as he paffed, and foon after joined the fleet under the command of Lord Hood, with the welcome account of his adventure and fortunate efcape.

Goliath, who had, as I before obferved, anchored alongfide of the Conquerant, fhot away her opponent's mafts in ten minutes after. The third fhip that doubled the van of the French line was the Orion, commanded by Sir James Saumarez.[s] A frigate, La Sirrieufe, fired upon him as he paffed, and Sir James ordered a few guns to be pointed at her; a broadfide, however, was difcharged, and the frigate inftantly funk. He then proceeded and took his ftation on the larboard bow of the Franklin and quarter of the Peuple Souvrain, receiving and returning the fire of both. The Audacious, commanded by Captain Gould,[t] next followed, and dropped anchor on the bows of the Conquerant, where he commenced a fpirited and galling fire. Captain Millar, in the Thefeus, was the laft that anchored between the French line and the fhore. Paffing between the Guerrier and Zealous, he could not refift the opportunity which offered, as he brufhed the Frenchman's fides, of pouring in an effective broadfide: he then took his ftation on the larboard fide of the Spartiate. The Vanguard, diftinguifhed by the flag of Admiral Nelfon, now entered the battle. Aware of the impoffibility of the rear of the enemy (being to leeward) coming

---

[s] This officer has had the good fortune, repeatedly, to diftinguifh himfelf. Early in this war, he commanded the Circe of 36 guns. Being on a cruife off Cherbourg, he fell in with the Crefcent, French frigate. After a clofe action of more than two hours, during which the enemy loft 120 men, killed and wounded, he captured her without the lofs of one man in his own fhip. For this gallant action he received the honour of knighthood. He commanded the Orion in Lord Bridport's action off Port l'Orient, 3d June 1795. And in Lord St. Vincent's unrivalled victory over the Spaniards, he alfo, in the fame fhip, had a fhare in the glory of that day. On June 6th, 1801, he was made a Baronet.

[t] At the capture of the ifland of Corfica he commanded the Cyclops frigate, of 28 guns.

to the affiftance of their van, he determined to redouble his efforts to conquer one part before he attacked the reft. In purfuance of that refolution, he himfelf fet the example to the reft of his fleet, and anchored withoutfide of the enemy's line, who were, in confequence, completely between two fires. The Vanguard anchored within half-piftol-fhot on the larboard fide of the Spartiate, and began fuch a fevere and well directed fire, that, totally difmafted, and having loft a great number of her crew, the Frenchman was obliged to call for quarter, which was immediately granted. Captain Louis,[u] in the Minotaur, anchored next ahead of the Admiral, and engaged the Aquilon, which was alfo obliged to ftrike to his fuperior fire. The Bellerophon, commanded by Captain Darby, now entered the conflict, and running down the line, dropped anchor alongfide of l'Orient of 120 guns, bearing the flag of the French commander in chief, Admiral Brueyes. The Defence, Captain Peyton, followed clofe, and took his ftation, with great judgment, ahead of the Minotaur, by which the line remained unbroken; he engaged the Franklin of 80 guns on the ftarboard bow. This fhip bore the flag of Contre-Admiral Blanquet Du Chelard, fecond in command. The Majeftic, commanded by Captain Weftcott, next came into action, and clofely engaged the Heureux on the ftarboard bow, receiving alfo the fire of the Tonnant, an 80 gun fhip, next aftern of l'Orient. The fupe-

---

[u] He commanded this fhip alfo at the recapture of the ifland of St. Lucia in the Weft Indies, in 1796.

rior weight of metal pouring in from thefe two fhips, foon made dreadful havoc in the Majeftic. Captain Weftcott[x] fell by a mufket fhot at the time he was exerting himfelf with great gallantry to counteract the advantages poffeffed by the enemy in fize and number, by the energy and vivacity of his fire. Mr. Cuthbert, the firft lieutenant, continued to fupport the unequal conflict with determined courage and refolution. The Alexander and Swiftfure now came in for their fhare of glory. Having been (as I before obferved) prevented affifting at the commencement of the battle, by bearing down to reconnoitre Alexandria, and afterwards being obliged to alter their courfe to avoid the fhoal that had proved fo fatal to the Culloden, it was eight o'clock before they came into action, and total darknefs had enveloped the combatants for fome time, which was difpelled only by the frequent flafhes from their guns; the volumes of fmoke now rolling down the line from the fierce fire of thofe engaged to windward, rendered it extremely difficult for the reft of the Britifh fhips who came in laft to take their ftation: it was fcarcely poffible to diftinguifh friend from foe. To remedy this evil, Admiral Nelfon directed his fleet to hoift four lights horizontally at the mizen-peak as foon as it was dark. The Swiftfure was bearing down under a prefs of fail, and had already got within range of the enemy's guns, when Captain Hallowell perceived a fhip ftand-

---

[x] In Lord Howe's action with the French fleet on the 1ft June 1794, Captain Weftcott commanded the Impregnable of 98 guns, the flag fhip of Rear-Admiral Caldwell.

ing out of action under her foresail and foretopsail, having no lights displayed. Supposing that she was an enemy, he felt inclined to fire into her; but as that would have broken the plan[y] he had laid down for his conduct, he desisted: and happy it was that he did so; for we afterwards found the ship in question was the Bellerophon,[z] which had sustained such serious damage from the overwhelming fire of the French Admiral's enormous ship l'Orient, that Captain Darby found it was necessary for him to fall out of action, himself being wounded, two lieutenants killed, and near two hundred men killed and wounded. His remaining mast falling soon after, and in its fall killing several officers and men, (among the former was another of his lieutenants,) he was never able to regain his station. At three minutes past eight o'clock the Swiftsure anchored, taking the place that had before been occupied by the Bellerophon; and two minutes after began a steady and well directed fire on

---

[y] Captain Hallowell being aware of the difficulty of breaking men off from their guns when once they have begun to use them, determined not to suffer a shot to be fired on board the Swiftsure till the sails were all clued up and the ship anchored in her station. As the British fleet bore down towards the scene of action, they were first saluted by a shower of shot and shells from two batteries on the island, and were then obliged to receive the whole fire from the broadsides of the French line full into their bows. The men being employed aloft in furling sails, and below hauling the braces, ranging the cables, and preparing every thing for placing the ships in the best situation at anchor, it is a providential circumstance that greater slaughter was not the consequence; especially, as it is but justice to observe, that the French received us with cool deliberate courage, and did not open their fire till we were within half-gun-shot distance of them, when both sides hoisted their colours. A shot striking the larboard bow of the Swiftsure several feet below the water mark, was a considerable annoyance; the chain-pumps were obliged to be kept constantly at work, nor could the leak be kept completely under; she had four feet water in the hold from the commencement to the end of the action.

[z] The lights which had been hoisted, must have gone overboard when the mizen-mast fell.

the quarter of the Franklin and bows of l'Orient. At the fame inftant the Alexander paffed under the ftern of the French Admiral and anchored withinfide on his larboard quarter, raking him, and keeping up a fevere fire of mufketry on his decks. The laft fhip which entered the bloody conflict was the Leander. Captain Thompfon bore up to the Culloden on feeing her ftrike, that he might afford any affiftance in his power to get her off from her unfortunate fituation, but finding that nothing could be done, and unwilling that his fervices fhould be loft where they could be moft effective, he made fail for the fcene of action, and took his ftation with great judgment athwart hawfe[a] of the Franklin; by which manœuvre he was enabled to do confiderable damage to the enemy without expofing his own fhip to the greateft danger. In the van, four of the French fhips had already ftruck their colours to the Britifh flag. The battle now raged chiefly in the centre. The Franklin, l'Orient, Tonnant, and Heureux, were in hot action, making every exertion to recover the glory that had been loft by their comrades. At three minutes paft nine o'clock a fire was obferved to have broken out in the cabin of l'Orient; to that point Captain Hallowell ordered as many guns as could be fpared from firing on the Franklin to be directed; and, at the fame time, that Captain Allen of marines, fhould throw in the whole fire of his mufketry into the enemy's quarter, while the Alexander on the

---

[a] A fea term, meaning acrofs the headmoft part of a fhip as fhe lies at anchor.

other side was keeping up an incessant shower of shot to the same point. The conflagration now began to rage with dreadful fury: still the French Admiral sustained the honour of his flag with heroic firmness; but at length a period was put to his exertions by a cannon ball, which cut him asunder: he had before received three desperate wounds, one on the head, two in his body, but could not be prevailed on to quit his station on the arm-chest. His Captain, Casa Bianca, fell by his side. Several of the officers and men seeing the impracticability of extinguishing the fire, which had now extended itself along the upper decks, and was flaming up the masts, jumped overboard; some supporting themselves on spars and pieces of wreck, others swimming with all their might to escape the dreaded catastrophe. Shot flying in all directions, dashed many of them to pieces; others were picked up by the boats of the fleet, or dragged into the lower ports, of the nearest ships: the British sailors humanely stretched forth their hands to save a fallen enemy, though the battle at that moment raged with uncontrolled fury. The Swiftsure, that was anchored within half-pistol-shot of the larboard bow of l'Orient, saved the lives of the commissary, first lieutenant, and ten men, who were drawn out of the water into the lower deck ports during the hottest part of the action. The situation of the Alexander and Swiftsure was perilous in the extreme. The expected explosion of such a ship as l'Orient, was to be dreaded as involving all around in certain destruction. Captain Hallowell, however, determined not to move from his devoted station, though repeatedly urged to do so. He perceived the advantage he possessed of being to windward of the burning ship. Captain Ball was not so fortunate; he twice had the mortification to perceive that the fire of the enemy had communicated to his own ship. He was obliged therefore to change his birth and move a little further off.

Admiral Nelson, who had received a very severe wound on his head, and was obliged to be carried off the deck, was informed by Captain Berry of the situation of the enemy. Forgetting his own sufferings, he hastened on deck, impelled by the purest humanity, and gave directions that every exertion should be made to save as many lives as possible. All the boats of the Vanguard, and of the nearest ships that could swim, were sent on this service, and above seventy Frenchmen were saved by the exertion of those so lately employed in their destruction. The van of our fleet having finished for the present their part in the glorious struggle, had now a fine view of the two lines illumined by the flames of the ill-fated foe; the colours of the contending powers being plainly distinguished. The moon, which had risen, opposing her cold light to the warm glow of the fire beneath, added to the grand and solemn picture. The flames had by this time made such progress that an explosion was instantly expected, yet the enemy on the lower deck, either insensible of the danger that surrounded them, or impelled by the laſt paroxyſms of deſpair and vengeance, continued to fire upon us.

At thirty-ſeven minutes paſt nine the fatal exploſion happened. The fire communicated to the magazine, and l'Orient blew up with a craſhing ſound that deafened all around her. The tremulous motion, felt to the very bottom of each ſhip, was like that of an earthquake; the fragments were driven ſuch a vaſt height into the air that ſome moments elapſed before they could deſcend, and then the greateſt apprehenſion was formed from the volumes of burning matter which threatened to fall on the decks and rigging of the ſurrounding ſhips.

Fortunately, however, no material damage occurred. A port-fire fell into the main-royal of the Alexander, and ſhe once more was in danger of ſharing the ſame fate as the enemy, but by the ſkill and exertions of Captain Ball it was ſoon extinguiſhed. Two large pieces of the wreck dropped into the main and foretops of the Swiftſure, but happily the men were withdrawn from thoſe places.

An awful ſilence reigned for ſeveral minutes, as if the contending ſquadrons, ſtruck with horror at the dreadful event, which in an inſtant had hurled ſo many brave men into the air, had forgotten their hoſtile rage in pity for the ſufferers. But ſhort was the pauſe of death: vengeance ſoon rouſed the drooping ſpirits of the enemy. The Franklin, now bearing the French Commander's flag, opened her fire with redoubled fury on the Defence and Swiftsure, and gave the signal for renewed hostilities; the latter being disengaged from her late formidable adversary, had leisure to direct her whole fire into the quarter of the foe that had thus presumed to break the solemn silence; and in a very short time, by the well directed and steady fire of these two ships, and the Leander on her bows, the Franklin called for quarter, and struck to a superior force.

The Alexander and the Majestic, and occasionally the Swiftsure, were now the only British ships engaged; but the commander of the latter finding that he could not direct his guns clear of the Alexander, who had dropped between him and the Tonnant, and fearful lest he should fire into a friend, desisted, although he was severely annoyed by the shot of the Tonnant which was falling thick about him. Most of our ships were so cut up in their masts and rigging that they were unable to set any sail or move from their stations. About three o'clock on the morning of the 2d of August the firing ceased entirely, both squadrons being equally exhausted with fatigue. At four, however, just as the day began to dawn, the Alexander and Majestic recommenced the action with the Tonnant, Guillaume Tell, Genereux, and Timoleon. The Heureux and Mercure had fallen out of the line and anchored a considerable distance to leeward.

Captain Miller, perceiving the unequal contest, bore down to assist his friends, and began a furious cannonade on the enemy. The Theseus had as yet fortunately received but little damage in her masts and rigging, and that had been repaired by the active exertions of her commander as soon as the first part of the action in the van had terminated in our favour.

L'Artemise frigate, stationed on the left of the centre of the French line, fired a broadside at the Theseus, and then struck her colours. Captain Miller dispatched an officer to take possession of her, but just as the boat had come within a short distance, she burst into a flame, and soon after blew up.

This unofficer-like conduct, replete with treachery, will reflect eternal disgrace on the name of Estandlet, who commanded her. After having surrendered his ship by striking his ensign and pendant, and conscious that he was then secure from immediate danger, he set fire to her, and with most of his crew escaped to the shore.[a]

[a] The fate of the Artemise frigate is rather peculiar, a former commander having displayed a still more atrocious and deliberate act of villany. Citizen Charbonniere, commanding the Boudouse, being in company with another French frigate, fell in with and captured a British merchantman, which, of course, made no resistance. He took the captain and crew out of the vessel, and brought them on board his frigate, and there, in cold blood, put them all to death. The captain of the other French frigate humanely remonstrated against this needless act of blood; but Charbonniere urged a decree of the convention, which ordained that all British prisoners should be put to death; the other argued that at least he might take them to Toulon (near which port they were), as it would never be too late to put the decree in execution, which had probably been passed in a moment of frenzy, and would undoubtedly soon be repealed. These humane arguments had no effect on the sanguinary monster, for he caused them all to be taken on the forecastle and shot to the number of eleven, among whom was the captain's son, a lad of twelve years old, who in vain interceded for his father's life, as the unhappy father did for mercy towards his child. This anecdote was related to me by an officer of the strictest honour and veracity, who assured me he was in the Bay of Tunis at the time Charbonniere was there also, and having heard this story of him, and wishing to ascertain the truth or falsehood of it, he waited on the French Consul for that purpose, who

At six o'clock the Leander, having as yet received little damage, was ordered by signal from the Admiral to assist the ships engaged, which she accordingly obeyed. At this time the action between our three ships Alexander, Majestic, and Theseus, and the Guillaume Tell, Genereux, Tonnant, and Timoleon, had become very distant, as the latter continued imperceptibly to drop to leeward, and the Theseus was obliged to veer on two cables to keep within reach of them.

At eight a. m. the Goliath bore down and anchored near the Theseus, the French ships having brought to again. The fire of our ships was now chiefly turned on the Heureux and Mercure, which were soon obliged to surrender. The Timoleon was ashore, and the Tonnant was rendered a complete wreck. Thus circumstanced, and perceiving that few if any of our ships were in a condition to make sail, Rear Admiral Ville Neuve, in the Guillaume Tell of 80 guns, resolved to lose no time in escaping from the certain fate that awaited him. About noon he got under weigh, as also did the Genereux of 74 guns, and La Justice and La Diane frigates. The instant

---

candidly acknowledged that the fact was too true, and that the deed was reprobated by the whole French nation; yet how could that be, when we find that the French government soon afterwards removed this assassin from the Boudouse to the command of the Artemise, a fine new frigate; and afterwards promoted him to the command of a line of battle ship? The account further adds, that the fishermen's wives, apprehensive lest their husbands might, by way of retaliation, suffer a similar fate if they fell into the hands of the English, were so enraged against Charbonniere, that they insulted him grossly as he was proceeding from Toulon to Marseilles, and his life was in such danger from them that he was allowed an armed force to guard him. We have since heard that this cruel monster has gone to answer for the bloody act before the most just of tribunals.

Sir Horatio Nelson perceived what they were about, he dispatched the Zealous, by signal, to intercept them. Unfortunately none of the windward ships were in a condition to second his attempt to stop the fugitives. He did, however, all that could possibly be done; as they passed by him he received and returned the fire of each in succession: the damage he sustained in this contest prevented him from tacking, and the Admiral, with his usual judgment, gave the signal of recall. In the morning of the 3d of August there remained in the Bay only the Timoleon and Tonnant of the French line that were not captured or destroyed. The former being aground near the coast, the Captain (Trullet) with his crew escaped in their boats after setting fire to her, and in a short time she blew up. A flag of truce had been sent to the Tonnant, but she refused to submit; on which the Theseus and Leander going down to her, and the Swiftsure following, she struck without further resistance. This completed the conquest of the French fleet in the Bay of Aboukir, and the British flag rode triumphant on the Egyptian seas.

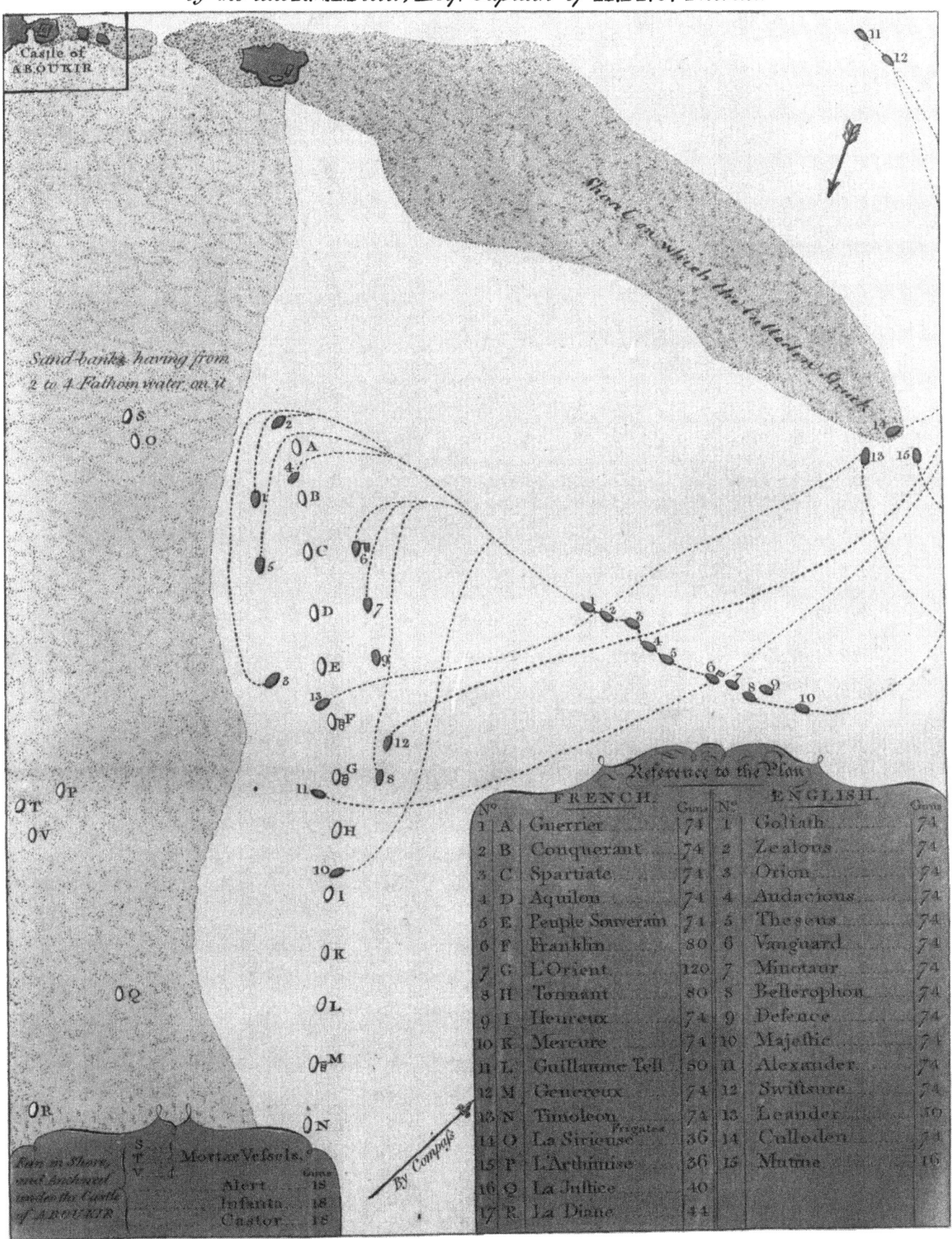

CHAPTER V.

>........................ Porte
> Al mar tributo di cœlesti umori
> Per sette il Nilo sue famose porte,
> E per cente altre ancor foci minori.
> E naviga oltra la città, dal forte
> Greco fondata a i Greci abitatori:
> Et oltra Faro, esola già che lunge
> Giacque dal lido, al lido or si congiunge. TASSO, can. 15, v. 16.

HAPPILY impreſſed with early ſentiments of religion, Sir Horatio Nelſon did not, in the moment of victory, forget to whom that victory was firſt to be attributed. The finger of Providence had been viſible from the entrance of the Britiſh fleet into the Mediterranean to the concluſion of the important action in the Bay of Aboukir. For though we ought not perhaps on every trivial occurrence of life to look for a particular mark of Divine ſuperintendency, yet both ſcripture and hiſtory give us authority to attribute thoſe great events of life, by which kingdoms and nations to future generations are affected, to the particular and immediate ordinance of the Almighty, acting upon apparently natural cauſes, but ſo combined as to produce effects moſt beneficial to the general welfare of mankind.

The French nation, collectively and individually, had thrown off all religion, and had openly declared to the world, that man was free to think and act for himself; that God, if God there was, could not, or would not, controul him. In their public assembly of the representatives of the people, it had been deliberately argued, and at length decreed, that the existence of a Deity was unfounded, and consequently that all worship towards him was absurd; and, what was hardly less impious, it was afterwards decreed by a fresh law, that a God did exist, and that homage might be paid to him. Christianity, that mild system of true and disinterested philanthropy, was however entirely laid aside, or made a butt for impious witlings to scoff at. Death was declared to be nothing more than eternal sleep. This doctrine, subversive of all social order, and destroying all the well regulated systems of long established principles, was the favourite topic of every Frenchman, and to disseminate it was his prime object. And as in former times fire and sword were employed to propagate particular dogmas of religion, now the same means are exercised to root out all religions from the face of the globe. Wherever the French armies came, religion felt the blow; being first degraded in the persons of its ministers, it was afterwards, by every means, rendered odious or contemptible to the people. On some occasions, indeed, policy dictated another mode of action, and a seeming respect was at first paid to the established religion of the place; but this seldom lasted long, or was rendered nugatory by the general avowed disbelief in all religion, openly expressed by the French armies.

Many heretofore powerful governments had been overturned by these destroyers, who, flushed with repeated conquests, looked forward to the entire subjection of the world to their arms. The British nation had hitherto proved the forest hindrance to all their prospects: to destroy that power was the principal object of their wishes. Great Britain had long been unrivalled in its commercial engagements; whatever therefore would destroy the principal source of its commerce must ultimately involve the nation itself in destruction.

India had for some time presented itself to the French nation as the desired object through which the British commerce might receive the deepest wound; and the well known hatred which Tippoo Sultaun bore to this nation, afforded to the French the most flattering prospects of success, could they but convey a well disciplined army of their own to aid their sanguinary ally. It appears from various subsequent events, that Egypt was the road through which they proposed to march to India. And Buonapartè seems to have entered into all the schemes of the French government on this head, with his usual activity and enterprize.

When, therefore, he found himself perfectly master of that rich country, and no obstacle of importance intervening; when a junction with the firm ally of France in the Mysore seemed certain; the object of his ambition appeared almost within his grasp. He now only waited for a further reinforcement from France, which was to be sent to him as soon as the government was assured that he had established himself in Egypt. Admiral Brueys, it appears from various documents, was anxious to return to France with his fleet, that he might be ready to revisit the shores of Egypt with the promised reinforcement. But Buonapartè did not choose to be left without a means of retreat, and therefore he insisted upon his remaining on the coast till farther orders.

The Admiral's ship, l'Orient, being too large to cross the bar of the old harbour of Alexandria, it was found necessary to anchor his fleet in the Bay of Aboukir; where, protected by every precaution of art, and aided by the nature of the place, flanked by batteries, sand-banks, rocks, and shoals, he appeared to bid defiance to every hostile attack.

The victory obtained over this fleet at once destroyed all the pleasing dreams of future conquests in the East, which Buonapartè had hitherto indulged. Cut off from a possibility of receiving the promised reinforcements from France, by the annihilation of its fleet, he foresaw that the utmost he could now hope for, was to secure a safe situation for his army in the country where he was. The great change of opinion among his newly acquired subjects, occasioned by the event of this battle, which convinced them that their invaders were not invincible, made his situation sufficiently uneasy, without any other circumstances to render it more so; but of them too he had a sufficient share.

Had the storm which damaged Rear-Admiral Nelson's ship, when first he came into the Mediterranean, continued longer than it did, he would in all probability have been disabled from further exertions at that time; by this gale the Toulon fleet was detained longer in port, which gave an opportunity to Commodore Troubridge to form a junction with the Admiral. At length the French fleet sailed from Toulon, and proceeded by Sardinia to Malta; but we made our course for Naples, and missed them. Had our squadron fallen in with the enemy previous to the capture of Malta, and had a battle been fought, though it had terminated in our favour, as, in all humility, we may suppose, the utmost that we could have done would have been to have captured several of their men of war, and dispersed the rest; but as we well know, in such an event, our own ships must have suffered much, the rest of the convoy with troops might have escaped, and proceeding to its destination, would have effected its purpose; in which case the natives of Egypt would have been ignorant of the naval defeat of their invaders, and would have had no hopes of future succour from us; and from the crippled state of our ships, without a port to go to for repairs, the French would have been enabled to pour in fresh supplies of men and ammunition, and the fertile banks of the Nile would, without opposition, have been completely subjugated by the power of the invader. The same may be said had the two fleets met, as was expected, on the 22d of June, when they crossed each other in the night. But now their fleet, which was to have fecured to them a fafe retreat in cafe of failure, or if fuccefs had crowned their efforts, was to have convoyed frefh fupplies from the mother country, was annihilated, all hopes of retreat were cut off, all profpect of reinforcements was deftroyed.

The Admiral faw the grand effects that muft refult from the victory he had obtained, and with his mind filled with gratitude to that God whofe arm had been ftretched out to fave his fleet from the numerous dangers that furrounded it, iffued the following order, that does equal honour to his head and heart.

Vanguard, off the mouth of the Nile, 2d *Aug.* 1798.
" Almighty God having bleffed his Majefty's arms with victory, the Admiral intends returning public thankfgiving for the fame at two o'clock this day; and he recommends every fhip doing the fame as foon as convenient."

Accordingly, he fet the example on board his own fhip immediately, having the proper prayers and thankfgivings offered up on the quarter-deck by the chaplain, himfelf, officers, and crew, attending. The other fhips that were leaft difabled did the fame; fome of the fleet were fo bufily employed in knotting and fplicing their rigging, or fifhing their tottering mafts, that they were obliged to poftpone it till with greater eafe and fecurity this neceffary duty could be performed. The French prifoners on board the Britifh fhips were aftonifhed at the folemnity with which the officers and men offered up their orisons to the Almighty at such a moment. When flushed with a conquest so important, the mind of man is too often prone to forget the hand that preserved him through past dangers. Some of the French officers observed, " that it was not surprising we could preserve order and discipline, when we could impress the minds of our men with such sentiments after a victory so great, and at a moment of such seeming confusion."

The Admiral next issued the following memorandum to each of the ships of his fleet.

Vanguard, off the Mouth of the Nile, 2d Aug. 1798.

" The Admiral most heartily congratulates the captains, officers, seamen, and marines, of the squadron he has the honour to command, on the event of the late action; and he desires they will accept his most sincere and cordial thanks for their gallant behaviour in this glorious battle. It must strike forcibly every British seaman, how superior their conduct is, when in discipline and good order, to the riotous behaviour of lawless Frenchmen.

" The squadron may be assured, the Admiral will not fail, with his dispatches, to represent their truly meritorious conduct in the strongest terms to the Commander in Chief."

This flattering testimony of approbation from the Admiral, was truly acceptable to the several individuals that composed his fleet; and the important advantages so lately obtained by an inferior over a superior force, could not fail to make a strong impression on the minds of all, that the benefits arising from a strict obedience, and steady discipline, can alone ensure success on the sea.

It is to be hoped that the glorious event of this day may have its due influence on future generations of our brave seamen; who must be convinced that the honour of the British navy can alone be supported and maintained by a steady adherence to the first of military and naval duties, *Obedience*.

The fleet, which under the command of Sir Horatio Nelson had achieved this important victory, had been trained in the school of a Noble Admiral,[b] whose exertions to support the discipline of that part of the navy under his command, have been eminently successful, particularly during that eventful period when the machinations of our domestic enemies, in almost every other part of our marine, had but too well succeeded; I say domestic enemies, for I do not believe that our republican neighbours had any hand in the business, but that it originated and extended itself solely from the baleful exertions of a set of vultures who seem to exist only to torture and destroy the country that protects and supports them. It is now well known that hardly a ship of our fleets, either abroad or at home, was

[b] Several deep laid schemes, of the most sanguinary tendency, were detected and defeated, and the ringleaders brought to immediate punishment, in the fleet blockading Cadiz, under command of the Earl of St. Vincent.

[c] It is certain that a similar mutiny existed at the same time in the marine of our enemies, which prevented them from taking advantage of the confusion and disorganized state of our fleets.

without an emiffary from the correfponding focieties. Many of them, who have fince fuffered for their crimes, have confeffed that they were employed for the horrid purpofe of diforganizing our fleets, and opening, through the defection of our navy, a way for the entrance of every fpecies of anarchy and deftruction. Certain it is, that in every mutiny that has been fuccefsful, we have reafon to believe that a very fmall part of the crew have influenced and directed the operations of the whole. A thoroughbred Britifh feaman is by no means inclined to refift the orders of his fuperiors, or to wifh the deftruction of that profeffion to which he owes his livelihood and fupport. It has been almoft univerfally found, that every mutiny has originated among the waifters or landfmen on board; who, from having more opportunities and leifure, get together and plot mifchief, while the feaman is either bufily engaged in repairing the damages time or hard weather has made in his wardrobe, or during his watch, in knotting, fplicing, and many other avocations to which he well knows how to turn his hand.

May the event of the day I have had the honour to commemorate, be deeply engraved on the mind of every feaman—May future ages emulate the glorious example by following the fteps that led to it—May Britifh failors be convinced that their hardy courage, without the aid of difcipline and fubordination, will never give them the palm of victory—May they ever be affured that by a cheerful obedience to the commands of their officers, in whofe courage and fkill they may always confidently rely, they are attending to their own truest interests: and then, with the blessings of that Providence who has hitherto supported them against the united powers of the universe, they may look forward to a continuance of the same eminent situation they now hold; and on their proper element, may bid defiance to the world in arms.

On the 5th the Leander sailed from the Bay; in her went Captain Berry of the Vanguard, bearing the dispatches of Sir Horatio Nelson to the Commander in Chief the Earl of St. Vincent, off Cadiz, giving an account of the glorious victory he had accomplished: unhappily this ill-fated ship was not destined to convey the wished-for intelligence; for on her passage she fell in with the Genereux of 74 guns, which had escaped from the action, and had received very little damage in it. The Frenchman was more than completely manned, her usual complement being 700, she had now 900 men on board; whereas the Leander was short of her complement, which at the most never exceeded 343. After gallantly defending the honour of the British flag till resistance was no longer allowable, the ship being perfectly unmanageable by the loss of her masts, and to save a further useless effusion of blood, Captain Thompson was obliged to surrender to a superior force; the dispatches were previously destroyed by Captain Berry[d]. The enemy, on taking

---

[d] The particulars of this action are so well detailed in a letter from Captain Thompson to Evan Nepean, Esq. that I shall here give it at length, as it must be highly interesting to those who have not seen it, and those who have, will not think it time misspent to re-peruse it.

poffeffion of the Leander, did not follow the example that had fo recently been fet them; for no fooner had the French crew

Copy of a letter from Captain Thompson, of his Majesty's late ship the Leander, to Evan Nepean, Esq.

SIR, On board the Lazarette, at Trieste, October 14, 1798.

It is with extreme pain I have to relate to you the capture of his Majesty's fhip Leander, late under my command, by a French 74 gun fhip, after a clofe action of fix hours and a half. On the 18th of Auguft laft, being within five or fix miles of the weft end of Goza, near the ifland of Candia, we difcovered at day-break a large fail on the fouth-eaft quarter, ftanding directly for the Leander; we were then becalmed, but the ftranger bringing up a fine breeze from the fouthward, we foon made him to be a large fhip of the line. As the Leander was in officers and men upwards of eighty fhort of complement, and had on board a number which were wounded on the firft, I did not confider myfelf juftified in feeking an action with a fhip that appeared of fuch confiderable fuperiority in point of fize; I therefore took every means in my power to avoid it: I however foon found that our inferiority of failing made it inevitable, and I therefore, with all fail fet, fteered the Leander a courfe which I judged would receive our adverfary to the beft advantage, fhould he bring us to battle. At eight o'clock the ftrange fhip (ftill continuing to have the good fortune of the wind) had approached us within a long random fhot, and had Neapolitan colours hoifted, which he now changed to Turkifh; but this deception was of no avail, as I plainly made him to be French.—At nine he had ranged up within half a gun fhot of our weather quarter; I therefore hauled the Leander up fufficiently to bring the broadfide to bear, and immediately commenced a vigorous cannonade on him, which he inftantly returned. The fhips continued nearing each other until half paft ten, keeping up a conftant and heavy firing. At this time I perceived the enemy intending to run us on board, and the Leander being very much cut up in rigging, fails, and yards, I was unable, with the light air that blew, to prevent it. He ran us on board on the larboard bow, and continued alongfide us for fome time: a moft fpirited and well directed fire, however, from our fmall party of marines (commanded by the ferjeant) on the poop, and from the quarter-deck, prevented the enemy from taking advantage of his good fortune, and he was repulfed in all his efforts to make an impreffion on us. The firing from the great guns was all this time kept up with the fame vigour, and a light breeze giving the fhips way, I was enabled to fteer clear of the enemy, and foon afterwards had the fatisfaction to luff under his ftern, and paffing him within ten yards, diftinctly difcharged every gun from the Leander into him. As from henceforward was nothing but a continued feries of heavy firing within piftol fhot, without any wind, and the fea as fmooth as glafs, I feel it unneceffary to give you the detail of the effects of every fhot, which muft be obvious from our fituation; I fhall therefore content myfelf with affuring you, that a moft vigorous cannonade was kept up from the Leander, without the fmalleft intermiffion, until half paft three in the afternoon. At this time, the enemy having paffed our bows with a light breeze, and brought himfelf on our ftarboard fide, we found that our guns on that fide were nearly all difabled by the wreck of our own fpars that had fallen on this fide. This produced a ceffation of our fire, and the enemy took this time to afk us if we had furrendered. The Leander was now totally ungovernable, not having a thing ftanding but the fhattered remains of the fore and main mafts, and the got on board the Leander, than all hands were employed in the moſt rapacious plunder; Captain Thompſon had received a ſevere wound in the action, yet was he by no means ſafe from the rough treatment of the ferocious plunderers.

The Genereux, with her prize, proceeded to Corfu; from whence Captains Thompſon and Berry were ſent to Trieſte, and after performing quarantine there, were permitted to return to England on their parole of honour, where the ſentence of a

bowſprit, her hull cut to pieces, and the decks full of killed and wounded; and perceiving the enemy, who had only loſt his mizen-top-maſt, approaching to place himſelf athwart our ſtern; in this defenceleſs ſituation, I aſked Captain Berry if he thought we could do more? He coinciding with me that further reſiſtance was vain and impracticable, and, indeed, all hope of ſucceſs having for ſome time vaniſhed, I therefore now directed an anſwer to be given in the affirmative, and the enemy ſoon after took poſſeſſion of his Majeſty's ſhip.

I cannot conclude this account without aſſuring you how much advantage his Majeſty's ſervice derived during this action from the gallantry and activity of Captain Berry, of the Vanguard; I ſhould alſo be wanting in juſtice, if I did not bear teſtimony to the ſteady bravery of the officers and ſeamen of the Leander in this hard conteſt, which, though unſucceſsful in its termination, will ſtill, I truſt, entitle them to the approbation of their country. The enemy proved to be the Genereux, of 74 guns, commanded by M. Lejoille, Chef de Diviſion, who had eſcaped from the action of the 1ſt of Auguſt, and, being the rearmoſt of the French line, had received little or no ſhare of it, having on board 900 men, about 100 of whom we found had been killed in the preſent conteſt, and 188 wounded. I encloſe a liſt of the loſs in killed and wounded in the Leander, and have the honour to be, &c.

THOMAS THOMPSON.

A return of officers and men killed and wounded on board his Majesty's ship Leander, on the 18th August, 1798.

Officers killed: Mr. Peter Downs, midſhipman; Mr. Gibſon, midſhipman of the Caroline; Mr. Edward Haddon, midſhipman; 24 ſeamen killed.—Marines killed: Serjeant Dair, and 7 privates.—Total: 3 officers, 24 ſeamen, 1 ſerjeant, 7 marines, killed.——Officers wounded: Captain Thompſon, badly; Lieutenant Taylor; Lieutenant Swiney; Mr. Lee, maſter; Mr Mathias, boatſwain, badly; Mr. Lacky, maſter's mate; Mr. Nailor, midſhipman.—41 ſeamen; 9 marines.—Total, 7 officers, 41 ſeamen, 9 marines, wounded.

THOMAS THOMPSON.

court-martial did ample honour to the gallant conduct of thefe two officers[e].

[e] At a court-martial affembled and held on board his Majesty's fhip America, on Monday, December 17th, 1798, at Sheernefs:

The Court, in purfuance of an order from the Commiffioners for executing the office of Lord High Admiral of Great Britain and Ireland, &c. dated the 13th of the prefent month, December, proceeded to inquire into the conduct of Captain Thomas Thompfon, commander of his Majesty's fhip the Leander, and fuch of the officers and ship's company as were on board of her at the time fhe furrendered, and was taken poffeffion of by the Genereux, a French fhip of 74 guns, and to try them refpectively for the fame accordingly. And the Court having heard the evidence brought forward in fupport of Captain Thompfon's narrative of the capture of the faid fhip, and having very maturely and deliberately confidered the whole, is of opinion—That the gallant, and almost unprecedented defence of Captain Thompfon, of his Majefty's late fhip the Leander, againft fo fuperior a force as that of the Genereux, is deferving of every praife his Country and this Court can give; and that his conduct, with that of the officers and men under his command, reflects not only the higheft honour on himfelf and them, but to their Country at large: and the Court do therefore moft honourably acquit Captain Thompfon, his officers, and fhip's company; and he and they are hereby moft honourably acquitted accordingly.

Signed by the Court.

The Prefident, after the fentence was read, addreffed Captain Thompfon nearly as follows: "Captain Thompfon, I feel the moft lively pleafure in returning you the fword with which you have fo bravely maintained the honour of your King and Country; the more fo, as I am convinced, that when you are again called upon to draw it in their defence, you will add frefh laurels to the wreath you have already fo nobly won." The thanks of the Court were alfo given to Sir Edward Berry, who was prefent on this occafion, for the gallant and active zeal he manifefted, by giving his affiftance on board the Leander, in the combat with the Genereux: and upon the return of Captain Thompfon to the fhore from the court-martial, he was faluted with three cheers by all the fhips in harbour at Sheernefs.

It is with concern we contemplate the contraft of French manners with our own. Inftead of that humane attention to the wants and diftreffes of the prifoners which has always been fhewn by us to thofe that fall into our hands, we find by a variety of inftances that they feldom or ever treat their prifoners with common humanity. By a letter from Captain Berry, publifhed foon after his return to England, we learn that the French, on taking poffeffion of the Leander, not only plundered the officers and crew of every thing they poffeffed, but afterwards by their cruelty and neglect expofed the fick and wounded to almoft certain death.—Mr. Stanley, the Britifh Conful at Triefte, in a letter to the Lords Commiffioners of the Admiralty, ftates, that forty of the crew of the Leander arrived at that port in a dreadful ftate, having been forced by the Commander at Corfu into fmall veffels, in which, wounded and difeafed, expofed to the inclemency of the weather for feventeen days, and with a very fcanty allowance of bad food, they fcarcely furvived the feverity of their treatment.

But to return to the victorious fleet in the Bay of Aboukir. The utmost exertions were now to be made, to render the captured ships fit for a voyage, that they might be transported to the harbours of Britain as memorials of the prowess of her sons. Our own ships too, required repair; most of them were severely crippled in their masts and rigging, many of them damaged in their hulls, and all so completely shaken, that much was to be done before they could with safety venture on so long a voyage. Sir Horatio Nelson sent Captain Troubridge and Captain Hallowell with a flag of truce to Aboukir to offer an exchange of prisoners; and it was agreed on the part of the French commander, that receipts should be given for all the French prisoners sent on shore, who should also engage not to serve, or bear arms against us, until regularly exchanged. They were also to find boats to transport them from the ships to the shore, as most of the boats of the two fleets were destroyed or damaged in the action. Accordingly the treaty on our part was put in execution without delay; the wounded, who had been treated with the utmost humanity and kindness, were first landed, and the rest followed; but no sooner had they reached the shore, than, by orders from the Commander in Chief, they were formed into a battalion, and called the Nautic Legion. It is needless to comment on this breach of a solemn engagement: none but the abettors of French principles will attempt to justify it; that such there are on British ground is melancholy to reflect; but if they had witnessed, as I have done, the various mifchiefs arifing from them, they furely would blufh to think they could ever have defended fuch conduct!

On the 8th the ifland was taken poffeffion of; as it was obferved that fome of the enemy had made towards it, Captain Hallowell brought off two brafs thirteen-inch mortars made by General Gomier, and two brafs twelve-pounders. The iron guns he threw into the fea, and deftroyed the platforms. This ifland is fituated to the northward of Aboukir about two miles. In the evening of the fame day, Captain Troubridge, who had now fucceeded in getting the Culloden off the rocks, and had in part repaired the damages fhe had fuftained, captured a boat in which was a courier bearing difpatches and letters from Buonapartè at Cairo, which place he left ten days fince. Thefe intercepted letters form the firft part of the curious collection which have fince been publifhed in England, and which, as they contain the undifguifed fentiments of the writers, may be faid to give the beft infight into the hiftory of this famous expedition, by which France got rid of more than forty thoufand of her beft foldiers. Moft of thefe letters, which were of a private nature, have very properly been fuppreffed; they contained a melancholy proof of the depravity of morals which prevails throughout the new republic; the writers of them, though complaining of the perilous ftate in which they were, feemed to lament it only becaufe they were deprived of the power of continuing in the fame courfe of debauchery they had before indulged in; several letters disclosed the most treacherous dispositions; being to the wives or sisters of friends with whom the writers held illicit correspondence; all, however, concurred in expressing an abhorrence of their present forlorn situation; in want of every comfort, and deprived of many necessaries; in a burning climate, exposed to the worst of diseases, and surrounded on all sides by ferocious enemies, whose numbers they daily increased by their insolent and rapacious conduct; so that they could not stir a few yards from their camp without being murdered by the wandering Bedouins, who constantly hovered round their rear ready to cut off every straggler. On the 10th a square-rigged vessel was discovered in the offing; the Swiftsure was ordered, by signal, to chace, and immediately got under weigh: in the evening we came up with, and took her; she proved to be the French national corvette La Fortune, of 16 guns and 70 men, commanded by Citoyen Marchand, Lieutenant de Vaisseau. On board of her were several officers, and amongst the rest a surgeon on the staff, who, it seems, had suffered his sense of the dangers and difficulties he was exposed to by the expedition, to get the better of his prudence, and had expressed his disapprobation of it with so much acrimony, that the Commander in Chief had, by way of punishment, put him into the corvette bound on a cruise off Damietta. When captured by us he was ignorant of the event of the battle in Aboukir Bay; as soon as he was informed of it, and that his brother was killed on board l'Orient, his grief knew no bounds, he threw his snuff-box overboard, and expressed the most lively sorrow; when suddenly recovering himself with the observation, " c'est la fortuna de la guerre," he turned to the spectators and said he would amuse them, and instantly pulled from his pocket a ludicrous figure of a monk, with which he so entertained himself and the company, that in a few moments all care for his brother, his country, or himself, now a prisoner, was forgotten. How perfectly characteristic of the inhabitants of the soi-disant *great nation!* a few moments serve for grief of the most poignant nature, and their buoyant minds turn with double relish to frolic and folly. In the evening of the same day we descried three sail which we supposed to have been our frigates, so long wished-for and expected, but they did not venture near enough to let us into the secret. On Saturday we anchored with our prize in the fleet; some of the prisoners were sent on board the Guerrier to take their passage for Europe, and the next day the surgeon, of whom I have given some account, was sent on board the Majestic, to his great joy, as he was in fear of being returned to the army on shore; but was now to attend some of the wounded Frenchmen who were to go home in the Majestic. On the 12th the Swiftsure again got under weigh, and sailed towards Alexandria to watch the motions of the enemy in that port; in the evening she returned to the fleet, but instantly sailed again after three sail in the offing, which first made towards the Bay and then retreated with expedition: the whole ship's company therefore were obliged to remain at quarters, although we suspected them to be our frigates, as it is always proper to be prepared for the worst. At seven o'clock the next morning we again descried the strange sails, and made the private and several other signals to them. At length one of them bore down to us: she proved to be the Bonne Citoyen; and the others, who then joined, we found to be the Emerald and Alcmene. We all returned to the Bay to the great satisfaction of the Admiral, who had been greatly distressed for want of frigates. On the 13th the Admiral dispatched the Mutine brig with the Honourable Captain Capel to Naples, bearing duplicates of the dispatches sent by the Leander to the Earl of St. Vincent. Captain Capel came by land from thence to England, and on the 2d of October 1798 arrived at the Admiralty with the wished-for intelligence of the defeat of the French fleet on the coast of Egypt.

This work would by no means answer the expectations of the public, should I omit to insert the very excellent letter of the noble Admiral to the Earl of St. Vincent; I have therefore given it with the other letters brought to the Admiralty by Captain Capel.

Admiralty-Office, October 2d, 1798.

The Honourable Captain Capel, of his Majesty's sloop Mutine, arrived this morning with dispatches from Rear-Admiral Sir Horatio Nelson, K. B. to Evan Nepean, Esq. secretary of the Admiralty, of which the following are copies:

SIR, *Vanguard, Mouth of the Nile, August 7th, 1798.*

Herewith I have the honour to transmit you a copy of my letter to the Earl of St. Vincent, together with a line of battle of the English and French squadrons; also a list of killed and wounded. I have the pleasure to inform you, that eight of our ships have already top-gallant-yards across, and ready for any service; the others, with the prizes, will soon be ready for sea. In an event of this importance, I have thought it right to send Captain Capel with a copy of my letter (to the commander in chief) over-land, which, I hope, their lordships will approve; and beg leave to refer them to Captain Capel, who is a most excellent officer, and fully able to give every information; and I beg leave to recommend him to their Lordships' notice. I have the honour to be, &c.

HORATIO NELSON.

P.S. The island I have taken possession of, and brought off the two thirteen-inch mortars, all the brass guns, and destroyed the iron ones.

To Evan Nepean, Esq.

MY LORD, *Vanguard, Mouth of the Nile, Aug. 3d, 1798.*

Almighty God has blessed his Majesty's arms in the late battle, by a great victory over the fleet of the enemy, whom I attacked at sunset on the 1st of August off the mouth of the

Nile. The enemy were moored in a ftrong line of battle for defending the entrance of the Bay (of fhoals), flanked by numerous gun-boats, four frigates, and a battery of guns and mortars on an ifland in their van; but nothing could withftand the fquadron your Lordfhip did me the honour to place under my command. Their high ftate of difcipline is well known to you, and with the judgment of the captains, together with their valour, and that of the officers and men of every defcription, it was abfolutely irrefiftible. Could any thing from my pen add to the characters of the captains, I would write it with pleafure, but that is impoffible.

I have to regret the lofs of Captain Weftcott, of the Majeftic, who was killed early in the action; but the fhip was continued to be fo well fought by her firft lieutenant, Mr. Cuthbert, that I have given him an order to command her till your Lordfhips' pleafure is known. The fhips of the enemy, all but their two rear fhips, are nearly difmafted; and thofe two, with two frigates, I am forry to fay, made their efcape; nor was it, I affure you, in my power to prevent them. Captain Hood moft handfomely endeavoured to do it, but I had no fhip in a condition to fupport the Zealous, and I was obliged to call her in.

The fupport and affiftance I have received from Captain Berry, cannot be fufficiently expreffed. I was wounded in the head, and obliged to be carried off the deck, but the fervice fuffered no lofs by that event. Captain Berry was fully equal to the important fervice then going on, and to him I muft beg leave to refer you for every information relative to this victory. He will prefent you with the flag of the fecond in command, that of the commander in chief being burnt in l'Orient.

Herewith I tranfmit you lifts of the killed and wounded, and the lines of battle of ourfelves and the French.

I have the honour to be, &c.
HORATIO NELSON.

To Admiral the Earl of St. Vincent,
Commander in Chief, &c. &c. off Cadiz.

LINE OF BATTLE.

Ships Names.	Captains.	Guns.	Men.
Culloden	T. Troubridge	74	590
Thefeus	R. W. Miller	74	590
Alexander	Alexander J. Ball	74	590
Vanguard	Rear-Adm. Sir H. Nelfon, K. B. / Edward Berry	74	595
Minotaur	Thomas Louis	74	640
Leander	T. B. Thompfon	50	343
Swiftfure	B. Hallowell	74	590
Audacious	Davidge Gould	74	590
Defence	John Peyton	74	590
Zealous	Samuel Hood	74	590
Orion	Sir James Saumarez	74	590
Goliath	Thomas Foley	74	590
Majeftic	George B. Weftcott	74	590
Bellerophon	Henry D. E. Darby	74	590
La Mutine, Brig	T. M. Hardy	14	110

HORATIO NELSON.

Vanguard, off the Mouth of the Nile, Aug. 3d, 1798.

FRENCH LINE OF BATTLE.

Ships Names.	Captains.	Guns.	Men.	
Le Guerrier	——————	74	600	Taken.
Le Conquerant	——————	74	700	Taken.
Le Spartiate	——————	74	700	Taken.
L'Aquilon	——————	74	700	Taken.
Le Souverain Peuple	——————	74	700	Taken.
Le Franklin	Blanquet, firſt Contre-Admiral	80	800	Taken.
L'Orient	Brueys, Admiral and Commander in Chief.	120	1010	Burnt.
Le Tonnant	——————	80	800	Taken.
L'Heureux	——————	74	700	Taken.
Le Timoleon	——————	74	700	Burnt.
Le Mercure	——————	74	700	Taken.
Le Guillaume Tell	Villeneuve, ſecond Contre-Admiral	80	800	Eſcaped.
Le Genereux	——————	74	700	Eſcaped.

HORATIO NELSON.

Vanguard, off the Mouth of the Nile, Aug. 3d, 1798.

FRIGATES.

Ships.	Guns.	Men.	
Le Diane	48	300	Eſcaped.
Le Juſtice	44	300	Eſcaped.
L'Artemiſe	36	250	Burnt.
Le Serieuſe	36	250	Diſmaſted and ſunk.

HORATIO NELSON.

Vanguard off the Mouth of the Nile, Aug. 3d, 1798.

A return of the killed and wounded in his Majesty's ships under the command of Sir Horatio Nelson, K. B. Rear-Admiral of the Blue, in action with the French, at anchor, on the 1st of August 1798, off the Mouth of the Nile.

	KILLED.			WOUNDED.			
Ships Names.	Officers.	Seamen.	Marines.	Officers.	Seamen.	Marines.	Total.
Theseus	0	5	0	2	24	5	35
Alexander	1	13	0	5	48	5	72
Vanguard	3	20	7	7	60	8	105
Minotaur	2	18	3	4	54	6	87
Swiftsure	0	7	0	1	19	2	29
Audacious	0	1	0	2	31	2	36
Defence	0	3	1	0	9	2	15
Zealous	0	1	0	0	7	0	8
Orion	1	11	1	5	9	2	15
Goliath	2	12	7	4	28	9	62
Majestic	3	33	14	3	124	16	193
Bellerophon	4	32	13	5	126	17	197
Leander	0	0	0	0	14	0	14
Total	16	156	46	37	562	78	895

OFFICERS KILLED.

Ships Names.	Officers Names.	Rank.
Vanguard	—— Taddy	Captain of Marines
————————	Thomas Seymour	Midshipman
————————	John G. Taylor	Ditto
Alexander	John Collins	Lieutenant

Orion	—— Baird	Captain's Clerk
Goliath	William Davies	Master's Mate
———	Andrew Brown	Midshipman
Majestic	George B. Westcott	Captain
———	Zebedee Ford	Midshipman
———	Andrew Gilmore	Boatswain.
Bellerophon	Robert Savage Daniel	Lieutenant
———	W. Launder	Ditto
———	George Joliffe	Ditto
———	Thomas Ellison	Master's Mate
Minotaur	J. S. Kirchner	Master
———	Peter Walters	Master's Mate.

OFFICERS WOUNDED.

Vanguard	N. Vassal	Lieutenant
———	T. Adie	Ditto
———	J. Campbell	Admiral's Secretary
———	M. Austin	Boatswain
———	J. Weatherstone	Midshipman
———	George Antrim	Ditto
Theseus	—— Hawkins	Lieutenant
Alexander	Alexander J. Ball, Esq.	Captain
———	J. Creswell	Captain of Marines
———	W. Lawson	Master
———	G. Bully	Midshipman
———	Luke Anderson	Ditto
Audacious	John Jeans	Lieutenant
———	Christopher Font	Gunner

Orion	Sir James Saumarez	Captain
———	Peter Sadler	Boatfwain
———	Philip Richardfon	Midfhipman
———	Charles Miell	Ditto
———	—— Lanfefty	Ditto
Goliath	William Wilkinfon	Lieutenant
———	Law Graves	Midfhipman
———	P. Strachan	Schoolmafter
———	James Payne	Midfhipman
Majeftic	Charles Seward	Midfhipman
———	Charles Royle	Ditto
———	Robert Overton	Captain's Clerk
Bellerophon	H. D. Darby, Efq.	Captain
———	Edward Kirby	Mafter
———	John Hopkins	Captain of Marines
———	—— Chapman	Boatfwain
———	Nicholas Betfon	Midfhipman
Minotaur	Thomas Irwin	Lieutenant
———	John Jewell	Lieutenant of Marines
———	Thomas Foxten	Second Mafter
———	Martin Wills	Midfhipman
Swiftfure	William Smith	Midfhipman

Vanguard, off the Mouth of the Nile,
Aug. 11, 1798.

Sir,

Herewith I fend you a copy of my letter to the Earl of St. Vincent of this date.

I have the honour to be, &c.

HORATIO NELSON.

Evan Nepean, Efq.

Vanguard, off the Mouth of the Nile,
Aug. 11, 1798.

My Lord,

The Swiftsure brought in this morning La Fortune, French corvette, of 18 guns and 70 men.

I have the honour to be, &c.
HORATIO NELSON.

Earl St. Vincent.

Sir Horatio Nelson was aware of the designs the enemy had formed to attack our East Indian possessions in case their Egyptian expedition was crowned with success; he therefore instantly dispatched intelligence of the invasion of Bonapartè, his probable object in it, and the event of the naval combat in the Bay of Aboukir. Lieutenant Duval, of the Zealous, was selected to convey this important intelligence to the East Indies, which he accomplished in time to put the government there sufficiently on its guard, and to counteract the machinations of the enemy, by a sudden and unexpected attack upon Tippoo Sultaun. Thus, at one blow, all the fine projects the French had formed for establishing themselves, and driving us out of India, were destroyed. I cannot better illustrate what has been said on this subject, than by quoting part of a letter from a celebrated Frenchman, Citizen E. Pouffielgue[f], Comptroller of

---

[f] They who have read the first part of "the Intercepted Letters," will recollect an excellent account of the battle of the Nile by this officer. The circumstantial detail he has given of the action, and the accurate description of the situation and appearance of the two fleets on the morning of the 2d of August, is the more to be admired, when we consider that he was at the distance of eleven or twelve miles from the scene of action. The tower of Abou Mandour, from whence he viewed the conflict, is situated on an eminence half a league to the southward of Rosetta.

the Expences of the Army, and Administrator-General of the Finances in Egypt; this letter was, with many others, intercepted by the British Fleet in the Mediterranean, and afterwards published. He thus expresses himself: " But the fatal engagement of Aboukir ruined all our hopes; it prevented us from receiving the remainder of the forces which were destined for us; it left the field free for the English to persuade the Porte to declare war against us; it rekindled that which was hardly extinguished with the Emperor of Germany; it opened the Mediterranean to the Russians, and planted them on our frontiers; it occasioned the loss of Italy, and the invaluable possessions in the Adriatic, which we owed to the successful campaigns of Bonapartè; and finally, *it at once rendered abortive all our projects, since it was no longer possible for us to dream of giving the English any uneasiness in India*; add to this, that the people of Egypt, whom we wished to consider as friends and allies, instantaneously became our enemies, and, entirely surrounded as we were by the Turks, we found ourselves engaged in a most difficult, defensive war, without a glimpse of the slightest future advantage to be derived from it."

On the morning of the 14th the Orion, Majestic, Bellerophon, Defence, Minotaur, Audacious, and Theseus, with the prizes, consisting of the Tonnant, Spartiate, Peuple Souverain, Franklin, Aquilon, and Conquerant, sailed for Gibraltar, but brought-to at single anchor in the mouth of the Bay. The prizes being supplied with jury-masts only, and very weakly manned from our fleet, were so unwieldy that they could with difficulty get out of the Bay, some of them drifting very much to leeward. In the afternoon a brig arrived from Tunis, with some of the officers and crew of l'Aigle frigate, Captain Tyler, lately lost off that port, as she was conveying dispatches and letters from England and Gibraltar, to Admiral Nelson and his fleet. Our mortification was excessive at being thus deprived of the pleasure of hearing from our friends and country after so long a voyage, during which no tidings of either could reach us. On the 15th the ships above mentioned, with their prizes, once more got under weigh, and proceeded on their voyage to Europe. Sir James Saumarez, in the Orion, commanded this division, and we find they all arrived safe at Gibraltar, to the joy and astonishment of the garrison, and the infinite satisfaction of the Earl of St. Vincent. On the 16th the Heureux was burnt, as it was found impracticable to refit and render her capable to undertake a voyage of any length, notwithstanding the exertions of Captain Ball, who had entertained a sanguine hope of repairing all the captured ships, sufficiently to enable them to reach the ports of Britain; and two days after, the Admiral was obliged to burn the Guerrier and Mercure; the former having, at the commencement of the action, received the fire of several of our ships, and having been so severely handled by the Zealous, that there remained no possibility of refitting her for a voyage; the latter being aground and so much damaged, that nothing could be done to save her.

The French, as their cuftom ever has been, have ftated the fuperiority in point of numbers and weight of metal in this action to have been on our fide; how falfely, will appear when the whole is fairly ftated. The French fleet confifted of thirteen fhips of the line, of which one was of 120 guns, and three of 80 guns each; the reft were feventy-fours, befides four large frigates, and many fmaller veffels, fuch as bombs, and gunboats. Our fleet confifted of fourteen fail of the line; one of them, the Leander, (which on this occafion was taken into the line) had only 50 guns, and the reft were feventy-fours, and the Mutine brig of 16 guns. It is needlefs to obferve, that the accident which befel the Culloden, reduced our numbers to thirteen fail of the line, the fame as the French, but by no means equal either in weight of metal, or number of guns and men, as the following ftatement will fhew. The Britifh fleet of fourteen fail of the line, and the Mutine brig, having in all 1026 guns and 8178 men, from which deduct for the Culloden 74 guns and 590 men, and Mutine of 16 guns and 110 men, and the amount of thofe actually engaged will be 936 guns and 7478 men. The French line of battle of thirteen fhips engaged, confifted of 1026 guns and 9610 men; and the four frigates, which alfo were in action, carried 164 guns and 1100 men; total 1190 guns, 10,710 men; making a fuperiority in point of numbers on their fide, of 254 guns and 3232 men: a great difproportion, when the other circumftances of the attack are alfo taken into the fcale.

On the 17th the Swiftsure, on a cruize off Alexandria, descried a square-rigged ship in the offing; she was soon made out to be an English frigate, the Seahorse of 36 guns. On coming within hail, her commander, Captain Foote, inquired what news of the French fleet? Captain Hallowell, in a few words, told him the event of the late action. The astonishment and pleasure expressed by all on board the frigate gave us singular satisfaction: instantly the shrouds were manned, and a salute of three hearty cheers was given us, which we as warmly returned. Captain Foote, on coming on board the Swiftsure, informed us, that he was dispatched by the Earl of St. Vincent to reinforce Lord Nelson's fleet: and that he had lately fallen in with, and captured, La Sensible, French frigate of 36 guns, having General Baraguay d'Hilliers and his staff on board, returning from Malta; and after a chase of twelve hours, and close action of eight minutes, he captured her. The Sensible had 18 killed and 36 wounded, in which latter number was the captain: the loss of the Seahorse was only two killed and 16 wounded. After the Frenchman had struck, one of the crew treacherously threw a grenade into one of the ports of the Seahorse, by which one man was killed and several badly wounded. Captain Foote remonstrated with the French commander on this shameful act; he caused an inquiry to be made to find out the culprit, and an American was reported to be the person: what became of him, I do not know, but that he richly deserved to be run up to the yardarm.

On the 19th a Greek veffel came out of Alexandria, and, purfuant to the orders of Admiral Nelfon, fhe was burnt, and her crew fent on fhore. The Zealous joined us on the 20th, with the information that the Admiral, in the Vanguard, and the Alexander, Captain Ball, had failed for Naples, leaving the Goliath, Zealous, and Swiftfure, with the Seahorfe and Alcmene frigates, and Fortune corvette, to guard the coaft of Egypt, and prevent the efcape of Bonapartè and his army, if they fhould make any attempt to effect it. Captain Hood was now our Commodore. The Goliath and Fortune remained at anchor in the Bay, while the Commodore and the reft of his fquadron cruized off Alexandria. On the 23d the Alcmene captured a veffel from Toulon bearing difpatches for General Bonapartè, and letters for his army and navy. The difpatches being thrown overboard, two of the crew of the Alcmene perceiving it, inftantly jumped into the fea and faved them, for which they have received, as they richly merited, a very ample reward in a penfion for life. The veffel captured, called La Legere, was a gun-veffel carrying fix guns.

On the 25th the boats of the Goliath, commanded by Lieut. W. Debufk, attacked and carried the Torride, a ketch of feven guns, anchored under the guns of the Caftle of Aboukir: the bufinefs was ably conducted, and gallantly performed. The boats got along-fide under cover of night, when an obftinate refiftance took place. Lieutenant Debufk, for fome time, fought hand to hand with the French officer commanding the Torride; feveral were badly wounded on both sides, and the vessel was brought off in triumph.

In the evening of the same day the Thalia frigate arrived, and the next day the Lion of 64 guns, Captain Manly Dixon, with a Portuguese squadron of four line-of-battle ships joined us: they came with an intention of strengthening Admiral Nelson's fleet. When the Portuguese found the business had been ably executed without them, they sailed the next day for Gibraltar; we were not, however, the less obliged to them for their friendly intentions. The Thalia sailed also with them for the fleet off Cadiz. On the day following a French Colonel (whose name I forget) was brought to the Commodore; he had been captured in a vessel endeavouring to escape from Aboukir. It appeared that he was a respectable officer who was worn out in the service of his country, and being probably disgusted at the service he was now engaged in, had requested leave to resign his commission, which was granted, and he was returning to his country with clean hands and the consolation of an honest heart. When the Commodore understood how he was circumstanced, and that his cloaths and other articles were at Alexandria, he humanely sent him in, on his parole, with a flag of truce, and on his return he was sent home in the Goliath.

We now cruized close off the mouths of the Old and New Harbours of Alexandria; the former is to the N. E. and the latter to the S. W. We perceived the enemy were busy in constructing batteries to command the entrance of each, as well as towards the

Lybian deserts, to check the attacks of the Bedouins. They also were converting a high sand hill, which rises behind the town, into a strong fortification. The French threw several shells at us without effect. On the 30th the Goliath joined us from Aboukir Bay, and Captain Foley having sent the prisoners who were captured in the Torride, consisting of one lieutenant, two guard marines, and forty-one seamen, on board the Swiftsure, sailed for Naples. On the 1st of September a Turkish vessel arrived from Constantinople bound for Alexandria: the Captain of her being informed of the state of affairs here, put himself under the direction of our Commodore, who sent him with a message to Dgezzar Pacha, Governor of St. Jean d'Acre in Syria.

The next day the Emerald made a signal for a sail bearing E. by S. We accordingly gave chace, and off the Tower of Arabs saw a cutter standing towards the shore; the Emerald fired several shot to bring her to, but she persisted, and at length ran aground a little to the west of the Tower of Marabou; our boats, and those of the Emerald, were sent to bring her off: the French, in the mean time, made good their landing; but a high surf soon destroyed the cutter. At this moment nothing was to be seen but barren uncultivated sands as far as the eye could reach; but in a short time we descried several Arabs advance, some on horseback, others on foot. The French now perceived their error, but it was too late; some of them indeed were so fortunate as to get on board our boats which pulled towards the shore in hopes of saving their unfortunate enemy, and a midshipman from the Emerald, with a noble spirit of humanity, threw himself into the water and swam through a high surf to the shore; having a rope in his hand, by which the French captain and four seamen were saved. From him we learned, that the cutter was called l'Anemone, of 4 guns and 60 men, Citizen Gardon commander; having on board General Carmin, and Captain Valette, aid de camp of General Bonapartè; also a courier with dispatches, and a party of soldiers; that the cutter sailed from Toulon on the 17th of July, and touched at Malta, from which place she had taken her departure six days. Perceiving there was no possibility of escape from us, the General ordered Captain Gardon to run the cutter ashore, who urged the dangers of a high surf, and the numerous hordes of wild Arabs that infested the coast. The General said he would cut his way through them to Alexandria, which was not more than two or three leagues off, the towers and minarets being plainly to be seen. No sooner had he landed, however, and perceived the Bedouins, who till this time were hid behind the sand-hills, but now began to shew themselves, than dismay and terror seized on all: nor could we behold their distress without commiseration, although they had so entirely brought it on themselves by refusing to surrender to us, and had fired on our boats when escape was no longer in their power. Our people approached the shore as near as the breakers would permit them, and were repeatedly hailed by the French to be taken on board; but only Captain Gardon and four men were brought off. We perceived that the officers and men suffered themselves to be stripped without resistance. Many were murdered in cold blood, and apparently without any cause; and among them the unfortunate General, and Aid de Camp, who, on their knees, entreated for mercy. An Arab, on horseback, unslung his carbine and drew the trigger, but the piece did not go off; he renewed the priming, and again presented at the General, but the shot killed the Aid de Camp, who was on his knees a little behind him; he then with a pistol fired at the General, who instantly fell. The courier also, who endeavoured to escape, was pursued and murdered. An Arab who got possession of his dispatches instantly rode away with them, and we have since learned, that they were afterwards recovered by the French for a sum of money. We now perceived a troop of horse from Alexandria marching along the strand, and the Arabs retired into the desart with their surviving prisoners. The French troops proceeding towards the scene of action, at length arrived on the spot where lay the remains of one of their murdered countrymen; but, probably, fearing that they should be surrounded with superior numbers, they wheeled about and retreated to the city. The commander of the vessel, who was brought off, most gratefully acknowledged the humane treatment he met with from our people, and extolled the gallantry of the young midshipman who had thus saved his life at the risk of his own; but mark the conduct of his countrymen! when afterwards a flag of truce came off from the French Governor of Alexandria with a message to our Commodore, after extolling the bravery of General Carmin in rather risking his safety to the mercy of Arabs, than surrender to us *the slaves of despotism*, he cast an unmerited reproach on Captain Hood for detaining those as prisoners who had so lately owed their lives to the humanity of our seamen.

On the 7th of September, being off the Tower of Marabou, we perceived two boats endeavouring to escape: two of our boats were sent after them, and captured one, which had several Italians on board, who were detained. The next day two large vessels endeavoured to make their escape, but were stopped and sent back again.

In the afternoon of the day following, the Swiftsure stood close in towards the Tower of Marabou, which is situated on a small rocky island, and commands the entrance of the New Harbour, from whence a reef of rocks extends into the sea to this place. Perceiving the enemy were busy erecting batteries there, a broadside was fired at them from the Swiftsure and Emerald, which for that time drove them from thence, but as soon as we retired they renewed their exertions, and in a short time erected two strong batteries.

On the 10th a boat bearing a flag of truce came off to us from Alexandria; in her were a number of masters of merchant ships and some Moors who had returned from a pilgrimage to Mecca. They requested permission to depart, but it being contrary to the

E.R.S. del.

Tower of Marabout, Egypt.

London, Pub.d by I. White, Fleet Street 1801.

I.C. Stadler sculp

Moors on board the Anystieure

London, Pub. by I. White, Fleet Street, 1801.

orders received on this head, they were all sent back. On the 13th three more boats were captured endeavouring to get away, two of which were burnt. On the 15th a Neapolitan came off to us in a little boat by himself; being much irritated at the treatment he had received from the French, he offered his services in any way: Captain Hallowell took him on board the Zealous, to the Commodore, who sent him again on shore in the evening to procure intelligence. Standing in near the city as usual, we saw two boats seemingly at anchor, on which Captain Hallowell dispatched two of ours manned and armed, who found them only to be Greek fishermen, and the next day they were sent back. The enemy, as usual, threw many shells at our ships, but without effect. The following day, however, we captured a boat endeavouring to escape, in which were many French and German officers; among the rest a young Russian, who gave so plausible an account of himself as induced Captain Hallowell, at his earnest request, to detain him: the rest were sent back, although they entreated to be permitted to remain as prisoners, or any thing but relanded; this, however, could not be complied with. The young Russian informed us " that he was the son of Baron Knorring of Livonia, that he was travelling in quest of knowledge, and being unfortunately at Cairo at the time of the arrival of the French, he was compelled to remain there till this time; that at length he had received from General Bonapartè leave to quit the country, but the strictness of the blockade had hitherto prevented him; he had tried before, and had failed; if he was not permitted to remain with us now, he would again repeat his attempts to get away, as he would not abandon himfelf to defpair." The franknefs of his manners was fo prepoffeffing that Captain Hallowell treated him with every attention and hofpitality, and the youth feemed to be entirely grateful for it.[g] On the 19th of September the Emerald failed for Naples, and the Swiftfure anchored in the Bay of Aboukir.

[g] I am concerned to ftate, that he did not treat his Englifh friends with that candour and regard for truth which his external manners and deportment seemed to promise; for we have fince learned from feveral people of rank and character, who had met him at the Court of Naples and other places in Italy, that from love of French principles, he had actually accompanied General Bonapartè on his expedition to Malta, and from thence to Egypt; and very probably he was charged with fome fecret commiffion by that General, in cafe he could elude our vigilance, and reach Conftantinople.

CHAPTER VI.

Suave, mari magno turbantibus æquora ventis,
E terra magnum alterius spectare laborem;
Non quia vexari quemquam est jucunda voluptas,
Sed, quibus ipse malis careas quia cernere suave est.   LUCRET. lib. ii. v. 1.

To repair the damages his ship had sustained in the late action, Captain Hallowell employed his crew to fish up as much of the wrecks of the ships that had been destroyed, as could be serviceable either in repairs or as fuel: the frigate that was sunk, as well as the wreck of l'Orient, supplied him with many useful pieces of timber; but as all the ships of our fleet had been employed in the same way while we were cruizing off Alexandria, it required more labour and industry to procure what we wanted. He also weighed up some small anchors, which, with other iron found on the masts, was sold afterwards at Rhodes, and the produce applied to purchase vegetables and tobacco for the ship's company; by these means the people were kept from idleness, and by their labour procured what was conducive to their comfort and health. While we lay here an Arab called Hadji Hassan, came off to us, as he pretended, with a message from Mourad Bey, the great leader of the Mamelukes; at length he gave us to underſtand that he came from Minich, beyond Cairo, where Murad was. He undertook to bring off a leader of Bedouins named Haſſan d'Har, but in this he failed, or deceived us. His companions, in their little boat, were ſent on ſhore near the Arabs Tower, and he remained on board with us.

The iſland Aboukir, of which mention has been made, now ſerved us as a place of relaxation and exerciſe, and our ſeamen were allowed to go thither without danger of hurting their conſtitutions in wine-houſes, as the place was without any inhabitants but quails,[h] and they were ſoon driven from thence. At this ſeaſon of the year great quantities of them flew on board our ſhips. Whether they were migrating to the north or ſouth, we could not aſcertain for a certainty, though, as ſome of them were quite exhauſted when caught, we imagined they had croſſed the Mediterranean from Europe, but that might alſo have been the caſe in paſſing over the ſandy deſarts of Egypt. We alſo found many hoopoes on the iſland. There are no trees on it, but it is covered with a low ſhrub bearing a round black berry. There were likewiſe a great quantity of bulbous roots, which our ſeamen at firſt took for onions, and were highly delighted with the diſcovery, but on cutting them they ſoon diſcovered their miſtake; we afterwards

[h] Called by the Arabs wheuz.

[i] The hoopoe is a beautiful bird about twelve inches long; its head is ornamented with a large creſt, which it has the power of erecting or laying back at pleaſure. The neck is of a reddiſh brown, the belly white, the wings and back ſtriped black and white in broad bars. The Egyptian or Arab name for it is afphour.

Aboukir Castle from the Island.

London, Pub. by L. White, Fleet Street, 1801.

found that this root bore a flower something like a hyacinth, but without the smell. We discovered several small caverns, in one of which were many human bones; another was like a passage to a dungeon, about three feet wide and six high, terminating with a small square chamber ten or eleven feet high. On the walls, which were of mortar, we perceived many Greek characters, probably inscriptions of names, but we could only make out a few of the letters. We could not guess for what purpose these caverns were formed, though, from many circumstances, we conjectured that the whole island, as well as the reef of rocks that extended into the sea from it, had been the foundations of extensive buildings. The stones, that were seen when the water was clear, were laid regularly in the form of chambers, and in general cut square. Probably it might have been the citadel or castle of the ancient Canopus, with a pier extending from it to form a commodious harbour for shipping. Between the island are seen a range of rocks, some above, and others just covered by the water; and it appeared to us as if this island had been formerly joined to the main land.

On the 25th we weighed again, and proceeded off Alexandria; and the next day the Flora cutter, Lieutenant Yawkins, arrived from the Earl of St. Vincent, then at anchor off Cadiz: he gave us the pleasing intelligence that he had spoke Admiral Nelson near the Faro of Messina. The next day the Alcmene took several wine vessels from Cyprus attempting to enter Rosetta.

On the 27th Captain Hood ordered the Swiftsure to proceed to Rhodes for wine and fresh provisions; accordingly we made sail, and arrived off the town of Rhodes in six days, but a heavy gale of wind prevented our anchoring, the road being entirely exposed. Several messengers came off to us with an invitation from the Governor; a Greek pilot also came on board. During the night we had much wind, accompanied with rain, thunder, and lightning; and in the morning the gale increasing, Captain Hallowell, after consulting the pilot, who declared he knew it well resolved to run for shelter into the Bay of Cavallero, on the coast of Natolia. The gale increased, accompanied by a thick mist, and the most awful thunder and lightning, during which the pilot ran us past the bay we intended to enter. At this part of the Archipelago numerous small islands are scattered in all directions, which rendered our situation extremely perilous.

At length the haze cleared up a little, and we perceived the entrance of a large bay, into which we ran, and found it spacious, and surrounded with high mountains. It is called the Gulf of Symea, and is on the coast of Natolia. At the furthest end of it, by a narrow channel, we entered a smaller bay, where the pilot declared there was good anchorage: the anchor was accordingly let go, but owing to a rocky bottom it did not hold, and we perceived that the ship was rapidly driving on the rocks. Captain Hallowell, who saw that not a moment was to be lost, instantly ordered the sails to be loosed, and ere the anchor could be weighed we were once more under way and ran farther up the bay The pilot again infifted upon anchoring; the fhip was only a few yards from the fhore, and frightful precipices hung almoft over us; the lead was hove, and no bottom was found at 70 fathoms. The wind was continually fhifting to all quarters, fometimes blowing in violent gufts, at other times calm for a few moments; but, fheltered by the furrounding mountains, the furface of the water was perfectly fmooth. By the exertion of officers and men fhe was again put about, and we made fail out of this place of danger, but with imminent hazard of being loft on the rocks which prefented themfelves on all fides as we worked out; and fo narrow was the channel in fome places, that it feemed hardly poffible to manœuvre the fhip fo as to efcape the one, without ftriking on the other.

On the projecting brows of the mountains, that feemed directly over our heads, we perceived wild goats fkipping about among the fhrubs, which covered the foil and fent forth a fragrant odour that in other circumftances would have been highly delightful, but at this moment the danger of our fituation entirely occupied our thoughts. The pilot, alarmed at the danger he had occafioned, was on his knees in an agony of terror, putting up fervent prayers for deliverance, but entirely incapable of giving the leaft affiftance. By the time we had gained the entrance of the Gulf, the weather cleared up and prefented a fine profpect of the furrounding wild country, and the dangers we had escaped. The sailors, forgetting their late peril, facetiously called the place *No Bottom* Bay.

As we sailed along between the shores of the island of Rhodes and the main land, we were gratified by a great diversity of picturesque and varied scenery. On the continent high blue mountains, softened by their distance, seemed to blend their summits with the sky; on the other side we beheld the fertile soil of Rhodes, with some places that seemed still to retain marks of its former splendour. When possessed by the gallant Knights of St. John of Jerusalem, it bade defiance to the Pagan world, and was a rallying point for the Christian heroes of those days of chivalry. One place, in particular, appeared to have been highly ornamented both by nature and art, and gave us the idea of an English park, in which, on the brow of a hill, we saw the remains of a ruined castle. At length, on the evening of the 5th, we anchored off the town of Rhodes and instantly the Governor sent an invitation to Captain Hallowell to come on shore; the next morning he went, accompanied by several of his officers and the young Russian stranger, Knorring. There are two harbours, one of them capable of holding only small vessels; the other, at the further end of which stands the Bey's palace (if it deserves that name) in former times was reckoned a very commodious harbour, but by the customary negligence of the Turks, it is now rendered fit only for small vessels; though they have a dock-yard there; and at this time a line of battle ship was on the stocks, intended as a present from the Bey to the

Grand Seignior.[k] The entrance of each harbour is guarded by a caftle of curious form: one is fquare, with fmall turrets, the other circular, with a lantern or light-houfe on the top. We proceeded to the great harbour; at the entrance we perceived the foundations of a pier that feemed to have been deftroyed by an earthquake, and we conjectured from that and feveral other circumftances, that it muft have been the fite of the far-famed Coloffus, which, from its fize and fhape, was juftly reckoned among the wonders of the world. We landed clofe by the gate of the Governor's palace. On entering the council-chamber we found Haffan Bey furrounded with many Turks of diftinction; he rofe to receive us, and conducted us to a couch at the upper end of the chamber, and feated Captain Hallowell on his left hand. This council-chamber was about twenty feet fquare, with fmall latticed windows on three fides of it, under which, againft the walls, were low fofas or mat-treffes; the bottom of the room was parted off by rails and a ftep; below thefe ftood the guards, formidable looking fellows, with large muftachios, and ftuck round with as many arms as they could well carry; the walls alfo of this part of the room were decorated with fire-arms, fabres, and fpears. The only diftinction that marked the feat of the Bey was a leopard fkin fpread on the fofa in a corner of the room, and over his head

---

[k] When a fhip of the line is built in this dock-yard, it is obliged to be taken into the road before any ballaft can be put on board, as there is fcarce water fufficient to float her in the harbour when fhe is quite empty.

was a board on which were Turkish characters and a golden crescent on it. The dragoman[1], or interpreter, on his knees, explained the object of our visit. The Governor promised to grant us his assistance to procure what we were most in need of, wine and bullocks for the squadron; we were then treated with pipes and coffee: the latter was brought in small cups set on silver filligree stands in the form of egg-cups; it is drank by the Turks hot, and without cream or sugar. Custom soon renders the omission of those auxiliaries very easily borne, as this coffee is of the first quality, and made in a peculiar manner that is very palatable. Hassan Bey is a venerable old man, decorated with a flowing grey beard: he is rather tall, and robust for his age; formerly he had been a slave, but by a series of events by no means uncommon in the Turkish dominions, he became governor of this island, and possessed of great wealth. We were informed that he had once been a Mamaluk, and afterward lived with a Bey, who died and left him his riches, which he had the foresight to conceal. Those who from their situation and power thought they had the best claim to the wealth of the deceased Bey, and suspecting that his slave knew where it was concealed, put the unfortunate Hassan to the torture in order to extort confession of the place where it was; but in vain, he endured it all without making any discovery:

[1] This interpreter we soon discovered to be a Frenchman who had resided for some time on the island. On the revolution, being in danger of losing his former situation, and deterred from returning to his own country for fear of suffering the penalties of emigration, he entered into the service of Hassan Bey.

afterwards he had the command of a Turkish ship of war, and for some achievement was promoted to his present rank; and it is but justice to observe, that he conducts himself with much humanity towards those whom he has under his command. We found him, however, very tardy in procuring the promised supplies, and if Captain Hallowell had not exerted himself with much industry to obtain them, we never should have procured any. The wine, which is in general good and wholesome, is made only by the Greeks, and as the Bey had put a price upon it which they thought inadequate to its real value, a very small supply could at first be obtained. However, when the cause of the impediment was discovered, our Commander insisted on making his own agreement with the people, and promised they should be faithfully paid for it by himself. On this their wine stores were freely opened to us, and the best kind that the island produced was procured at a very moderate expence. The wine is taken out of the casks and put into goat skins, the hair of which is on the inside, and gives a peculiar taste and flavour, that, from use, is not unpleasant; in these it was brought down to the boats and started into our own casks, and conveyed on board. We also obtained water with equal facility, the fountain from which we drew it being a few yards only from the landing place in the smaller harbour; the boats were placed alongside the wharf, and hoses, or leathern pipes, extended from the cocks of the fountain to the casks in the boats, which thus, in a manner self-filled, were conveyed on board without the tedious procefs of rolling the cafks to and from the boats; but during this operation we had nearly been involved in a quarrel with the inhabitants, who, accuftomed to fetch water from this fountain, could ill brook to be deprived of that privilege by ftrangers whom they looked upon as infidels. By the friendly care, however, of an old Turkifh officer who attended conftantly at the watering-place, our people were fuffered to proceed unmolefted with their work, which was completed in a very fhort time. Here we met with our poor friend Hadji Haffan, the Arab, who had been fent to Rhodes by the Commodore, under fufpicion of his being an agent for the French. It appears, that a little Turk named Achmet (who was found by Captain Hope in one of the veffels he had captured) in order to make himfelf of confequence, and to render his attachment to our caufe apparent, had accufed poor Haffan of being a fpy. Achmet, it feems, had been for fome time in France, and had engaged to accompany the expedition from Toulon; but, perhaps, the French finding that he was not to be depended on, had treated him in a manner that raifed his anger againft them, and he pretended to efpoufe our caufe with warmth and fincerity. With this man, therefore, Hadji Haffan was fent to Rhodes, to be forwarded as a traitor to Conftantinople, but the innocence of the poor fellow being difcovered, he was liberated. His joy at feeing us was very expreffive; he entreated to be taken back with us, as he was afraid of being left at Rhodes, although the Bey feemed inclined to

Cooper Williams del.
I. C. Stadler sculp.

The Arsenal at Rhodes.

London: Pub. by I. White Fleet Street 1801.

serve him; he was accordingly again received on board the Swiftsure.

The city of Rhodes no longer presents that splendid appearance that it formerly did when under the dominion of the Knights of St. John of Jerusalem, though many of its buildings recall them to the traveller's recollection. Over one of the gates is still to be seen a stone shield with the Cross of the Order; and the buildings are of that kind we denominate Gothic, and discover many traces of their former beauty. The ridiculous display of artillery, which the Turks are fond of, evidently demonstrates their ignorance of its proper use: the castle that commands the entrance of their harbours is loaded with guns of every description, and even every small hole and window has some fire-arms sticking out of it, such as blunderbusses, trombones, muskets, and pistols. On a platform between the two gates are several Colossal pieces of ordnance, not on carriages, but resting on stones, or on the ground, so that no alteration can be made in their elevation or direction; from these are fired large balls of marble, made from the statues and other pieces of sculpture which formerly adorned the city. Within the walls is a building which still retains the appearance of a monastery; it is a quadrangle surrounded with cloisters, and is now converted into a guard-house and arsenal, where we saw large piles of marble bullets of various dimensions, from the size of a twelve-pounder, to that of an eighteen-inch shell. The folding-doors of this building are of oak, and highly ornamented with carved work of the same Gothic or

Saracenic order which is to be feen in our ancient cathedrals. Near this place, in a wretched hovel, were crowded the officers and crew of a French frigate lately captured in the port. Our commiferation for the fate of thefe men, thus reduced to the moft abject flavery, was ftrongly excited, and they experienced from us that compaffion and affiftance their wretched condition demanded, and we were enabled to afford them. We next went into the bazar, or market-place, where nothing but dirt and indolence feemed to reign; from thence we proceeded to the land-gates, and were furprifed at the ftrength of the fortifications in that quarter, but we found them in a ftate of dilapidation which plainly difcovered that the prefent poffeffors were not the founders.

Croffing the bridge, we perceived a party of people in the foffe (which is now a dry lawn) amufing themfelves with the athletic game of wreftling. A ftout negro and a fmall white man were at this time the combatants. They were both ftripped to the fkin, having only leathern drawers on well faturated with oil, with which alfo their bodies were fmeared. Although they exhibited very little fkill in the exercife, yet the method of preparing themfelves for it, brought to our recollection Virgil's defcription of the fame paftime.

>Exercent patrias oleo labente palæftras
>Nudati focii[m] . . . . Æn. lib. iii. v. 281.

[m] Our youth their naked limbs befmear with oil,
And exercife the wreftler's noble toil. Dryden's Tranf. Æn. iii. l. 364.

In all probability the prefent inhabitants of this ifland derived the cuftom from the Romans, who were formerly mafters of it and the neighbouring ftates.

From thence we entered into an open place of great extent which is ufed as a burial ground. The multitude of fmall ftone pillars, fome of them furmounted with turbans, which denote them to be the tombs of men, and others plain, for thofe of the women, have a very ftriking appearance. Beyond this we entered on the fuburbs, which rife on the fide of a hill that entirely commands the city. The long narrow alleys furrounded with high walls, the houfes having no windows vifible, and the folemn filence that conftantly reigns there, made us happy to emerge into the country, and there we had no great caufe to admire the character of the prefent poffeffors of this once juftly admired place, as cultivation is fadly neglected: indeed the only people who feem to have any activity or induftry are the Greeks, and they are kept in fuch fubjection that all fpirit of commerce muft be cramped, if not entirely fmothered.

The ifland of Rhodes has ever been celebrated in hiftory from the earlieft times, and has been diftinguifhed by various appellations: it now retains a name which it was fuppofed to have derived from the Greek word Rhodon, a rofe, which flower is faid to have been in great abundance there; but Athenæus tells us that it was called fo from a rofe-bud of brafs which was found in laying the foundations of the ancient city of Lindus. I have a silver coin of the diameter of a sixpence, but confiderably thicker, which reprefents on one fide the face of the fun finely executed, on the reverfe a rofe burfting into bloom, with a fmall bud iffuing from the ftem; on the left of the rofe is a ftar: the infcription over the rofe is ΡΟΔΙΟΝ, and the face of the fun is faid to have been a likenefs of that of the Coloffus, which we are told was caft in brafs by Chares, of the city of Lindus, who learned his art under the famous Lyfippus, about 300 years before Chrift. Diodorus Siculus gives an account of a fiege that was carried on againft this city by Demetrius, the fon of Antigonus, who had in vain endeavoured to excite the Rhodians to affift in his war againft their ally Ptolemy Sotor, king of Egypt. After incredible exertions of valour and ingenuity on both fides, Demetrius was at laft compelled to raife the fiege, and by way of amends for the injury he had done the citizens, he prefented them with the engines and ftores employed againft them: thefe they fold, and with the money arifing from the fale, with fome additional fums of their own, erected this famous Coloffus. It was feventy cubits high, and the ftride was fifty feet wide: in one hand it held a light-houfe, which was feen from a great diftance. The artift was twelve years before he completed this enormous ftatue, and in about fixty-fix years after it was thrown down by an earthquake, which terribly fhook the whole ifland: it lay where it fell for the fpace of 894 years, when Moawias, the fixth Caliph, or Emperor of the Saracens, having captured the ifland, fold the brafs of the Coloffus to a Jew, who broke it to pieces and tranfported it to Alexandria, where he loaded nine hundred camels with it. The ftatue was hollow, and in the feet and legs were immenfe piles of ftones, by which the artift conceived he had fecured it againft the injuries of tempefts, and violence of the waves. In thofe days Rhodes was celebrated for the excellency of its government, the magnificence of its buildings, the convenience of its harbour, and the falubrity of the climate. The inhabitants were reckoned the moft expert navigators in the world, fo that for many years they held the fovereignty of thofe feas. After various reverfes of fortune, we find the Rhodians reduced to a Roman province, the city having been firft taken and plundered by Caffius: this happened forty-two years before the birth of Chrift. In 1308 of the Chriftian æra, Rhodes became the afylum of the Knights of St. John of Jerufalem, or, as they are fometimes called, of St. John d'Acre, from the laft place they poffeffed in the Holy Land; when they retired to this ifland, which was given to them in that year by Emanuel the Greek Emperor; but in the year 1522 they were compelled to furrender it to the arms of Soliman the Magnificent, (Philippe de Villiers de l'Ifle Adam being at that time Grand Mafter of the Order) when they retired to Malta. During the time it was in the poffeffion of thefe gallant Knights, great expence and labour were beftowed on the fortifications of the city, which ftill retain traces of its ancient confequence, particularly towards the land fide, where we found a deep and wide ditch faced with masonry, flanked by strong bastions, and the walls of great thickness, and supplied with heavy artillery. There are several handsome mosques in the city, one of which I entered, and was permitted to stay there for some time, having previously taken off my shoes. This indulgence has only been allowed since the late action, as christians formerly were not suffered to enter the places of worship sacred to the faith of Mahomet. The Governor has, besides his house of audience, another in the suburbs, and one in the centre of the city, appropriated to his haram: but he does not follow the general fashion of his country in maintaining a plurality of women, having one wife only. During our stay the plague made its appearance in a slight way; those who were infected, or suspected of being so, were instantly transported to the continent, where, in the wilds of Caramania, there was less danger of its spreading. As I walked in the bazar one day I perceived a man in the crowd with a black mark across his face. I was informed it denoted that he belonged to an infected house; but the people appeared perfectly unconscious of any danger from coming in contact with him: my own feelings, I confess, were not so placid; as he brushed near me, it was some time before I could recover from the uneasy sensation of dreading the effect. Mr. Cilgrin, the Swede, informed us there is plenty of game in the country; I saw several partridges, whose plumage and appearance are so different from ours, that I should not have classed them under the fame head. They are larger than ours, their colour grey, with red legs, and a red circle round each eye like a pheafant. As the governor neglected to perform his promife of procuring from the continent a hundred bullocks for our fquadron, Captain Hallowell determined to proceed with the fupply of wine and bread, which he had at length, with much labour and difficulty, obtained. Previous to our failing from Rhodes two Ruffian frigates and ten gunboats arrived from Conftantinople: they brought intelligence that a large army of Turks was on its march towards Egypt; that the Emperor of Ruffia had entered into a treaty of amity with the Sublime Porte, in confequence of which, the former was permitted to fend a fleet from the Black Sea through the Dardanelles, to cooperate with the Britifh and Turkifh fquadrons in the Mediterranean, againft the common enemy. This was an event of great importance, and quite a new epoch in the hiftory of thofe two powers. The Fortune brig, commanded by Lieut. Davis, arrived here from Smyrna, where the plague raged, and prevented his receiving any fupply of provifions: he failed from Rhodes, accompanied by Achmet[n] as interpreter, and intended to proceed to St. Jean d'Acre, to intreat Dgezzar Pacha, Bey of Syria, to fupply us with provifions, of which our fquadron now began to fear they fhould foon be in want. At the

---

[n] This man being afterwards convicted of various frauds, he was turned out of the Britifh fhips and put under the care of Haffan Bey, from whom, however, he contrived to efcape.

fame time we loſt our gueſt, the young Ruſſian Baron Knorring, who ſailed in a veſſel bound to Conſtantinople, bearing with him letters of recommendation from the Captain to our miniſter there.

I miſſed a curious ſcene the day before we departed. Captain Hallowell was invited to dine with the Bey, and ſent for me to be of the party; but unfortunately I had ſtrolled into the ſuburbs. As the ſcene would have deſerved the pencil, I have reaſon to regret my abſence from the repaſt, though in other reſpects perhaps my loſs was not great. I ſhall beg leave to give a deſcription of it as it was related to me: the gueſts ſat down on the floor round a ſmall table or ſtand, about two feet high, on this was placed a large circular metal diſh, which was heaped up with a pillau, conſiſting of boiled mutton, fowls, and rice; having no knives or forks, they inſtantly proceeded to pull the joints to pieces with their fingers, cramming their mouths with eagerneſs, and then offering a piece they had torn off to their gueſts. As ſoon as they had ſatisfied their hunger they all got up and returned to their ſofas, and their places were taken by the domeſtics, who ſoon finiſhed what their maſters had left, and were then ſupplied with a ſort of pudding like pancakes, which they in like manner tore to pieces and devoured. In ſhort a Turkiſh repaſt is by no means agreeable to an Engliſh palate; beſides which, the only beverage is water. As ſoon as the higher orders had dined, they were supplied with pipes° and coffee, with which, in a torpid state, they passed the rest of the evening.

Late in the evening of the 11th of October, having in vain waited for a further supply of cattle, we left Rhodes with only fourteen small bullocks, each about the size of a calf.

At day-break, on the 14th, we descried our squadron, and by noon anchored near the Zealous off the tower of Marabou.

° The pipes made use of in this country are formed of slender sticks of the cherry-tree or other wood, perforated, and are from three to four feet long. The mouth-piece is of amber, or ivory, according to the taste or fortune of the possessor. The rich and dignified bestow much cost on this part, which they stud with diamonds, rubies, and other precious stones. The bowl of the pipe is of fine clay. The Turkish tobacco is remarkably mild, and leaves very little smell behind it.

CHAPTER VII.

> Quis nescit, ... qualia demens
> Ægyptus portenta colat? crocodilon adorat
> Pars hæc; illa pavet saturam serpentibus Ibin.
>
> JUVENAL, Sat. xv. lib. v. ver. 1.

On joining the squadron under Commodore Hood, we learned that during our absence nineteen vessels of various sizes, attempting to escape from Alexandria, had been captured and burnt. This may at first sight appear an useless severity; but it was not so, for it was known that most of these vessels, particularly the Danes and Swedes, had volunteered to transport the French troops to Egypt; and, had we suffered them to depart, in all probability they would again have served for the same purpose, and would have conveyed fresh supplies to Bonapartè's army. It was equally our duty, at that moment, to prevent the French army (if they had been so inclined) departing for Europe, as we knew that Italy was at this time threatened, and, as it since appeared, was actually overrun by the French armies. If Bonapartè's army had returned to Europe, it would have given a decided bias to the war, and the Emperor, already severely harassed, would have been completely driven out of the field. The Arab, Hadji Hassan, having volunteered to open a communication for us with Mourad Bey, one of the Mamaluk chiefs, was accordingly, at his own defire, fent on fhore among fome ruins between Alexandria and Aboukir, being previoufly armed with a mufket and a pair of piftols; the Captain gave him a fmall boat, which had belonged to the French, in which he paddled himfelf afhore. The fame day feveral veffels were permitted to depart from Alexandria, particularly Neapolitans, as they had been forced into the fervice of the Republic. In the morning of the 19th two Turkifh corvettes arrived and anchored aftern of the Zealous. In the evening a fmall boat was defcried making towards us; in it was Hadji Haffan, who had fucceeded in procuring a man willing to take any meffage to the Mamaluk army in Faioume: he had alfo brought off his nephew, who could write, and by the aid of an interpreter a letter was addreffed to Mourad Bey, informing him that a Britifh fquadron was on the coaft, and ready to co-operate with him againft the common enemy.[p] Captain Hood giving his confent to the meafure, Maffoud Abdullah, the Arab, was fent on fhore armed only with a mufket, and he faithfully executed his commiffion, as I fhall have occafion to relate hereafter.

On the 21ft of October we were joined by a Ruffian and Turkifh fquadron, confifting in all of four frigates, an armed

[p] The annexed plate reprefents the three Arabs in their ufual dreffes, which will give a pretty accurate idea of the appearance of thefe people. The man in black is Maffoud delivering a letter to Hadji Haffan, who is fitting down; near him ftands his nephew Halleel, who acted as fecretary.

Turks on board the Transport

Casper Williams del.

J C Stadler sculpt.

London, Pub. by J. White, Fleet Street. 1801.

brig, two armed veffels of eight guns, and ten gun-boats. The two Ruffian frigates were remarkably fine veffels; one, named the Michael, of 50 guns, was commanded by Captain Alexander Sorokin: the other, called the Kazanfki, of 48 guns, was commanded by Captain Meffer, an Englifhman, who at the clofe of the American war, being a midfhipman in our fervice, and having no chance of promotion, with feveral other young men volunteered his fervices to the northern powers. He entered into the Ruffian navy, and in the courfe of fervice rofe to the command of this frigate. The Turkifh frigate was alfo a very fine fhip; fhe was built by a French builder at Conftantinople, as the Turks feldom, if ever, employ their own people to conftruct their men of war. On board of one of the corvettes was a Dragoman from the Sublime Porte, bearing the diamond aigrette and peliffe which Sultan Selim had fent for Admiral Nelfon. The Sultan, as foon as he heard of the victory of the Nile, took the former out of his turban, and fent it with other things of value to Sir Horatio Nelfon; and wrote to the King to requeft his permiffion that it fhould be worn by the Admiral as a mark of his Highnefs's approbation; which of courfe was granted.

On the 22d Captain Hallowell received orders from the Commodore to proceed to Aboukir Bay with the Turkifh gun-boats and one Ruffian frigate; and that evening he anchored there with the frigate and one gun-boat, and the next day five more gun-boats joined. In the night two dgermes[q] came alongside the Swiftsure: they were loaded with corn from Rosetta, and bound for Alexandria, and were therefore detained. Captain Hallowell having prepared every thing for attacking the Castle of Aboukir with the Turkish gun-boats, proceeded the next day to put the courage of our new allies to the proof, but having no very high opinion of their zeal he took the precaution to put five British seamen into each boat: yet, notwithstanding their example and exertions, it was impossible to make the Turks do their duty. Our commander, in a small boat, called a gig, bearing a white flag with a red cross, led them in, and rowed from gun-boat to gun-boat, in vain endeavouring to instil some ardour into their minds, and, at length, by occasional coaxings and threatenings, he drew them near enough to batter the castle; and it would have been with more effect, but the motion of the vessels prevented certain aim. Here locks to the guns would have been of great service, as with a long laniard, or cord tied to the trigger, an exact aim might have been taken; but they were not provided with this useful invention; nor were their guns properly adapted to it, as they had no breechings, but run in a groove, and frequently recoiled with great force from the stem to the main-mast. Whenever the Turks heard the whistling of a shot, down they fell, or

[q] Dgermes are the boats used for transporting merchandize from the Nile to Alexandria: they are strong built, and draw little water, so that they can in tolerable weather pass the bar at the mouth of the river. They are without decks, and have two or three masts, according to their size, with very large latine sails. When the sailors wish to furl the sails, they are obliged to climb up the yard, which cannot be lowered, being made fast to the head of the mast.

Cooper Williams del.^t   I. C. Stadler sculpt.

The Attack of the Turkish Gun-boats on the Castle of Aboukir.

London, Pub.^d by I. White Fleet Street 1801.

sneaked below into the hold. One of our row-boats having a wounded Turk in it, and the surgeon being willing to put on a temporary dressing, immediately rowed out of the line towards the wreck of a vessel lying about a cable's length from the shore. As the boat approached, several heads were seen peeping from behind it: at first it was imagined that the French had taken possession of this post, but, on closer inspection, turbans were perceived; and we found that the worthy commanders of the Turkish frigates had retreated behind this breast-work, in order coolly to enjoy their pipes. Some of the Russian row-boats were also there, but on our coming up, and ashamed of their companions, they returned to the scene of action.

The annexed plate is a view taken on the spot.

This day one Turk was killed and five wounded; among the latter was one whose arm being broke by a splinter, the tourniquet was applied to stop the hæmorrhage; and as the Turks assured us they had a surgeon on board the frigate, he was sent thither, with a request that the tourniquet might be returned. The next morning a boat rowed alongside the Swiftsure with the wounded man in it, whom they tumbled into one of our boats, without any ceremony, and rowed away. As soon as he was brought on board, the surgeon discovered that nothing had been done to him, and the tourniquet was absolutely buried in his flesh: he died in a few minutes after he was taken down below.

It will hardly be believed that such ignorance and inattention to their wounded companions could be met with among the most barbarous nations; but such is Turkish humanity!

The next day, resolving to remedy the evil of the former, the Captain put fifteen British, and (with the consent of Captain Messer) five Russian seamen into each gun-boat.[r] The Turks had nothing therefore to do but to use their oars; unwilling, however, to get within the reach of the enemy's shot, they made such bad use of them that it was found necessary to take them in tow with our row-boats. The Turkish commander of the frigate, in his barge, also took a share in this duty, but no sooner did he hear the first shot, than he cast off the tow-lines, and retreated with all expedition towards the island, where he laid perdúe till the action was over.

This day one Turk was killed and two wounded: as the boats were frequently within the range of grape-shot, it is rather surprising they did not sustain more damage. Towards the close of the day the fire of the enemy began to slacken, and, at length, was completely silenced; but as night approached, and we began to retire, they again commenced a heavy fire on us with more effect, as our unwieldy gun-boats were slow in their motions, and when they put about to return

[r] The Russian seamen are neat in their persons and remarkably patient of fatigue and hardship. They were entirely obedient to command and fearless of danger. They did not appear to receive so much attention to their wants and comfort from their officers, as they deserved. I have known a boat's crew remain alongside the Swiftsure from dawn of day to sun-set without any food, except what the humanity of our sailors afforded them from their own store. When the circumstance was known to our commander, they were always supplied from his table.

to their anchorage were expofed to the fire of the enemy, without a power of returning it. Such veffels fhould always be fupplied with a long gun out aftern. The launch of the Swiftfure, commanded by the Honourable Lieutenant Eylmer, had a heavy carronade, which was placed on a groove reaching from the ftem to the ftern, fo that it could be made ufe of either advancing or retreating; the other boats alfo had different pieces of ordnance according to their fize, and were commanded by officers of the Swiftfure. A dgerm, that had fallen into our hands, was prepared as a mortar-boat, and a fmall mortar, or howitzer, mounted in her, from which fhells were thrown with tolerable precifion, and the tower and minaret of Aboukir were ftruck feveral times. The day following the gun-boats again got under way, but owing to a heavy fwell and frequent fqualls of wind, they drove fo far to leeward that it was late at night before they could be brought to the anchorage off the ifland, which, in compliment to our Admiral, we denominated Nelfon's ifland. The next day proved more favourable to our operations, and the whole fleet of gun-boats and row-boats proceeded towards the mouth of the Lake Maadie, and from thence our line extended along the fhore to the foot of fand-hills, on the fummit of which was the French camp; near the bottom of the hill was a grove of palm or date-trees, and fome high bufhes, which proved highly ufeful to the enemy. The Ruffian failors had been withdrawn from the gun-boats, but the launch, and fome of their fmaller boats, manned and armed, attended, as alſo the Toridè gun-veſſel, carrying four heavy guns, commanded by Mr. Autride, midſhipman of the Zealous. The enemy had formed a low battery on the neck of land leading to the entrance of the lake, and placed ſome field-pieces on the ſand-hills above; the buſhes, and every little ſand-hill, were lined with infantry. Our ſmall mortar-veſſel threw ſhells into the camp, which, to our ſurpriſe, twice broke into a flame, and the enemy were ſeen in apparent confuſion endeavouring to extinguiſh it. Captain Hallowell perceiving a large gun-boat of the enemy cloſe to the ſhore, rowed in with his barge to attack it; the French retreated from it: as it was faſt aground, and expoſed to a heavy fire of muſketry, he was obliged to deſiſt from his attempt to bring it off: a marine was ſhot cloſe aſide him.[s]

Some of the Turkiſh gun-boats were now brought ſo near the battery as to uſe their muſkets, and the buſineſs was beginning to grow very ſerious, when, from the daſtardly conduct of the Turks in one of the boats, which threw ſome of the reſt into confuſion, the action was obliged to be diſcontinued. Captain Hallowell had directed Lieutenant Witts of the marines,

[s] The annexed plate repreſents the barge making towards the French gun-boat, which is evacuated. The head of a Turkiſh gun-boat is ſeen on the left, our people on board of it are firing muſketry on the French battery. On the neck of land, beyond which is the Lake Maadie, or as ſome call it, the Lake of Aboukir, a poor camel is ſeen tied to a palm-tree, unconſcious of the danger of his ſituation: an accidental ſhot from one of the boats ſtruck him on the hump and killed him. Above is the French camp on fire, below which are the heads of the ſoldiers peeping above the ſand-heaps, from whence they annoyed us with their muſketry, being themſelves ſecurely ſheltered. Near this place General Abercromby landed his troops on the memorable 8th of February 1801.

Cooper Williams del.

Attack on the French Camp near Aboukir.

London. Pub. by I. White Fleet Street, 1802.

J. C. Stadler sculp.

to anchor his gun-boat, which he was in the act of doing, and his seamen busy about the anchor, when the Turks, made desperate by their fears, rose upon our unarmed people, and with their sabres began to cut them down. Our sailors in the launch, as well as a Russian boat, seeing the situation of our men, some of whom had jumped overboard to avoid the strokes of the Turkish scymetars, immediately flew to their assistance, and first throwing in arms to them, were preparing to follow them, when fortunately Captain Hallowell, who perceived the confusion, boarded her, and soon put an end to the fray; the Turks being now as mean in their humility as before they were ferocious in their attack upon unarmed men. All this time the vessel was drifting towards the shore, but was fortunately put about before she grounded. An English seaman seeing one of his comrades cut down by a Turk, instantly attacked the Mussulman with a wooden handspike and beat out his brains: the commander of the gun-boat was also wounded.

Seemingly ashamed of their conduct on the former day, the Turks behaved better on the following, as they suffered their vessels to be anchored in a line before the castle, distant about a cable's length, and began to batter it with some effect, when unfortunately one of their guns burst, killing one, and desperately wounding two more of our people.'

' One of them, named Sunderland, was equally ingenious as brave. He had lately completed a set of leaden aprons, which fitted neatly on the locks of the guns, and secured them from every injury, so that they were always dry and ready for service. He lost both his legs, and died the following night.

This was, on the whole, an unfortunate day for us, as we loft three men killed and five wounded, two of whom died in the evening: among the wounded was Mr. Harpur, boatfwain of the Swiftfure, who commanded one of the gun-boats; he was hurt by a cable in letting go the anchor.

On the 29th of October feveral Arabs came off to the Swiftfure from Rofetta; one of them, named Huffein, was Tfourbadgi of Rofetta. They were remarkably well-made men, tall, and handfome, with black beards and dark complexions; over their common habit they wore long gabardines of black horfe-hair. They feemed anxious to exprefs their gratitude for our endeavours to free them from their invaders. One of them was a pilot for the Bar of the Nile. He engaged to remain with us to conduct our watering parties to the proper place, where we might obtain a fupply of that neceffary article.

Through the medium of Hadji Haffan and his nephew, we were taught to believe, that thefe people announced the approach of a large army of the country powers to co-operate with us. As, however, it did not make its appearance, fufpicions naturally arofe unfavourable to the veracity either of thofe who came to us, or of our interpreters: at length, by the aid of Mr. Simeon, the dragoman or interpreter of Haffan Bey (who had arrived in the Bay) it was difcovered that our hitherto fuppofed faithful Arab Hadji Haffan, had given us falfe intelligence. The Tfourbadgi of Rofetta, and the other Arabs, neither did or could promife that the Arabs in that quarter would assemble a large army. Yet I cannot think that this poor fellow did it from a treacherous motive, or with any intention of leading us into mischief; but as he saw that our hopes of inducing the natives to join us in our attacks upon the French were very high, he, to make himself and countrymen of consequence, repeatedly assured us that they were on their march, and would undoubtedly attack the rear of the French camp while we were annoying their front. His conduct had, however, been very unjustifiable, inasmuch as he had always been treated with kindness and humanity, and told that the sure way to gain our esteem was to relate the truth; he was therefore sent on board a large Turkish ship called the Haptap in disgrace.

About this time we learned that a man of the name of Abdullah Basha, had come to the squadron off Alexandria: he was a person well known, and possessed of property in the country. He came from Cairo, and brought intelligence that Mourad Bey had gained a victory over the French. The account he gave was, that the latter were 12,000 strong, the former only 7 or 8,000. That the French made the attack, and lost 3,000 men; the Mamaluks only 300, with several wounded; and among the latter Elib Mahommed Bey, Osman Bey, Selim Bey, Ebudiab Bey, and other persons of consequence. That this action happened on the 21st September, near Rickfiè, a place about a league distant from Cairo; that Mourad had retired into Faioume, not having a sufficient force to support a second attack; but that, in revenge, he had sent 300 French prisoners to Cairo, after having deprived them of sight and cut off their noses and ears; that Bonapartè had sent these unfortunate men to Rosetta, that the sight of them might not dispirit his troops.

This account, though evidently exaggerated, corroborated others, that induced us to believe the French were by no means in that security they pretended. The difficulties, they had to encounter in this country, which they affirmed in their official details to be entirely subjugated, were very apparent, as we frequently saw convoys of provisions and ammunition parading along the shore escorted by large bodies of horse and foot. When they came to the entrance of the Lake Maadie, and were obliged to halt in order to pass in boats, our boats had an opportunity of attacking them with great advantage, and considerably retarded their progress.

The French could not send either for water or provisions to any distance from their army without a strong detachment of troops. Small parties, that had attempted to procure those necessaries, had repeatedly been destroyed by the natives.

On the 5th of November two Egyptian Chiefs named Ibrahim Sheik and Massoud Sheik, came off to the Haptap: they informed us that Mourad Bey was within three days march of the coast with his Mamaluks. Captain Hallowell took them with him to Captain Hood, who was cruising off Alexandria. In the evening a French boat, bearing a flag of truce, accompanied by a Turkish boat, came into the Bay. The pretended object of their visit was, that the Turkish Admiral, who had been hitherto detained by the French in the harbour of Alexandria, wished to be informed whether the Sublime Porte was at enmity with the French or not. The Turkish officers were referred to Hassan Bey for an answer, who, irritated at their pretended ignorance of a fact so well known, disdained to give them any, and they returned as wise as they came. A heavy squall of wind came on the next day, which had nearly proved fatal to the unwieldy Haptap; in a short time she rolled away her main-top-mast, which perhaps saved her from driving from her anchors, and the gale fortunately subsiding, by the aid of our carpenters the damage she sustained was soon repaired.

This was a sufficient specimen of the imbecility of Turkish sailors, and they too seemed perfectly sensible of it, and were anxious to sail for a more sheltered port.

On the same day Massoud Abdullah arrived with letters from Mourad Bey. This honest fellow must have run much hazard in penetrating by himself through the deserts as far as the province of Faioume, where Mourad then was. The French being masters of all the intermediate country, he ran great risk of falling into their hands, and the consequence would have been certain death, if he had. They made no scruple of destroying the natives on the slightest pretence, and any attempt to convey intelligence from us to the Bey, would have been cause sufficient for the extirpation of a district.

As our water was nearly expended, the Torride gun-brig was sent to the mouth of the Nile, and returned with a supply. She was sent again on the same duty, and I received permission to go in her. We sailed by day-break on the 9th, and as it was calm did not make much way, but drifting near the coast, were obliged to anchor: the next day, however, we reached the nearest entrance of this famous river. A French gun-boat, that was anchored there, got under weigh, and retired further up, leaving us unmolested to prosecute our business, which is thus performed. The waters of the Nile, being considerably lighter than the sea, floated on the top like oil. Our people had only to dip their pails, or place their pumps near the surface, and the water was perfectly fresh; but if, through carelessness, they dipped a little deeper, the salt water mixed with it and spoiled the whole. The water, thus obtained, had a red appearance, and seemed of the consistence of cream, but we found that it purged itself after remaining a short time in the casks, and was both palatable and wholesome. While the people were thus employed, I accompanied Mr. Autridge in a boat to a small sandy island in the mouth of the river, where we saw a large flock of pelicans; but having only bullets in our muskets, we did not succeed in killing any of them. From this island we had a pleasant view up the Nile towards Rosetta, whose towers and minarets, appearing above the groves of palms, had a pleasing effect. We also observed a handsome mosque, where the French had established a post, as we could perceive the tri-coloured flag waving on it. A little to the right, on an eminence, was an old tower, which we conjectured to be that of Abou Mandour, from whence Monfieur Pouffielgue viewed the combat on the 1ft of Auguft, of which he gave fo accurate and well written a defcription, as may be feen by referring to the firft part of the intercepted correfpondence. We alfo found a fkeleton of a camel, probably wafhed there by one of thofe ftorms which frequently do much damage on this coaft.

The Torride did not come unattended to this bufinefs; no fooner did fhe fail from the fleet, than feveral of the Turkifh armed veffels got under weigh, not daring to truft themfelves fo near a French poft, without being protected by fome Britifh veffel. We went on board one of them, at the requeft of her commander, and found her to be a handfome veffel, mounting twenty guns, fix and nine-pounders. The captain (who was from the ifland of Candia) informed us, that though under the command of the Grand Signor, the veffel was his own property. Being willing to entertain us in the beft manner poffible, he ordered fupper inftantly to be brought in: it confifted of boiled fifh and cheefe fwimming in clear oil. As I had my cue, I fell to work with my fingers, and pinching a piece out, prevented our entertainer from doing it for me; and in a fhort time this curious difh was difpatched. He then, in defiance of the laws of Mahomet, fet before us fome excellent Candiote wine, of which he fwallowed fuch large potions as plainly indicated his contempt for the ordinances of his prophet. That our entertainment might be complete, he refolved to treat us with a concert: a wretched ragged Greek made his appearance, bearing a little guitar with three ftrings, and another accompanied it with his voice; but the mufic (if it deferved the name) was fo intolerably bad, that none but Turkifh ears could be delighted with it, and we were glad to retreat from fuch a medley of difcordant founds. Our veffel having obtained her cargo of water, gave us an opportunity of doing fo without giving offence. We accordingly got on board, and failed for the fquadron, and our Turkifh convoy made hafte to follow us.

The bottoms of the Turkifh gun-boats being very foul, Captain Hallowell determined to employ their crews, affifted by fome of his own, to haul them on fhore on the ifland, and careen them; but found that it was firft neceffary to dig a dock level with the water for that purpofe; and with incredible labour he fucceeded in getting one of them into it. Sea weeds two yards long were found fticking to it, and the whole bottom was incrufted with mufcles; many bufhels of which were taken off. No wonder, therefore, that they proved fo unwieldy and unmanageable in their late attacks on the caftle.

In digging the docks feveral Egyptian reliques of great antiquity were found; the plate annexed is an exact reprefentation of fome of the principal of them. No. 1 reprefents the Ibis, a bird worfhipped by the ancient Egyptians, becaufe it deftroyed the ferpents, that were bred in the mud left by the over-

Antiques from Aboukir Island.

flowing of the Nile: it is of copper, and the body is five inches and a half in length, the head and beak three inches three-fourths, the neck three inches, and the legs three and a half; there were two of thefe in tolerable prefervation. No. 2 is alfo of copper, of the fize of the engraving; it reprefents fome animal in a fitting pofture, but what cannot be difcovered, as the fculptor does not feem to have a good idea of nature. No. 4 is alfo of copper, and rather larger than the drawing; it reprefents the Ibis with the figure of a man before it. Thefe two laft appear, from the hollow part at the bottom, to have been fixed on ftaffs. No. 3 is an alabafter figure of the fize reprefented; and from a fmall hole drilled at the back, appears to have been worn round the neck as an amulet; from the lock of hair on the right fide of the head, it probably reprefented Ofiris. It was found near the fkeleton of a man, and with it a great quantity of fmall bones of birds. The little alabafter figure I afterwards prefented to Sir William Hamilton at Palermo, the others I have now in my poffeffion, together with a copper coin found in another part of the ifland, which is of the date of Bafilius.

On this ifland we turned our little bullocks, thinking they would thrive better there than on board; but left the French fhould land in the night and take them off, a guard of failors was left with them. Had the French poffeffed the enterprife, which our people have fo often fhown, they certainly might have taken them in fpite of the Turkifh gun-boats at anchor in the Bay, as we could never difcover that any watch was kept on board them. Amongft our crew were feveral Cornifh miners; they were employed to dig wells on the ifland in hopes of difcovering a frefh fpring; but when they came to water, it proved always very brackifh, being only falt water filtered through the fand.

On the 21ft a Mamaluk came off to us from Utko: he had been difpatched by Mourad Bey in confequence of the letter conveyed by Maffoud Abdullah. I accompanied the captain on board the Haptap, where Haffan Bey, two Arab Sheicks, and fome Turkifh commanders, were affembled in divan, when Selim delivered his meffage from Mourad Bey. This Mamaluk was a Kiachef, or officer of rank, under Mourad, and prefented a more pleafing appearance than any of the turbaned race we had yet feen. He related that his mafter had haraffed the French in the province of Faioume with fome fuccefs, and that he would be ready at any time to co-operate with us, could we mufter 500 men, and the Arabs bring 1000 into the field to affift him; but, fortunately, this could not be accomplifhed, as fubfequent events have proved that a much larger force would have been requifite for fuch an enterprife.

The plate annexed reprefents Selim Kiachef on his legs delivering his meffage to the Britifh, Turkifh, and Arab chiefs, who are feated on fofas round the cabin. The old man on the left, looking down, with his hand on his grey beard, is Haffan Bey, the Governor of Rhodes. The Turk on the right

A Mamaluke delivering a message from Mourad Bey.

London: Pub. by I. White, Fleet Street, 1801.

of the picture is Hamet, the Captain of the Haptap, and the second beyond Haffan Bey is Ibrahim, an Arab Sheick.

On the 25th the Haptap failed for Conftantinople; this unwieldy ship was in conftant danger of being loft, and her commander requefted she might be allowed to depart.[u]

In the night of the 27th a Turkifh boat rowing guard between the ifland and the caftle, fell in with a large dgerm having feventeen Arabs on board, which fhe brought off: this was thought a great feat, and they were not a little proud of the exploit.

On the 4th of December Haffan Bey failed for Rhodes, taking with him the Turkifh gun-boats and frigates. For the former he had for fome time paft been greatly alarmed, on account of the expofed fituation of the Bay of Aboukir, the nature of the veffels, the unfkilfulnefs of the mariners, and the heavy gales which prevail at this feafon. Captain Hallowell had fuffered great inconvenience from them, as in all emergencies they applied to him for affiftance and advice: they frequently had expended all their provifions and water, and the captain of the large frigate, whofe province it was to furnifh them with thofe articles, was always very unwilling to do fo, and nothing but threatening to write againft him to the

---

[u] The Haptap is a large Turkifh built fhip, intended for war or commerce; and is nearly as large as one of our feventy-fours, but very much undermafted. She traded from Conftantinople to Alexandria, and her commander Hamet, an Arab, bore an excellent character. On each fide of the poop of this curious fhip an alcove juts out in the Chinefe tafte; indeed her whole appearance indicates the builder was a native.

Porte could induce him to act honeſtly by them. This conduct on his part begat mutiny and diſaffection on theirs, and he ſometimes had to prefer his complaints againſt the commanders of thoſe veſſels for their conduct. At one time the crew of his own frigate exhibited ſymptoms of mutiny; he came on board the Swiftſure in great trepidation, requeſting the aid of the captain, who aſſured him that he would ſoon reduce them to obedience by running alongſide and pouring a broadſide into the ſhip. This threat not only quieted the inſurgents, but equally alarmed the captain for the fate of his frigate, and order was reſtored. We had a guard boat every night rowing about the Bay, as well to prevent any attempt of the enemy againſt us, as to intercept their boats when endeavouring to tranſport proviſions from Roſetta to Alexandria.

On the 16th the ſhip's company was put to a ſhort allowance of proviſions, for we had received no ſupply ſince we left Syracuſe in July: and that there might be no cauſe for complaint, it was reſolved, both by the captain and officers, to put themſelves to the ſame allowance as the ſhip's company; and all their live ſtock was appropriated to the uſe of the ſick. This arrangement ſatisfied the people; and ſeeing their officers expoſed to the ſame difficulties as themſelves, they bore their privation with the utmoſt cheerfulneſs, to the no ſmall aſtoniſhment of the French; who, from ſeeing no ſhips arrive to relieve us, concluded that we muſt be under the neceſſity of quitting the coaſt from abſolute want. The truth was, that the blockaders were as badly off as those they were stationed to guard: if the French were without wine, and possibly sometimes badly supplied with provisions, they had at least the satisfaction of a little more liberty; but we were pent up in our ships, and, except the little island, had not a place to land on.

On the 29th we were relieved by the Seahorse, which took our station, and we joined the Commodore off Alexandria, after having been ten weeks stationed in Aboukir Bay.[x]

---

[x] I cannot omit mentioning the spirited conduct of the young midshipmen, who, during the conflicts between the gun-boats and the French in the Bay of Aboukir, as related in this chapter, eagerly volunteered their services, and always went with the boats.

On the 1st of August, also, these lads remained on the quarter-deck, or forecastle, during the whole of the action.

The other boys of the ship likewise evinced an equal spirit. One of them had brought a cartridge-box from the magazine to the quarter-deck, and had sat down on it to secure it from the sparks of fire that were flying about; a shot came in at the starboard gangway, and knocked away his combustible seat, and then dismounted a larboard gun. The boy recovered himself instantly, got up, and after carefully wetting the powder that was scattered on the deck, ran for another cartridge, brought it to the same place, and reseated himself with great composure, waiting till it was called for.

I do not mention these circumstances as peculiar to the boys on board of the Swiftsure only, (for I am well informed that the same spirit of emulation and courage is common on board all our ships) but as a proof of the general spirit of our youngsters, who thus, at an early age, give such ample promise of what may be expected from them when a few more years have matured their judgment.

I must here beg leave also to mention two instances, among many, of the healthiness of the climate on the coast of Egypt. On board the Majestic a man lost an arm and a leg, and suffered the operation of the trepan for a fracture on his skull; he recovered, and is now a pensioner at Greenwich hospital. A boy on board the Swiftsure was struck on the head by a grape-shot, and was obliged to be trepanned *twice*, yet he recovered; as did also several others who had been desperately wounded.

CHAPTER VIII.

> Posta in riva del mar, ed ha vicine
> Immense solitudini d'arena;
> Le quai, come Austro suol l'onde marine,
> Mesce il turbo spirante, onde a gran pena
> Ritrova il peregrin riparo o scampo
> Ne le tempeste de l'instabil campo. TASSO, Canto xvii.

On the 30th of December the Swiftſure fell in with the Zealous and Lion off the tower of Marabou. We learnt that during the time we were in the Bay of Aboukir, a grand illumination had been exhibited by the French at Alexandria. The pharos, the minarets, and even Pompey's pillar, were brilliantly lighted up, and fire-works were diſplayed; all this was in honour of their new feſtival, the anniverſary of the founding the Republic. We perceived a material difference in the works around the town; they now bore a formidable aſpect. A large ſand-hill, that appeared to be at the back of the city, was completely fortified; and from its commanding ſituation, ſeemed capable of refiſting any attack that could be made on it from inſurgents in the city. On Pompey's pillar the tricoloured flag was hoiſted, and a ſoldier conſtantly on guard, who could, from that height, give early intelligence of the approach of an enemy.

The annexed drawing reprefents the caftle at the entrance of the new harbour built on, or near, the fpot where formerly ftood the celebrated pharos, efteemed one of the wonders of the world. The caftle is a handfome building, adorned with towers at the corners, and a tall minaret, in the ftyle of moft of the Saracenic buildings in this and the adjacent country; behind it, on the right, is the fand-hill above mentioned. From the caftle to the main-land extends a long caufeway over arches, and on the right of the whole is Pompey's pillar, with the French flag difplayed on the top of it. On the left of the harbour, among the ruins of the ancient city of Alexandria, is the column known by the name of Cleopatra's needle. I could not but regret the circumftances of the times, which prevented a nearer infpection of thefe venerable remnants of antiquity; but they have all been ably defcribed by thofe celebrated travellers Norden and Pocoke, and by feveral fubfequent writers, as well as the French literati of the prefent day, fo that nothing new could be faid on them.

The French had been bufy in rendering the caftle more capable of refifting any attacks upon it; they had levelled the battlements on the lower part, and erected a battery of guns and mortars on the platform, with which they frequently annoyed us, as, in the courfe of our cruize, we fometimes approached within the range of their fhot.

The city is fituated in the middle of barren defarts of fand, having on one fide the lake Mariotis, which is nearly dry, and

The Pharos at Alexandria.
London: Pub. by I. White, Fleet Street, 1801.

a branch of the lake Maadie, or Aboukir, on the other. The appearance of the buildings of the new town is the same as is generally found where the Turks have been long settled, mean in their architecture, the streets narrow, dark, and dirty.

On the 3d of January a sail was discovered endeavouring to escape: she was pursued and captured by the Lion, and proved to be a French corvette of 10 guns and 77 men, named Le Chaseur: she bore dispatches from Bonapartè to the French Directory, which were thrown overboard and lost.

We now often experienced those heavy gales of wind that at this season of the year do so much damage on the coast. The new port, being open to the sea, is often a scene of dreadful devastation: if one ship drives from her anchors she is sure to run foul of another, which experiences the same fate, and communicates it to a third, till the whole are involved in the same destruction. The policy of the Turks was very inimical to the pursuits of commerce; for the old harbour, which is completely sheltered from the effects of the weather, was appropriated only to the ships of Mussulmen; the merchantmen of all other nations were obliged to run the hazard of the new and dangerous port.

On the 12th we fell in with the Fortune polacre from St. John d'Acre; from her we received a small supply of wine and onions, but she brought no live stock. Lieutenant Davis informed us that the plague had broke out afresh at Rhodes, and that a French vessel from Egypt, having on board her a brother of General Bonapartè, had been captured by the Turks, and taken to the ifland of Scio. During his ftay at Rhodes a flight fhock of an earthquake was felt there.

While on the Egyptian coaft we had frequent communications with the enemy. At one time the Commander in Chief fent two officers to offer us a fupply of vegetables: from our long cruize on this inhofpitable coaft, he concluded we muft be in want of fuch refrefhments; yet we had the ingratitude to think that his civility was only a cover for his curiofity; it was natural to fuppofe he wifhed to know the ftate we were in, and how we bore the privations attendant on fuch a long and unprofitable cruize. Being aware of this, all poffible civilities were fhown to the French officers; and that they might be the better able to judge of our abilities to continue on that ftation, they were conducted into the feveral parts of the fhip, even to the lower decks. They could not conceal their furprife at the healthinefs of our people, the cheerfulnefs that appeared on their countenances, and the regularity and good order that reigned throughout.

In the courfe of converfation after dinner one of them remarked, that we had made ufe of unfair weapons during the late action, by which, probably, the Admiral's fhip l'Orient was burnt; and that General Bonapartè had expreffed great indignation at it. In proof of this affertion he ftated, that; in the late gun-boat attacks, their camp had twice been on fire, occafioned by balls of unextinguifhable matter which were fired from one of the English boats. Captain Hallowell instantly ordered the gunner to bring up some of those balls, and asked him from whence he had them. To the confusion of the accusers, he related that they were found on board of the Spartiate, one of the ships captured on the 1st of August.

As these balls were distinguished by particular marks, though in other respects alike, the Captain ordered an experiment to be made in order to ascertain the nature of them.

The next morning I accompanied Mr. Parr, the gunner, to the island; the first we tried proved to be a fire-ball, but of what materials composed, we could not ascertain. As it did not explode, which at first we apprehended, we rolled it into the sea, where it continued to burn under water; a black pitchy substance exuding from it till only an iron skeleton of a shell remained. The whole had been carefully crusted over with a substance that gave it the appearance of a perfect shell. On setting fire to the fuse of the other, which was differently marked, it burst into many pieces; though somewhat alarmed, fortunately none of us were hurt.

People account differently for the fire that happened on board of the French Admiral; but why may it not have arisen from some of these fire-balls left, perhaps, carelessly on the poop, or cabin, where it first broke out? and what confirms my opinion on this head is, that several pieces of such shells were found sticking in the Bellerophon, which she most probably received from the first fire of l'Orient.

On thefe occafions we picked up fome curious anecdotes that attended the invafion and proceedings of the French armies in their progrefs up the country; among others, one that does not fpeak highly for French gratitude. When the news arrived at Cairo of the capture of Alexandria by the Republican troops, a great fermentation took place in that city. There were many Franks[y] at that time there. Againft the French, of courfe, the fevereft vengeance was denounced; and they would all inevitably have been murdered, but the humanity of the wife of Ibrahim Bey, a Mamaluk leader, faved them. Moved with pity for their fituation, fhe took them all to her houfe, and concealed them there till the arrival of the French army under General Bonapartè. The General, as well as the reft of his followers, expreffed their admiration at the conduct of this woman, but it did not fave her from a heavy contribution levied on her hufband, which, as he was abfent with his Mamaluks, fhe was obliged to pay.

An inftance of fummary juftice occurred foon after the landing of the army, which was by fome condemned, by others approved. A foldier was detected in taking a turkey from an inhabitant; General Bonapartè inftantly ordered him to be fhot. All this in military juftice is allowable, where the fame ftrictnefs is obferved towards the higher orders, but it is well known they plundered without controul.

---

[y] Chriftians of all countries, are fo called by the Mahometans.

A quarter-mafter of dragoons was tried for fome crime by a court-martial, and was condemned by it to the gallies for life, agreeable to the conftitutional law. When the fentence was reported to Bonapartè, he broke all the officers of the court-martial, and ordered another to be affembled to try the criminal, having firft made a law by which the crime of which the culprit was accufed, fhould be punifhed with death. Being as before found guilty, he was condemned on this (ex poft facto) law, and fuffered death accordingly!

We were told from good authority, that not long fince a confpiracy amongft the Turks was fufpected; General Bonapartè inftantly introduced the new fyftem of domiciliary vifits, and, on fearching the houfes, papers were found concealed in the trowfers of the ladies. Thefe papers, it was faid, difclofed a plot that had been formed to murder all the French that were at Alexandria; and on the fame day, the fame fcene was to have been acted at Cairo.

On their firft arrival at Alexandria, the French new modelled the laws and cuftoms of the Turks (as they have invariably done wherever they have gained a footing); they formed a municipality, confifting half of Turks and half of French. It may be furmifed, that the ftory of the treafonable papers found on the women was of the fame kind with thofe which have fo frequently been fabricated by the revolutionifts to anfwer particular purpofes; be that as it may, the French foldiers fearching the women, of courfe, gave great offence to the Mahometans.

Soon after the defeat of the French fleet in the Bay of Aboukir by Admiral Nelson's squadron, the army of General Bonapartè at Cairo broke out into open rebellion, and declared they would not march a step further; that they perceived they were brought to Egypt to be sacrificed; and they even threatened to massacre all their officers. In this emergency, Bonapartè called out all the troops, and addressed them to the following purpose.

"My comrades and fellow-soldiers! when this expedition was decreed in France, I requested, and obtained, leave to chuse my own soldiers. Whom did I chuse but you, with whom I had so often fought; you, the brave army of Italy! Let me, therefore, request you would not sully the character you have always borne in the face of the world, but act with that attention to good order and discipline that has hitherto made you the first army of France; and here I engage, that every one of you shall return to France in six months, *or let my head be forfeited to your revenge.*"[z] This, for the time, had its effect, and discipline and good order were re-established.

By the French we frequently were told of battles having been fought with the Mamaluks, in which sometimes thousands of the latter were stated to have fallen. This appeared very extraordinary to us, who had always been taught to believe that the greatest number of the Mamaluk cavalry never exceeded 8000; and since the French arrived in Egypt, they had been

---

[z] So it would have been, had they caught him before he ran away from them in the year following.

divided, part of them being with Ibrahim Bey, who retired into the deferts towards Syria, the reft with Mourad Bey in Faioume.[a] The mode of attack of thefe brave, but ill-difciplined troops, was extremely irregular; they advanced in fmall parties, at full fpeed, up to the bayonets of the enemy, who were drawn up in regular order to receive them. They firft difcharged their carbines, next their piftols, and then made the laft defperate attack

---

[a] The following tranflation of a letter, written by the unfortunate Admiral Brueys to his fleet, on receiving the news of the capture of Cairo, with the obfervations on it by an officer who was with the French army, will prove how widely they depart from the fact in relating the events of their fucceffes.

LIBERTY—EQUALITY—*On board l'Orient, the 10th of Thermidor, the 6th year of the French Republic, (29th July 1798, only three days before the action in Aboukir Bay). Admiral Brueys, commander of the naval forces of the Republic in the Mediterranean, to the Naval Army.*

Long live the Republic! my comrades, our brave brethren in arms have obtained poffeffion of the city of Cairo, the capital of Egypt, in the defence of which the Beys had placed all their hopes and exhaufted all their refources. *Ten thoufand* Mamaluk cavalry attacked our troops with impetuofity, but were brifkly repulfed; *a thoufand* of them were cut to pieces, a much greater number drowned in the river, and all the reft, ftruck with the greateft terror, put to flight, being almoft all wounded. We have taken all their baggage, *three hundred camels*, and *more than three hundred horfes richly caparifoned*. General Bonapartè and General Vial, attended by their brave foldiers, took *the fort by ftorm*. The city of Grand Cairo, which contains 400,000 inhabitants, has fent deputies to meet the army. General Bonapartè made his entry there in the midft of the acclamations of the people. The capture of this city infures to us the conqueft of Egypt, and adds one of the fineft palms to the trophies of our victories. May we, my companions, be fo fortunate as foon to find an opportunity of diftinguifhing ourfelves at fea by *a complete victory over the Englifh*. Long live the French Republic! Long live the French People!

Obfervations on this letter by an Officer who accompanied the army.

The city of Cairo *was not defended. Four thoufand Mamaluk cavalry,* under the command of Mourad Bey, attacked the different divifions formed in a fquare battalion, but were repulfed. Their lofs both in drowned and killed by the cannon and mufketry amounted to *four hundred*. I am ignorant of the number of the wounded, becaufe they carried them all away with them. A retrenchment, which was only a little ditch with fome cannon planted behind it, was taken, as were alfo about *ten camels and fifty horfes*. The army entered into the city of Cairo on the next day without meeting with any refiftance.

with the fabre; after which they wheeled about and retreated as faft as they advanced. In this defultory mode of attack they were open to every difadvantage: in the firft place, they had no covering artillery, but were themfelves expofed to that of the French, which is allowed to be the beft in the world; and on their near approach they were received by a fteady fire of mufketry, whilft their own aim on horfeback, and at full fpeed, muft be very imperfect; but if, efcaping thefe dangers, they came to clofe quarters, the bayonets of the French could not protect them from the force and fkill of the Mamaluk fabre, which bearing before it every refiftance, hewed down all that came within its reach. The French officers who came to us, reported that the ftories we had heard of the fkill and power of the Mamaluks with the fabre were literally true, and that if they were difciplined according to European tactics, they would be the fineft cavalry in the world. The mode in which they are exercifed to the ufe of the fabre is curious; bags ftuffed hard with cotton, are placed upright the height of a man, and till a foldier can cut through one of thefe with a fingle ftroke, he is not accounted a fkilful Mamaluk.[b]

On the 19th of January, the Commodore ordered the Swiftfure to proceed to St. Jean d'Acre to procure provifions, for

---

[b] The Mamaluk, in action, wears a metal helmet under his turban, having ftrong bars of iron to draw down and guard his face from the ftroke of the fabre. Under his cloak he has a quilted jacket lined with fteel net-work that will refift the fharpeft fword and almoft turn a bullet.

Cooper Willyams delt.

I. C. Stadler sculp.

A Street in Caiffa.

London: Pub. by I.White, Fleet Street, 1801.

which the whole squadron was now in great distress, and we accordingly made sail for that place.

On the 22d, by break of day, we descried Mount Carmel, and in the afternoon anchored in the centre of the spacious Bay of Acre. The plague, which raged at St. Jean d'Acre, prevented any further communication with the shore on that side than was absolutely necessary to procure provisions and water;[c] but I saw enough of that place to raise my astonishment at the gallant defence it made a few weeks after, when a band of British seamen and marines under Sir Sidney Smith, with the Turkish garrison, were successful in defending those rotten and ruined walls against the flower of the French army; and that army under the command of one of the most successful Generals of the age. The next day we anchored nearer the southern side of the Bay, about a mile and a half from the town of Caiffe, which is situated at the foot of Mount Carmel. This place has by far the most miserable collection of human habitations I ever beheld: it is nearly square, and surrounded with a high wall of no great strength; at the corners are square towers, and at the entrance from the sea-shore is a tolerably well built castle. The streets exhibit a frightful specimen of human misery, being very narrow and full of mud; and to add to the

[c] The Honourable Lieutenant Eylmer, who commanded the watering party, informed me, that in the crowd that came down to the shore, was our old acquaintance Hadji Haffan, the Arab, who was left here by the Haptap, which ship had sailed for Cyprus. Poor Haffan seemed very happy to see an officer of the Swiftsure; and, notwithstanding the orders to the contrary, pressed forward to shake him by the hand. He now gained a livelihood by selling sherbet about the streets.

disagreeable picture, dead carcasses of dogs, horses, or camels, were suffered to rot in the public ways without being removed. The houses are all flat-roofed; most of them have neither floors or windows, and, in fact, are no better than hovels. In a small area before the house of the Governor, was a train of artillery, chiefly howitzers, or carronades, mounted as field-pieces. They were of brass, and neatly finished.

We hastened to enjoy a ramble into the adjacent country: proceeding out of the western gate, we turned to the left, and ascended the hill which rises immediately behind the town. At the distance of a quarter of a mile we arrived at a square castle, with only one small entrance, and quite unornamented by architectural embellishments. It appears to have been formed more for the purpose of overawing the town than of defending it. From thence we continued to ascend through a grove of olives till we arrived at a steep and rocky path, by which we, at length, reached the top of Mount Carmel.

From this height we had a delightful view of the surrounding romantic country.[d] Directly under us appeared the town of Caiffe; to the right extended a level plain of apparently rich land, watered by the rivers Belus and Kishon, and bounded by the mountains of Nazareth.[e]

[d] I made a sketch of the scenery described; an engraving from which is here given.

[e] It was not possible to view this country without calling to mind the wonderful events that have occurred in it at various periods from the earliest times; more particularly, the sacred life and history of our Redeemer, pressed foremost on our minds. One thing struck me in the form of the houses in the town now under our view, which served to corroborate the account of former travellers in this country,

Copper Williams del.

The Bay of Tene, from the Top of Carmel

London Pub. by I. White, Fleet Street, 1801.

I. C. Stadler sculp.

On the northern side of the Bay, on the sea-shore, is situated the city of St. Jean d'Acre; above which, among the mountains, we perceived a large castle, but could learn no account to whom it belonged; it had very much the appearance of those strong holds we read of in romances. Over these mountains, at the distance of twenty miles, the towering heights of Mount Lebanon raised their snowy heads. The summit of Carmel, though perfectly wild and uncultivated, had its peculiar beauties. Small grafs-plots of the finest herbage were surrounded by flowering shrubs of various kinds; among which the arbutus and dwarf-oak bore a conspicuous character. The acorns of the latter feed the wild boars, which are numerous in this country. Of these animals we were fortunate enough to procure two, which, when brought on board, proved a delightful repast to men who had been at a short allowance of salt provisions for six weeks, and to our palates were preferable to the finest venison. Whether it was that circumstance or not, I cannot undertake to determine, but we certainly

---

explaining several passages of scripture, particularly the following. In Matth. ch. xxiv. v. 17, our blessed Saviour in describing the distresses which shortly would overwhelm the land of Judea, tells his disciples, that " when the abomination of desolation is seen standing in the holy place, let him (says he) which is on the house-top not come down to take any thing out of his house, but fly," &c. The houses, in this country, are all flat roofed and communicate with each other; a person there might proceed to the city walls and escape into the country without coming down into the street. Though I am aware that it may be objected that this and most of the places now existing are of a much later date than the times when this prophecy was pronounced; yet as the dress and appearance of these people have suffered little change, so, in all probability, the general form of the buildings has been transmitted, and, though meanly, copied.

x

thought the flesh had much more the flavour of venison than of pork.[f]

But to return to Carmel: the western extremity extends towards the sea, where it terminates in an abrupt point, on which is a monastery of Carmelite monks, that takes its name from the mountain. This monastery is the parent stock of the religious houses bearing the same appellation in Europe. Beyond this point, the Mediterranean sea presented an expanse of water farther than the eye could reach. After enjoying the prospect which the scenery around us so amply afforded, we descended towards the eastern side of the town; near the base of the mountain we came to several caverns, which by the natives are called the Seven Caves; they appear to have been the foundations and undercrofts of spacious buildings, of which, except these hollows, not a vestige remains. They are now the habitations of profligate women, who are never admitted within the walls of the town. As the Turkish army was collecting in the neighbourhood, we saw several of these women with the Turkish soldiers, and as they were the only Mahometan females we ever saw without their veils, they became objects of curiosity. Of two, that were near these caves, one seemed to possess a certain degree of beauty; but in order to render their eyes more brilliant, a dark line was drawn round the edge of each eye-lid: to our sight it had the con-

---

[f] The Greeks who were employed to procure these animals, having first cut off their heads, were obliged to cover them with a cloth as they brought them down to the boats, for the Mahometans hold them in the greatest abhorrence.

Caiffe and Mount Carmel.

Cooper Williams delt.

I. C. Stadler sculp.

London, Pub. by I. White, Fleet Street, 1801.

trary effect.[g] Their hair, which was very long and black, was braided in a curious manner, and the nails of their fingers were dyed of a pink colour.

We next entered into a spacious burial-ground, extending from the eastern gate of the town for several furlongs; from hence we walked through some gardens, or grounds that appeared occasionally to have undergone a partial tillage, and were watered by wells at short distances from each other, which supplied cisterns with fresh water, from whence it was conveyed by low aqueducts, or troughs, to the roots of the vines and fig-trees, which were in great abundance; as also some fine date-trees: at the foot of one of them I sat down and took the annexed sketch of the town of Caiffe, and adjoining scenery. The climate of this country may be estimated by the general appearance of vegetation at this season of the year.[h] The trees were again putting forth fresh buds, and the grass on the sides of the hills was in high verdure; the weather was warm and pleasant. Between the gardens and the sea is a sandy plain which surrounds the Bay; on which is the high road from Caiffe to Acre: the multitudes of passengers, chiefly soldiers, passing between us and the sea, some on horseback, others on camels, or on foot, formed a pleasing variety in the landscape. The plague, which I before said was now in the latter town, seemed to make little or no impression on the

[g] This mode of painting on the edge of the eye-lids is common throughout the East. By the Turks the composition used for that purpose is called surmè.

[h] The 25th January.

people of the country, who reforted thither as ufual, unconfcious or carelefs of the danger of infection. It is no wonder, therefore, that this dire fcourge fhould extend itfelf in a fhort time over the face of a country where fo little care is taken to prevent it. On our return to the town we paid a vifit to the monks of the monaftery of Carmel, who had been driven from their refidence by the Turkifh foldiery. We faw only two of them, who were Italians. The prior was juft dead of the plague; and thefe poor monks were in a miferable hovel, deftitute of every comfort. However miftaken may be the zeal of thefe men, we cannot but admire their fortitude. Banifhed from their homes, and refident among a favage people, by whom they are objects of fcorn and derifion for their faith; they are befides expofed to the rapacity of the government, which frequently raifes heavy contributions on them, at leaft, as much as they can pay; and oftentimes turns them out of their retreats to fuit its own convenience.

On our return on board the Swiftfure we found feveral large boats alongfide, loaded with rice and other articles, which Dgezzar Pacha, the governor, had fent as a prefent. We alfo received ample fupplies of live ftock,[1] fheep, and bullocks; and our boats were bufily employed procuring water at Acre, the Pacha having appointed a guard to protect them from any

[1] The Captain alfo procured feveral milch-goats, which had a very peculiar appearance: the ears are pendulous, and of an extraordinary length; I meafured one of them, and it was two feet long. The body was covered with fhaggy black hair like the goats of Europe, the head was like a fheep, the horns black, fhort, and bent downwards.

interruption from the natives; and when our officers waited on him, some Janissaries cleared the streets as they passed, that no infection might be communicated to them. The Pacha[k] is a venerable old man, with a beard as white as snow, yet he possessed great activity, both of mind and body, and seemed to be endowed with a much larger share of energy and spirit than characterised the generality of his countrymen; but, on the other hand, he was cruel and oppressive in the extreme: several circumstances happened at the time we were there, that sufficiently proved the former; and from Mr. Malagaba,[l] our consul, we learnt, that lately he had put to death the whole of the officers of his customs, whom he suspected of defrauding him in collecting his revenues. His mode of punishment was very summary; the unhappy objects of his suspicion, to the number of fifty-nine, were drawn up on the strand where his cavalry used daily to exercise; and on a signal given, the soldiers attacked them with their sabres, and slew them all, leaving their mangled carcases exposed on the beach. We were also told, that lately, in a fit of jealousy, he had put to death all his wives: a Frenchman having penetrated his haram was the cause; fortunately for him he escaped.

The city of Acre has at different periods borne various names, as Acco, Acca, and Ace. Having been enlarged and beautified by Ptolemy the First, it was called Ptolemais; but,

[k] Dgezzar had lately received the Grand Seignor's firman, creating him governor of all Syria, and commander in chief in Upper Egypt.

[l] The person acting as British vice-consul here is an Italian.

as it seems the Turks have invariably discarded both Greek and Roman names, it now goes by its ancient appellation of Acco, or Acra. The Knights Templars of St. John of Jerusalem were put in possession of this, their last retreat in the Holy Land, by Richard Cœur de Lion; from them it is now, by Europeans, called St. Jean d'Acre. They gallantly defended it for a long time against the Saracens; but, at length, oppressed by superior numbers, the place was taken by assault, and a most horrible carnage ensued.

It was in this city that our Prince, afterwards Edward the First, was wounded by a poisoned weapon, and, as we are told, owed his life to the affection of Eleanor his wife, who sucked the venom from the wound. It was here also that a convent of nuns immortalized themselves in defence of their virtue by an act of heroism scarcely credible: when the city was taken by the Mahometans in the year 1291, the lady abbess called her flock together, and proposed to them to excite horror rather than desire in the breasts of the Barbarians, who had just entered the town, by disfiguring their faces, and she herself set the example. When the soldiers entered the monastery, and instead of beautiful virgins, as they expected, found only objects of disgust, with faces mangled and deformed, their lust was converted into rage, and, in their disappointed fury, they put them all to death.

As Jerusalem was only three or four days journey from Acre, I obtained leave from Captain Hallowell to proceed thither, but it was firſt neceſſary to obtain permiſſion from the Governor. Mr. Malagamba, who acted as Britiſh conſul, was conſulted on the occaſion; he promiſed to ſpeak to Dgezzar on the ſubject: he ſucceeded in obtaining his approbation, and a promiſe that he would appoint two Janiſſaries to accompany me. I had provided a Turkiſh habit, and ſuffered my muſtachios to grow; and though I much wiſhed to have a companion of my own country, yet an eager deſire to behold a place ſo celebrated, determined me to proceed. The following day, however, the conſul prevented the journey; he had diſcovered that Dgezzar ſuſpected I was a Frenchman, nor could any thing he urged in my behalf, perſuade him to the contrary. This curious old man profeſſed magic, and declared he was not to be deceived; with ſuch a prepoſſeſſion againſt me it would have been madneſs to proceed, and I reluctantly gave up the attempt.[m] Indeed the many inſtances we daily ſaw of the ſeverity of the Pacha, afforded ſufficient cauſe to dread the worſt effects from his ſuſpicions. Among the people, who brought off rice and other proviſions to us, were many who bore the marks of his vengeance: ſome of them had ſuffered amputation of one hand, others were deprived of an eye, or had their noſes ſlit, or ears cut off; one poor wretch had recently been entirely deprived of his ſight.

---

[m] As, from ſubſequent events, it appears that the French army under Bonapartè was at this inſtant on its march to Syria, it is fortunate for me that I did not attempt the journey, as, in all probability, I ſhould have fallen into their hands, if I had eſcaped the poignards of my guides.

Being thus circumscribed in my progress, I was resolved, however, to see as much as was possible: accordingly, I again landed at Caiffe with Captain Allen and Lieutenant Witts of marines. We proceeded towards the promontory of Carmel, Signior Salina, the vice-consul's deputy, being with us. In our walk we passed by a field then under tillage: a neat old man, who seemed to be the farmer, was overlooking his plough, which was then turning up the glebe; at the same time a Turkish officer coming up and entering into conversation with Salina, I made the sketch which is here given. We proceeded by olive groves till we began to climb the rugged path leading to the monastery, which, I before observed, is situated on the western point of Carmel; we found it occupied by a detachment of the Turkish army, who had miserably defaced it: part of the chapel was destroyed, and only the walls remained. It is a large handsome building, capable of containing from thirty to forty monks. Under the chapel was the cave of Elijah, which we entered, and found it was in its original state, being a simple excavation in the rock; in one corner a small altar was erected by the monks: the Turks, who also respect the memory of Elijah, had left this place as they found it.

After taking on board a plentiful supply of rice, and also a number of oxen,[n] which, in general, were very small, we sailed from the Bay of Acre on the 28th of January. The wind

[n] These oxen were so small that ninety-seven were taken on board the Swiftsure; they were generally not so large as a common English calf. Many of them, though full grown, weighed only sixty pounds.

Agriculture in Syria.
London: Pub. by I. White, Fleet Street, 1801.

being unfavourable, it was ten days before we came in sight of our squadron off Alexandria; and, to our surprise, perceived no less than eight sail, five at anchor, and three under weigh. We were shortly joined by the Theseus, Captain Millar, who gave us the pleasing intelligence that Commodore Troubridge, in the Culloden, had arrived; and that the Zealous and Swiftsure were to be relieved from their long and weary cruize on this unproductive coast.°

° In the fifth chapter, page 90, I mentioned the arrival of his Majesty's ship Lion of 64 guns, off Alexandria. She was commanded by Captain Manley Dixon. This ship had been dispatched by the Earl of St. Vincent to reinforce Admiral Nelson's squadron.

On her passage up the Mediterranean on the 5th July, she fell in with a squadron of four large Spanish frigates.

At the time the enemy were first discovered, the Lion was steering east under a press of sail. Captain Dixon instantly resolved to bring them to action in the closest manner possible, and communicated the same to his officers and ship's company, which being received with the most cheering symptoms of satisfaction by all, he took in studding-sails and cleared for action. At a quarter past eleven the action commenced with a heavy cannonade on both sides. The third frigate from the van having lost her foretop-mast, Captain Dixon thought that by directing the principal aim of his attack against her he should secure a general action, supposing that the noble-minded Spaniard would never leave a friend in distress: steering therefore for the crippled ship, which was now become the sternmost in the line of battle, the other three frigates tacked in succession, and passed the Lion very gallantly within musket-shot; but as their line after tacking was by no means a close one, they each received a well-directed broadside from the Lion; the good effect of which was very visible by their standing a considerable time on the same tack.

Captain Dixon still continued to pursue the same ship he had before made his principal object; which sailing nearly as well as the Lion, did much damage to her rigging by her stern chases. The three other frigates made a second close attempt to support her, but not so close as the former, and were each fully repaid by an exchange of broadsides. At length the Lion closed with the crippled ship, pouring in a destructive broadside, the yard-arms being just clear of each other. At this period the Lion having all her braces, bow-lines, clue-garnets, &c. shot away, and her sails cut to pieces, was rendered totally ungovernable. The three frigates made one more effort to protect and cover their distressed consort, but in vain. The Lion being at length by great exertions and labour brought round on the same tack with the frigate, which had now struck her colours and substituted the English ensign in their place,

Captain Dixon took poffeffion of her in the face of the three remaining frigates, who were diftant about two miles on the weather-bows.

The frigate captured proved to be the Dorothea of 42 guns and 370 men, commanded by Don Manuel Gerrard. From the prifoners Captain Dixon learned that the frigates that efcaped were the Pomona of 42 guns and 350 men, Felix O'Neil commodore, Don Francis Villamil commander; Cafilda of 42 guns and 350 men, Don Deam Errara captain; Proferpine of 42 guns and 350 men, Diag Bial captain. They had all failed from Carthagena on the 8th inftant on a cruize.

CHAPTER IX.

> Illi robur & æs triplex
>   Circa pectus erat, qui fragilem truci
> Commisit pelago ratem
>   Primus .... Hor. lib. i. ode 3.

The ships that had arrived with Commodore Troubridge were the Theseus, Captain Millar, the Perseus, Captain Oswald, and the Bulldog, Captain Drummond; the two latter were bombardes, and were supplied with heavy iron mortars of a new construction.

On the 10th of February six vessels came out of the harbour of Alexandria and several dgermes; the latter escaped to Rosetta, the former were brought into the squadron by the Bulldog. The following day some of them were sent in again; from those detained, we learned that the French daily lost from thirty to forty men of the plague.

The Bulldog and Perseus[p] twice bombarded Alexandria, which so alarmed the ships in the harbour, that several of

---

[p] These vessels stood towards the town as the evening closed, and threw in their shells as they proceeded: by shifting their situation the enemy's shot never hit them; but in the attack on the second night, the mortar on board the Perseus burst, killed and wounded several of the crew, and nearly carried away the main-mast; she was of course rendered for the present unfit for further service of this kind.

them came out; among the reft, the Turkifh Caravella of 64 guns, bearing an admiral's flag. As intimation of fome Frenchmen being on board her had been communicated to our Commodore, the Turkifh Admiral was interrogated on the fubject,[q] and, at length, acknowledged that the pilot was a Frenchman, and that one of the fçavans charged with a fecret commiffion from Bonapartè, was alfo in the Caravella. Captain Hallowell was directed to bring him on board. On entering the fhip he found feveral perfons, apparently Turks, fmoaking their pipes in the cabin: from a hint he received, he feized one of them and declared he was a Frenchman; which, after fome hefitation, the other in great alarm confeffed; and he was taken on board the Culloden. He proved to be Monfieur Beauchamp, who had for a long time refided in different parts of the Ottoman dominions, and was perfectly mafter of the language. Bonapartè had directed him to ufe his endeavours to induce the Sublime Porte to enter into terms of amity with the French; and at the different iflands he fhould touch at, in his voyage to Conftantinople, he was to try to perfuade the governors to fend provifions and other neceffaries to the French army in Egypt, and to induce them to enter heartily into the French caufe. As his miffion was of fuch dangerous import, it was thought right to fend him to Conftantinople, and the

[q] The Turkifh admiral had engaged to convey Mr. Beauchamp, with fecrecy to Conftantinople, and had left his own fon and fome of his principal officers as pledges of his good faith; the perilous fituation in which he had left them, and the danger they were expofed to by the difclofure he made, feemed to have very little effect on his mind.

Swiftsure was directed to carry him to Rhodes, from whence he would be forwarded by Hassan Bey.

The same day that the Turkish line-of-battle ship came out, a flag of truce also came from Alexandria: Captain Barri, a French naval officer, was in the boat. As it was known that the plague was in Alexandria, the boat was not allowed to come alongside, and the communication was carried on by word of mouth from the stern of the ship.

On the 14th of February the Swiftsure sailed from the coast of Egypt, having the Turkish Caravella and two Greek vessels in company; but the Turk proved so bad a sailer, and leaky withal, that we were obliged to bear up for Cyprus.

On the 17th we anchored in the Bay of Limesol, to the eastward of Cape de Gatte; here we found our old acquaintance the Haptap: that unwieldy machine (for it hardly deserved the name of a ship) had first made the Bay of Acre, and next came to this place; but as the weather was now daily growing worse, and Hamet the captain had dispatches for the Porte, he left his ship here at anchor, and proceeded to the coast of Caramania, from whence he went by land to Constantinople. Soon after our arrival a Turkish ship came into the Bay, and anchored near us; her commander came on board, and reported that he was one of three ships which had sailed *three months ago* from Smyrna loaded with provisions and supplies for our squadron off Alexandria; he further stated, that four days since he was off Alexandria, but seeing nothing of our squadron, he had bore up for this iſland. The fact is, that long ere he made the coaſt of Egypt, and, conſequently, before he could diſcern our ſquadron, his fears had impelled him to return, leſt he ſhould meet a French cruizer. This is one among very many proofs we had of Turkiſh indolence, cowardice, and imbecility. Whenever Egypt is in their power again, unleſs they have better protectors than their own troops and navy, the French, or any other nation ſo inclined, may once more make themſelves maſters of it. As ſoon as we anchored in the Bay Mr. Gamble, the purſer, went on ſhore to procure wine and bread for the ſhip; heavy ſqualls prevented the ſupplies coming off with the uſual expedition.

On the 19th the weather grew worſe, there was a great ſwell, and the Turkiſh man of war rode heavily: at length ſhe gave the ſignal of diſtreſs by firing ſeveral guns; on which Lieutenants Eylmer and Mudge, with a carpenter, were diſpatched to her aſſiſtance. At three o'clock p. m. the gale increaſed, and we drove at our anchors; but, at length, brought up again in thirty-ſeven fathoms. In the evening the gale ſubſided, and we learned that the Caravella was ſafe, but as the leak gained upon her in the late gale, the Turk was ſo alarmed that he had given her up for loſt, and fired the ſignals of diſtreſs as before mentioned.

Limeſol is a ſmall town built of brick, or clay, that appeared to have been dried in the ſun; it has a ſquare caſtle, and a ſmall open battery on the beach. About two leagues to the eaftward of the town are fome ruins which now bear the name of Old Limefol, but are fuppofed to be the remains of the city called Amathus, in which was a temple to Venus, the tutelar goddefs of the ifland, and which was alfo the capital of the ifland. Hiftory tells us, that Richard the Firft of England being on his journey to the Holy Land, was refufed permiffion to take in water at this place. On his return he took Ifaac, king of the ifland, prifoner for this indignity, and fent him in filver chains to Tripoli. Mulberry trees and vineyards abound here, and the beft wine in the ifland is the product of the environs of Limefol.

On the 20th I landed with Captain Allen, and, after paying our compliments to the vice-conful, who was an aged blind Greek, we rambled into the country. Paffing the gardens and orchards immediately furrounding the town, we came to an open plain through which a fmall river glides; but, like moft of the rivers in this country, it was little more than a chafm formed by the torrents which, in rainy weather, are precipitated from the mountains. On thefe plains large flocks of goats and fheep were feeding; the former are very beautiful animals, fpotted like leopards, with fhorter hair than thofe of Europe. The latter are remarkable for the fize of their tails, which, near the body, are fometimes nine inches or a foot broad, and weigh from five to twenty pounds. The fat which compofes this mafs is firm and well tafted. The fhepherds attending them were Greeks. Beyond the plain arofe fome high mountains; and towards the centre of the ifland is one called Mount Olympus. But of the beautiful nymphs, celebrated by ancient poets, we faw none. The race, if not extinct, is carefully concealed from public view.

On the evening of the 19th we failed from Limefol, leaving the Turkifh Admiral in the Bay.

On the 22d the high mountains on the continent on the coaft of Caramania came in view, and the next day we faw Cape Celidonia.

On the 24th the ifle of Rhodes was defcried at a great diftance. The wind being unfavourable, we made but fmall progrefs. On the following day a fail appeared in fight, and proved to be the Tigre of eighty guns, commanded by Sir Sidney Smith, bearing a broad pendant. Captain Hallowell, who went on board and dined with the Commodore, informed us on his return, that Sir Sidney Smith was on his paffage from Conftantinople, where he had arranged a plan of operations with the Sublime Porte for a mutual co-operation againft the French in Egypt, whither he was going to take the naval command. He was alfo invefted with the rank of Minifter Plenipotentiary from England to the Porte. In the evening we parted company, he proceeding towards Alexandria, and we making fail for Rhodes, where we arrived on the 2d of March.

It being the faft of the Rhamadan, the city bore a very different appearance to what it did when we were there before: the fhops were now fhut up, and a general gloom appeared;

the mosques were daily crowded by the devotees of all ranks. After waiting on the Governor, and the Captain having informed him of the prisoner he had brought with him, we returned on board.

On the following day I accompanied Lieutenant Eylmer to Hassan Bey, taking Citizen Beauchamp with us. At first the old Turk seemed to be very much enraged against him; but his brow soon smoothed by the Frenchman entering into conversation with him in his native language, and we left Monsieur Beauchamp less oppressed with terror than he was at first; the idea of being put into the hands of the Turks having given him the greatest alarm. Captain Hallowell also humanely made interest with the Bey, that he should be treated with kindness till he could be sent to Constantinople. Monsieur Beauchamp had a large sum of money about him, which was concealed in his girdle, and amounted in gold sequins to about seven hundred pounds, which he declared was his private property. To secure it from the rapacity of the Turks, the Captain counted out the money before the Bey, and at the same time wrote a letter to Mr. Smith, the British minister at Constantinople, apprising him of the circumstance, that the prisoner might not be deprived of it on his passage, or be prematurely made away with for the sake of his treasure. I am sorry to add that we afterwards learned that the money was not his private property, but allowed him by Bonapartè for the purpose of inducing the Turks to declare against us, as it is well known that a bribe is a powerful stimulus to gain the friendship of the Turk.

We found the gun-boats (lately with us in Aboukir Bay) now laid up in the harbour. An alteration had been made in the construction of one of them at the suggestion of Sir Sidney Smith, in order that the gun might be lowered into the hold, to enable her to make a voyage with greater ease and safety; for it was found that the great weight of it in the fore part of the vessel made her very unsafe in a heavy swell. The Bey had promised they should all be altered to the same pattern, but nothing had been done; nor did it appear that any exertions were making to hasten the equipment of the promised flotilla, which the Turkish government had ordered to be immediately forwarded from hence, to act under the direction of the British commander. On Monsieur Cilgrin[r] remonstrating with the Bey on the subject, he replied, that it was true he had promised Sir Sidney Smith that every thing should be got ready with expedition, but, said he, the Porte promises me many things without performance, and I, in like manner, *promise* every thing.

While we were standing in the court-yard of Hassan Bey's palace two curious figures made their appearance; they were dressed in white woolen dresses, having caps of an odd form

[r] Monsieur Cilgrin is a Swede, who, with his countryman Major Klinthebert, is employed by the Porte to superintend the building of ships of war. They are both gentlemanly well informed men; and, during our stay at Rhodes, paid us the most marked and polite attention. The former wore the Turkish habit, but his friend was distinguished only by his mustachios.

Pasham Beys Palace at Rhodes.
London, Pub. by I. White, Fleet Street 1801.

ornamented with tufts of wool: each had a ſtaff in his hand, and a calabaſh for water at his girdle. We were told that theſe men were begging ſaints called Fakirs; they freely came into any houſe they choſe without invitation, and were always received with reverence, and difmiſſed with preſents. In the view annexed I have given a drawing of the figures as they ſtood before me while I made the ſketch.

Before we returned on board we called on Monſieur Beauchamp, who was comfortably lodged in the houſe of Muſtapha, the Viſier, or miniſter of Haſſan Bey. He expreſſed his gratitude to the captain for ſecuring him a ſituation ſo much eaſier than he expected, as the leaſt he feared was to be confined in irons.

Taking leave of him, we returned on board; ſailed from Rhodes, and ſhaped our courſe for Europe, after a cruize of ſeven months and four days in theſe ſeas, from the period of the action in Aboukir Bay. A fair wind bore us rapidly paſt the ſouthern coaſt of Candia, the high moutains of which, with Mount Ida in the centre of the iſland, were covered with ſnow. But ſoon the gale increaſed; and towards the evening of the 7th, the violence of the ſtorm was ſuch as to endanger the ſhip, which laboured much and rolled heavily in the trough of the ſea, that now roſe in mountains round us. The larboard quarter gallery was ſtove in during the night, and it was found neceſſary to put up the dead lights leſt the windows of the ward-room ſhould ſhare the ſame fate. We now lay-to under storm stay-sails, yet were rapidly carried forward to the westward. On the 9th the gale subsided, but towards evening again increased.

The following day, however, the weather cleared up, and we found ourselves off the entrance of the Adriatic, where we spoke a Swedish brig loaded with pepper, bound from Leghorn to Bari, a town of Naples, in the Gulf of Venice. The master of her said he had been boarded by the crew of a French row-boat privateer near Leghorn, who had plundered him of his charts and clothes. The day after land appeared in sight, which proved to be Cape Passero; and in the evening we entered the Bay of Syracuse. The son of the governor came off to us, and gave an account of the late revolution that had taken place at Naples, which was now in the possession of the French. Their Sicilian Majesties had retired from thence under the protection of Lord Nelson[*] to Palermo, where they held their court. The same day the Captain sent dispatches overland to Palermo, giving an account to Lord Nelson of his arrival in this port.

On the 18th the Culloden, with the Seahorse, came into the harbour; and the day following the Bulldog and Perseus arrived.

[*] Rear Admiral Sir Horatio Nelson, K. B. was now raised to the peerage by his Sovereign for his gallant services in the late action of the Nile, by the stile and title of Baron Nelson of the Nile, and of Burnham Thorpe, in the county of Norfolk; and his Majesty has since conferred on him the dignity of Viscount, with remainder of the barony, first to the issue male of his father, and afterwards to the issue male of his sisters, Mrs. Bolton and Mrs. Matchem. The remainder of the viscounty of St. Vincent has been in a similar manner extended to the sister of the Earl, and her sons and daughters.

On the 15th they all sailed for Palermo, leaving the Swiftsure to take in some bullocks and other live stock.

On the 16th the Swiftsure sailed from Syracuse, and had no sooner left the port than she was again assailed with heavy gales, accompanied by a thick fog.

In the morning of the 17th it fell calm, and, to our concern, we found the ship was driving by the currents towards the rocky shore near Catania,[1] where the sea breaking with violence on the iron-bound coast, presented a frightful prospect of speedy destruction. The water being of unfathomable depth, destroyed the hope of safety by anchoring; and we continued to approach the rocks, which were whitened with the foam of the sea breaking over them, to a far greater height than the tops of our masts. Providentially a breeze from the south sprung up just as we had given up all for lost; and with hearts elate, and grateful for our escape from the impending danger of shipwreck on such a terrific coast, we once more passed the straits of Messina. As we sailed by the port we saw the Bellerophon and three other English ships, with a Portuguese man of war, at anchor in the harbour.

In the morning of the 18th we passed by Point Melasso, over which, though at a considerable distance inland, the tower-

[1] A town at the foot of Mount Etna, celebrated for its coral and amber fisheries. It has also frequently suffered from the dreadful effects of eruptions from the mountain. The rocks, so terrible on this coast, are formed of liquid fire or lava, which rushing violently from the mountain, overwhelms every thing in its progress, and at length makes its way into the sea, forming new boundaries to that element. The castle of Catania was originally built on the coast; it is now at some distance from the sea by the accumulation of lava, which has created a promontory between them.

ing heights of Etna appeared covered with snow, as were also the summits of the neighbouring mountains. We now bore up with a favourable breeze under the lee of Volcano, one of the Lipari islands, on which two burning mountains were throwing up volumes of smoke and flame. The following day we beat to windward and passed the island of Stromboli, on which there is a constant volcano.

On the 20th of March we entered the Bay of Palermo, and found there the Vanguard, bearing Rear Admiral Lord Nelson's flag.

The Bay of Palermo presents the most beautiful view I ever beheld. On the west, Mount Pelegrino extends towards the promontory that encloses the right side of the Bay. The purple hue which decks the sides of this eminence, the curious arched road running in a zigzag direction to the summit, on which is a chapel and statue of St. Rosolia, the tutelar saint of the island; the white buildings, palaces, stores, forts, and turrets, extending from the mole along the strand to the extreme end of the promontory, form a picturesque and pleasing landscape. At the foot of this hill is seen the harbour defended by a pier, which has a circular light-house and battery at the extremity. From the harbour the city of Palermo extends along the bottom of the Bay, which, with its beautiful buildings, bears the noblest aspect. The form of the city is square, and is surrounded with high walls. At each of the four sides a handsome gateway leads to four principal streets,

Mount Pelegrino, near Palermo.
London: Pub. by I. White, Fleet Street, 1801.

which crofs each other at right angles in the centre of the city. The north fide of this beautiful place extends along the bottom of the Bay, having a fpacious road between the walls and the fea; on the edge of which is a low ftone wall and a broad pavement. This place is called the Marino; and in the evenings is the favourite refort of all ranks of people. At the further end of this walk are the gardens of Flora, which are alfo much frequented; in them are feats, fountains, temples, and fhady walks, that render them a delightful retreat during the heats of the mid-day fun; but the Palermitans never vifit them except in the evening. Torches are never permitted to difturb the myfteries of this place.

The walls of the city on this fide are furmounted with noble palaces belonging to the principal people of the ifland: at one of them Sir William Hamilton, the Britifh Ambaffador, refided; and at his houfe Lord Nelfon took up his abode, where alfo the officers of the navy were received with great hofpitality. From the gardens of Flora a fine gravel road leads to that point of the Bay oppofite Mount Pelegrino: it is called La Bagaria, and is decorated with beautiful palaces. The gardens have a very pleafing appearance from the Bay, and are apparently laid out with great tafte; but as I was prevented by various circumftances from vifiting them, I fhall not pretend to defcribe them, or the palaces to which they are attached.[u]

[u] The day after the Swiftfure had anchored in the Bay of Palermo, Lieutenant Edward O'Bryen, a nephew of the Earl of Inchiquin (now Marquis of Thomond) came on board as Firft Lieutenant in the room of Lieutenant Thomas Cowan, promoted to the rank of commander. At the fame time Captain

I had heard that Sicilian people of rank never walked in the streets: it surprised me, therefore, to perceive no carriages stirring; but I was informed, that during the last week of Lent the nobility and gentry laid aside their pomp, and paraded the streets on foot. The processions and solemn masses in the churches called on our attention; accordingly we proceeded to one of the churches most celebrated for the magnificence of its devotional pageantry. Here we saw the first nobility of the kingdom employed in carrying wax tapers in procession, and during the solemnization of high mass, without respect to persons, all were devoutly on their knees before the altar. But on Easter-day the whole city bore a very different aspect; the carriages of the nobility were continually passing, and all seemed to vie in the grandeur and elegance of their equipage and liveries.

On Easter Sunday I attended Lord Nelson, Sir William and Lady Hamilton, the Consul-General's lady, and Captains Troubridge, Hood, and Hallowell, to the Capuchins' monastery, about a mile from the south gate of the city. After viewing the chapel and upper apartments, we descended into a subterraneous cemetery of the dead, much larger, and therefore more extraordinary than that I visited near Syracuse. It is in the form of a cloyster; on each side of the

---

Allen of marines left the ship, being summoned to England to take possession of a large estate in Pembrokeshire, bequeathed to him by his uncle, —— Philips, Esq. whose name he has taken. His gain was our loss, as he was a valuable and highly respected officer.

alleys are niches for the dried monks. The number of them amounted, I was informed, to no lefs than five thoufand bodies; fome of which had been dead near two centuries. In a feparate chapel or aifle, were the bodies of the nobility and gentry who from pious motives chofe to be placed in this curious prefervatory. Among the reft, the capuchin our ciceroni fhewed us the body of a Moorifh prince, who had abjured his native religion and embraced the chriftian faith: he, of courfe, was a fort of demi-faint. Some of the bodies in this place were dreffed in their gala fuits; others were habited in the monaftic cowl. Our conductor took from a fmall coffin the remains of a young prince dreffed in the fafhion of his day, and prefented it to the ladies as a toyman in London would have fhewn a doll. Unfortunately the young gentleman, perhaps from too rough treatment at other times, dropped his head, which fell forwards, to the no fmall alarm of his fair vifitors. The monk then fhewed us a door of the oven in which thefe bodies were dried, and would fain have invited the ladies to fee the procefs; but on entering it they haftily retired: and well they might, for the firft object that faluted their eyes was the body of a fat officer, who had died only the day before in a fit of apoplexy as he was on duty at the mole. I wifhed to know fomething of the procefs, but could not underftand it: the body was extended on a low ftove, and covered with a fheet, feemingly preparatory to the operation. When the body is properly prepared the door of the oven is carefully closed so as to admit none of the external air. After remaining six months in this place, it is sufficiently dried to be placed in the niche or coffin as required; the skin then appears dry, shrivelled, and hard, apparently of the substance of tanned leather.

On the 26th of March Captain Hallowell gave a ball and supper to Sir William and Lady Hamilton. Several of the nobility of Palermo, Lord Nelson, and some of the principal officers of the fleet, were also of the party. The quarter-deck was decorated with the flags of different nations, as was also the poop; the former was the ball-room, on the latter the supper was served up, and the cabins were appropriated to cards. The novelty of the scene, which had a very brilliant effect, surprised and equally pleased the noble visitors, who did not depart until the morning, highly gratified with their entertainment.

From the marino, the entrance to the main street named Cassano, is through a handsome gate called Porto Felice. This street is the chief resort of the idle and the industrious. All the lower parts of the buildings are appropriated to commerce; even the ground floors of the palaces of the first people of the island are converted into shops. In the evening this street is crowded by carriages, and loungers of all descriptions.

There are many handsome churches and convents in the city; but the cathedral church, called La Matrice, or the mother church, claimed our particular attention from the beauty and magnificence of its external decorations. It is of Gothic architecture, and highly ornamented with ſtatues. The inſide was at this time under repair; but we ſaw enough of it to judge that it by no means correſponded with the outſide in taſte and ſymmetry, though the materials of which it is compoſed are of the moſt coſtly nature. The pillars that ſupport the roof are granite; one of the chapels is entirely encruſted with lapis lazuli; and in a receſs are four ſuperb ſarcophagi of red porphyry, three of which are cut out of ſolid blocks; they are ſaid to be the tombs of four emperors.

At the extremity of the main ſtreet is a large open ſpace, on the ſouth ſide of which, extending to the gate, is the palace of the Viceroy, which at this time is the reſidence of Ferdinand the Fourth, king of the two Sicilies, who with his family had retired from Naples in conſequence of the threatened approach of the French army.

Soon after the arrival of Lord Nelſon at Naples after the victory he had obtained over the French fleet off the Nile, his Sicilian Majeſty formed a deſign of driving the French from the frontiers of his dominions, as well as from Rome itſelf. Accordingly having collected a large army, amounting, it is ſaid, to a hundred thouſand men, he made rapid marches, and ſoon came up with the French forces; but though he might now have ſurrounded them, he contented himſelf with ordering them to evacuate his own territories and thoſe of the Holy Pontiff. Accordingly they retreated till they reached Rome; where, fortifying themfelves in the caftle of St. Angelo, they refolved to defend themfelves, and proceed no farther. From fome unknown caufe the king fuddenly retreated with much expedition to Naples, and his late numerous army difappeared. This caufe has been thus explained to me. His Majefty having embraced a plan of fetting up the commiffions in his army to fale, and many perfons having bought their rank, though they were known to poffefs no property, it is believed that the French loft not the opportunity to furnifh them with the money. The confequence is obvious. Of courfe they took good care not to act againft their benefactors.

CHAPTER X.

> Misenum Æoliden; quo non præstantior alter
> Ære ciere viros, Martemque accendere cantu.—
> At pius Æneas ingenti mole sepulchrum
> Imponit, suaque arma viro, remumque, tubamque,
> Monte sub aerio; qui nunc Misenus ab illo
> Dicitur, æternumque tenet per secula nomen. Æn. lib. vi.

On the 31st of March a squadron, consisting of the Culloden, Zealous, Minotaur, Swiftsure, a Portuguese man of war, the Seahorse and Perseus, and two brigs, sailed from the Bay of Palermo. The following day we saw the island of Ischia, and the coast of Naples. We had some rough weather this day, during which a man fell from the main-top of the Swiftsure and was killed. Several English gentlemen, who were on their travels in Italy, and had sailed in the British fleet to Palermo, now accompanied us. The Honourable Mr. Rushout[x] was a guest of Captain Hallowell, and being perfectly acquainted with this country as well as with the Italian language, proved of great service on many occasions.

The following day the squadron stood into the Bay of Naples. As it was known that many of the inhabitants were

---

[x] Now Lord Northwich.

desirous of returning to their allegiance, Captain Hallowell, accompanied by Mr. Rushout, landed on the island of Procida. They were received with enthusiastic joy, and amidst the acclamations of the people, ascended to the castle: the French tree of liberty was cut down, the tri-coloured flag destroyed, and the royal Neapolitan flag hoisted in its stead.

The squadron anchored between the town of Procida and Point Miseno.[y] A party of the marines under the command of Captain Knox of the Culloden were sent to Ischia to take possession of that island, and the castle of Ischia was given up to them without opposition.

In the evening one of our boats was sent to the low land between Point Miseno and the dead lake; but as it approached the shore some French officers with a party attacked it with musketry, and obliged it to return. The Culloden fired three lower-deck guns at them, and they dispersed; it was not judged prudent, however, again to attempt landing on that coast, as we had no troops, and the French were known to be in force there.

Commodore Troubridge in the meantime was preparing for future operations. On the 4th of April he dispatched the Perseus to Palermo with an account of the success that had hitherto attended the expedition.

---

[y] Misenus, one of the companions of Æneas, was drowned on his passage; Æneas performed funeral rites to his manes on this promontory, and it has ever since borne his name.

The people of Procida and Ischia being in great want of provisions, their supplies from Castelamare and Naples being now suspended, a request was made to the Neapolitan court at Palermo to send some corn to them.

On the 5th of April the Swiftsure got under weigh, and sailed towards Naples; and the Seahorse frigate standing towards Cape Sorrento and Massa, Captain Foote sent his boats to burn some vessels near the shore, which they effected without loss. At one place where they landed, a party came down to them with the royal Neapolitan flag, and expressed their joy at the prospect of being relieved from the French yoke. We learned also from other sources, that the people were in general anxious to return to their allegiance, and at Gaeta they were universally loyal. We were also told, that the French had put to death several priests and others for their attachment to the royal cause.

On the 8th the Swiftsure stood into the Bay of Baia, endeavouring to cut off eight large gun-boats that were proceeding along the coast from Naples, but they got under the protection of the castle of Baia, which being situate on a high rock, and having a very commanding position, prevented our nearer approach. Meanwhile General Macdonald, who commanded the Republican troops at Naples, sent a flag of truce to Commodore Troubridge with a message replete with abuse and invective: his insolence was treated by our gallant leader with the contempt it deserved.

The following day, perceiving a large barge from Naples standing into the Bay, we stood towards her, but she escaped to Puzzoli.

As the French were throwing up works on the isthmus of the dead lake to annoy the squadron, our gun-boats and launches were sent to impede their progress; and we learned from some loyalists that came off to us, that many of the enemy had been killed and wounded.

The people at Procida being now in the utmost distress for bread, some provisions were sent to them from the British squadron. On the 13th, however, several vessels arrived from Sicily with corn for the islands of Procida and Ischia; but instead of a free competition to supply them with it, a particular grant was issued from the Crown for Prince Strabia to issue it solely: the consequence was, that it came in too small quantities to be of essential service, and the Prince was so exorbitant in his demands, that the poor were literally starving.

On the 17th we again anchored in the squadron, and were informed that Cardinal Ruffo was collecting a large army in Calabria with which he meant to march towards Naples.

A curious proclamation of Macdonald's was at this time brought off to us; it threatened death to any who sided with their rightful sovereign, or the English, and made the bishops and priests answerable with their lives for the consequence of any insurrection or tumult that might arise in their districts. At the time this sanguinary proclamation was issued an insur-

Cooper Williams delt.

I.C. Stadler sculp.

The Castle and Town of Ischia.

London, Pub. by I. White Fleet Street 1801.

rection against the French usurpers took place at Trani, a town on the Adriatic side of the kingdom. But the French having soon made themselves masters of the place, put all the men to the sword, and then, in cold blood, shut up the women and children in a large house, set it on fire, and consumed them all!

As there was no likelihood that we should speedily quit this station, I obtained leave to pass some time at Ischia; and accordingly proceeded thither with Mr. Rushout. We took up our quarters in a small house about a mile from the castle, where our marines under Captain Knox were on duty.

The castle of Ischia has a very remarkable appearance; it is on a high rock at some distance from the land, and communicates with the town by a long and narrow causeway built on arches. In the precincts of the castle are no less than three churches or chapels, one of which belongs to a convent of nuns. The keep of the castle is on the summit, and commands a very extensive view; the ascent to it is very steep and winding under high arches formed by excavations through the natural rock, and defended at certain places by strong gates, and cannon commanding every avenue.

The town of Ischia, though small, has many good houses in it. The churches (of which there are several) are very respectable for their size and decorations.[z] About half a mile to the northward of the town is a handsome road across

---

[z] The view of the town and castle of Ischia, with a distant glimpse of the island of Capri, famous for the residence of Tiberius, was taken from the house we occupied, which was built on the lava.

a current of lava, which about five centuries ago iſſued from a crater on the ſide of the mountain. It ſtill bears the appearance of a freſh eruption, being nearly in the ſame ſtate as that at Torre del Greco.[a] It diſcovers no marks of vegetation, but lies in rude heaps of black and rugged rocks. From thence we paſſed along a fine road formed of lava to a pleaſant houſe on the margin of a ſmall lake where his Sicilian Majeſty uſed annually to paſs ſome time; then croſſing a high hill well wooded on each ſide, we paſſed an extenſive manufactory of earthen ware, and about a mile from thence arrived at the beautiful village of Lago, or Lacco, which is about five miles from the town of Iſchia. The annexed plate repreſents the approach to it: the rocks that jut into the ſea are compoſed of various ſtrata of lava of the moſt brilliant colours; and one of theſe rocks, which is ſeparated from the ſhore about a furlong, has much the appearance of a thatched hayſtack. In the environs of the village are ſeveral handſome houſes delightfully ſituated.

Returning to Iſchia, we made a circuit from the road to viſit the hot baths[b] of Caſa Michiola, where every accommodation is provided for invalids, and a noble inſtitution for the free admiſ-

---

[a] Torre del Greco, a ſmall town about five miles ſouth-eaſt of Naples, was deſtroyed in June 1794 by an eruption from Veſuvius, which iſſued from a crater at the baſe of the great cone. The people of the country, hardened by the frequency of theſe misfortunes againſt the fear of them, have already rebuilt the town on the ſame ſpot, and on the lava which covers the former town, out of which the ſteeple of the church is ſtill ſeen iſſuing.

[b] There are many hot ſprings on the iſland; which indeed ſeems to be compoſed entirely of volcanic materials.

Cooper Williams delt.

View at Fago, in the Island of Ischia.

London, Pub. by J. White, Fleet Street, 1801.

J. C. Stadler sculp.

sion of three hundred poor patients, who are provided with beds and provisions gratis. The building appropriated for this purpose forms a quadrangle. The area is planted with trees. We descended to the baths by a sloping passage, and found every thing requisite for the ease and convenience of the bathers. Round a long room are placed fifty cisterns, into which pipes convey both hot and cold water. Besides these, there are sweating rooms, into which we also went; but the heat was so overpowering that it obliged us soon to retire. We were told that the patient could not exist for more than four or five minutes shut up in the sudorific closets.

Another day I accompanied several gentlemen to the hermitage on the summit of Mount St. Nicholas; a mountain that rises in the centre of the island, and is higher than Vesuvius. We were mounted on asses, which are here called chuchus: the one I rode had been the favourite chuchu of Ferdinand the Fourth; for horses are seldom used on this island. Our road lay through a romantic country highly diversified by rich corn fields and enclosures; then thick woods and rocky ascents. Sometimes we passed over arched causeways reaching from one hill to another, across deep chasms formed by earthquakes or volcanic explosions. As we approached the top of the mountain a barren scene presented itself. A white tufa of erupted matter dazzled our eyes till we arrived at the hermitage, which is situated under the highest pinnacle of the mountain, and is excavated out of the rock. There is a small chapel and several cells; but the monks or hermits being abfent, we did not fee the interior of them.

From this height we had a fine bird's eye view of the Bay of Naples and the furrounding country. Directly under us was the town and caftle of Ifchia; beyond which, the iflands of Procida, Point Mifeno, the ifland of Nifida, and Point of Paufileppo, the city of Naples with the caftle of St. Elmo, and the majeftic heights of Somma and Vefuvius, and beyond thefe, the cloud-capt Appenines formed the fineft affemblage of interefting and claffic fcenery I ever beheld.[c]

On the 27th I returned to the Swiftfure, and learned that a perfon called Grande Diavolo, or Great Devil, had been on board the fquadron. This man was at the head of a large body of loyalifts in the diftrict of Gaeta. The news alfo of feveral defeats that had befallen the French in different parts of Italy, particularly at Mantua, gave us hopes of fuccefs in this quarter.

In the evening the Minotaur and Swiftfure failed from the fquadron, having fome Neapolitan and Swifs troops on board. At break of day on the 28th they were landed at Caftel-a-mare, and took poffeffion of the town, the French and revolutionifts having evacuated it; at the fame time a gallant foldier, who had been a corporal in the royal fervice, had advanced with a

[c] I took a fketch of this enchanting view, but as an accurate and well executed engraving of it has already been published in Sir William Hamilton's elaborate account of the Campi Phlegræi, I have not inferted it, as I do not wifh to give views that have already been offered to the public by more able artifts.

party of loyalists from the mountains. But in a short time the enemy appeared in great force and retook the place. Several of the Swifs fell in the attack; superior numbers obliged them at length to give ground, and many of them were brought off.

On our return to the squadron we found that the Zealous was returned from Salerno, where a party of marines and sailors had made good their landing, and had taken possession of the town. But the enemy, having recruited their numbers from the neighbouring places, had made a successful attack upon them, and obliged them to re-embark with the loss of three marines killed, several seamen wounded, and nine taken. Lieutenant Vivian of the marines distinguished himself in this affair for his gallantry in making good his retreat in the face of a very superior force. Lord Montgomery and Mr. Stephenson, who were with Captain Hood, also served as volunteers on this occasion.[e]

On the 1st of May I returned to Ischia, and found Mr. Rushout just arrived from the island of Capri, where the people were loyal and well-affected to the English. The remains of the

[d] The eldest son of the Earl of Eglinton. He was with several other Englishmen at Naples when the Court retreated from thence, and was obliged in consequence to quit it and embark for Palermo, from whence he accompanied our squadron on this expedition.

[e] Captain Darly of the marines, who was landed here from the Zealous, being well acquainted with the Italian language, volunteered to penetrate into the country to join Cardinal Ruffo. This he effected, and accompanied the Cardinal on his march to Naples, being invested by his Eminence with a superior command. He has since for his services been advanced to the rank of colonel in the Neapolitan army.

villa of Tiberius are still to be seen on that island, and valuable coins are sometimes picked up among the ruins. As our party was to receive an addition in Lord Montgomery and Mr. Stephenson, it was now necessary to look out for a larger house; accordingly we proceeded to Lacco, and engaged with Don Scipio, the agent of the Duke of Aqua Viva, to take the palazzo of that nobleman for a short time. We were told that the Duke was at this time imprisoned by the rebels at Naples.

This palace is delightfully situated about a quarter of a mile above the village of Lacco, and at the foot of the mountain of St. Nicholas. It commands a distant prospect of Vesuvius; and our squadron at anchor in the road of Procida was full in view. In this agreeable society and residence I passed my time very pleasantly: the weather was mild, the atmosphere clear and elastic, the surrounding country highly picturesque, and uncommonly varied. The gardens of the palace are peculiarly calculated to repel the heat which prevails in the summer months, being entirely shaded with vines extended over all the walks from stone pillars erected for the purpose. There are also two handsome summer-houses, which, with fountains and arbours, made it altogether a most agreeable retreat. From hence Vesuvius exhibited every evening a most beautiful appearance. As the sun declined the colour of the mountain changed from a light blue to a vivid rose colour; from that to a rich purple, which gradually became darker till at last it was enveloped in a black shade.

Palazzo di Aqua viva, near Lago.

In the quiet and repofe of this place we almoft forgot the fcenes of war and defolation in which we had fo lately been engaged, and which were acting at no great diftance from us.

The town of Furia is about two miles to the weftward of Lacco, but very irregularly built; it contains many good houfes, and handfome churches, and convents. Before the prefent troubles it was a place of confiderable commerce.

Flying reports of an intended attack upon the ifland, as well as fome apprehenfions of the difaffected on it, induced Captain Knox to fend fome fire-arms to us; and as we amounted, with the fervants, to eight, we thought ourfelves equal to refift an attack by our elevated fituation for a fhort time at leaft.

On the 7th Captain Hallowell fent us a prefent of wine and other neceffaries that money could not procure here; but unfortunately as the boat returned to the fhip it was overfet, and Dixon, the captain's coxfwain, a worthy and good feaman, was drowned.

On the promontory, that forms the little Bay of Lacco, is a fquare tower: as I was one day viewing it, I had an opportunity of witneffing the mode in which the people catch quails in this country. They extend long and deep nets acrofs a fmall valley, and the birds in their rapid flight are caught in great abundance. Having often tafted the tunny-fifh, which are plentiful both in this bay and at Palermo, I alfo wifhed much to fee the procefs of catching them, and my curiofity was now fatisfied. The nets ufed for the purpofe are of vast extent, and are spread in squares so as to form separate chambers. A man is always on the watch, as these nets are never removed. When he perceives a shoal of tunny approach, and that they reach the line of net, and proceed along it till they arrive at the first chamber, he instantly closes the entrance, and so on till they arrive at the last; which is called the camera di morte, or chamber of death. The boats now prepare for slaughter; the fish are harpooned with ease, and hoisted into large half-decked vessels, which in a short time have all the appearance of slaughter-houses, and the sea for a distance round is tinged with blood.[f] This species of fish, which is caught in great abundance in these seas, supplies the people with plenty of wholesome and nourishing food at a cheap rate; the flesh is firm, and of the colour and consistence of beef. There is also another sort of tunny whose flesh is much whiter.

As I landed near Lacco, I perceived a man scraping a small bason in the sand close to the water's edge, and, to my surprise, found that fresh water, almost boiling hot, came bubbling up, with which he was about to wash his clothes. But the whole of this, as well as many of the neighbouring islands, is a complete volcano, and, no doubt, will one day again give vent to the combustibles that never are extinguished.

On the 15th I received an order to return on board.[g] In

---

[f] At the time I am speaking of, twenty cantars of tunny were caught, each cantar consisting of 160 pounds weight.

[g] On my return to the squadron I learned that an officer of high rank had arrived from Palermo, and had failed in the Perseus to take the command at Orbitello, which place was invested by the French.

the evening the squadron got under weigh; and on the 17th we arrived off the Bay of Palermo.

On his arrival there he refused to land, but chose to go to some other place on the coast, the name I have forgotten. There, however, he found a probability of danger, and again refused to land. Captain Ofwald, though highly disgusted at the behaviour of this officer, brought him back to the Commodore, who, incensed at his pusillanimity, would not suffer him to remain any longer on board a British ship, but sent him back to Palermo with the account of his conduct. The Field-marshal, however, was received at Court as usual, and no punishment or disgrace inflicted on him.

CHAPTER XI.

*Fortuna, sævo læta negotio, et
Ludum insolentem ludere pertinax,
Transmutat incertos honores.*
    HOR. CARM. lib. 3. ode 29.

ON our arrival in the Bay of Palermo, we learned the news of the French fleet from Breſt having paſſed the Straits of Gibraltar. Our ſquadron did not anchor, but continued to ſtand on and off till the 20th, when Lord Nelſon, in the Vanguard, joined, and we ſtood to the weſtward. The fleet cruiſed near the iſlands of Levanzo and Maretimo for ſeveral days, during which time the Admiral received intelligence that induced him to return to Palermo; and on the 30th the fleet anchored off the Mole, in a line oppoſite the Marino. As it was the name-day of his Sicilian Majeſty, the fleet, in honour thereof, fired a royal ſalute.

At this time a ſtrange circumſtance occurred here. In the veſſel which brought to Palermo Mr. Wyndham, the Britiſh Miniſter at Florence, who had been driven from thence by the French, arrived Mr. A. an Iriſh gentleman, who was on his travels in Italy. Soon after Mr. Wyndham had left this vessel there came to Mr. A. a messenger, who requested he would accompany him to Sir William Hamilton. He accordingly left the ship; but the messenger, who was a Sicilian officer, instead of conducting him to the Ambassador's, brought him to the prison, which being a large handsome building, was at first unobserved by him. But when he entered, and the gates closed upon him, he found the nature of his lodgings. As he had never landed on any part of the Sicilian dominions, and had not made politics his study, he was at a loss to know on what pretence he was thus deprived of his liberty. After remaining two or three days in this uncomfortable situation, he was liberated by the exertions of Mr. Wyndham, Lord Montgomery, and his other friends; but without the satisfaction of knowing for what crime he had been so treated. Since he was permitted to live at his ease at Palermo, it may fairly be presumed that no dangerous matter was alledged against him; and for the services rendered by his fellow-subjects to the Sicilian monarchy, he was entitled at least to the satisfaction of knowing the accusation that must have occasioned such harsh treatment.

In the mean time news had arrived from Syria of the gallant defence made by the garrison of Acre. The events of this unparallelled siege, and the immortal glory gained by Sir Sidney Smith by the well disposed order of his small force, against a powerful army of French, hitherto unchecked in its career, and commanded by a General, who, till now, was deemed invincible, will adorn the hiftoric page, that recites it, to the end of time.[h]

But it is my bufinefs to dwell only on what I faw, or what was particularly atchieved by the fquadron in which I had the honour to be embarked. I fhall only remark, that the lofs of fome brave men well known to the world by their enterprifing exploits, accompanied the recital. Captain Wilmot, who commanded the Alliance frigate, and Major Oldfield of marines, fell glorioufly defending the outworks: the latter commanded the marines on board the Thefeus in the battle of the Nile.

After the retreat of the French army, the Thefeus failed from the Bay of Acre. On her paffage fome loaded fhells (that were for fecurity placed in the cabin) by fome accident exploded. Captain Miller, who commanded her, being then forward on the forecaftle, and perceiving the fire that had broke out abaft, immediately made towards the place of danger to animate by his prefence the endeavours of the people to extinguifh it. Unhappily fome fhells burft at the moment he

[h] By the fame channel we were informed of an act of cruelty exercifed by the French army on its march from Egypt into Syria that could fcarcely be credited, but which unhappily cannot be denied. Gaza was taken by ftorm, and the town was given up to plunder and deftruction. The garrifon in the fort *surrendered* and became prifoners of war. Notwithftanding which, the whole of them, amounting to more than four thoufand men, were put to death, becaufe fome of them were proved to have furrendered at El Arifh under an engagement not to bear arms againft the French. The bodies, collected in a heap, and weltering in their gore, foon brought on a peftilential diforder, which proved fatal to many of the French foldiers who were left to garrifon the place. Surely General Bonaparte muft have forgotten the circumftance of the prifoners landed at Aboukir from the Britifh fleet: they alfo had engaged not to bear arms till regularly exchanged, yet they were no fooner landed than they were formed into a regiment called the Nautic Legion, and inftantly began their operations againft us.

entered the cabin, and in an inftant this excellent officer was blown to atoms.[i]

Captain Ralph Willet Miller was born at New York in 1762. He was the fon of a loyal gentleman there, who loft all his property by his adherence to the royal caufe. During the early part of Captain Miller's life he ferved in the Weft Indies, and was in moft of the actions fought in that quarter by thofe naval heroes, Admirals Barrington, Hood, and Rodney, and was frequently wounded, particularly at the capture of the French Weft India iflands. He was at Toulon in 1793, and at the evacuation of that place was employed in the demolition of the French fleet, and twice nearly loft his life on that fervice. He was afterwards at the capture of the feveral ftrong pofts on the ifland of Corfica, and frequently was employed on fhore at thofe places; he afterwards volunteered the dangerous fervice of fetting fire to the French fleet in Gourgean Bay, and was appointed for that purpofe to the Poulette fire-fhip, but contrary winds prevented his exertions from taking effect. After various other fervices, we find him particularly noticed by Lord Minto for his eminent conduct at Corfica: foon after which he was appointed to the Unitè, and in a fhort time afterwards was advanced to the command of the Captain, at the particular requeft of Lord (then Commodore) Nelfon.

His conduct during the action on the 14th of February 1797, off Cape St. Vincent, was particularly mentioned by Sir Horatio Nelfon.

While Rear-Admiral Nelfon commanded the in-fhore fquadron at the blockade of Cadiz, and frequently headed the boats in their attacks on the Spaniards in the bay, being once in imminent danger from the fuperior number and force of his opponents, Captain Miller, in his barge, bore down to the fuccour of his Commodore, and had the happinefs to extricate him, and affifted him to capture the Spanifh Admiral.

On the expedition to Teneriffe he commanded the Thefeus, on board of which fhip Sir Horatio Nelfon's flag was flying. Though the attempt was unfuccefsful, it neverthelefs adds a brilliant wreath to the laurels of thofe engaged in it. Here the gallant Admiral loft his arm. Captain Miller, more fortunate, efcaped the fhowers of fhot that were poured on the Britifh boats, and landed with the firft at the town of Santa Cruz, which was completely in the poffeffion of the Britifh feamen commanded by Captain Troubridge, though from exifting circumftances they agreed to evacuate it.

Here too fell that gallant officer Captain Richard Bowen, who was raifed for his merit by the Earl of St. Vincent.

Captain Miller afterwards was twice engaged in fevere actions with the Spanifh gun-boats in Algeziras Bay. When Admiral Nelfon failed in purfuit of the French fleet to the fhores of Egypt, Captain Miller was one of thofe felected by the difcerning eye of the Earl of St. Vincent to compofe one of his fquadron, and moft ably did he acquit himfelf in that glorious action, as I have before related.

When Sir Sidney Smith failed up the Mediterranean, he requefted the Earl of St. Vincent to appoint Captain Miller to be under his command; accordingly at the fiege of Acre we find his fervices particularly noticed by Sir Sidney, who (whilft he directed the operations on fhore) appointed Captain Miller to command the naval department. Soon after which this brave man loft his life, a life that had always

As the fleet remained several days at Palermo, I took the opportunity of visiting several places that had escaped my observations before. Among the rest, the monastery of St. Martino, situated on the mountains about eight or nine miles from Palermo. Our road led through Monte Reale, a small town on an eminence which overlooks the capital, and is about three miles from it. The road to it is decorated at certain distances with fine marble fountains. At Monte Reale we saw the monastery of Benedictines. On the grand staircase is a good painting relative to the founding of the abbey. The cathedral, which is adjoining, is a great curiosity; the ornaments of the outside are Saracenic, as in part also is the interior, which presents a grand display of the taste and munificence of the founder. Part of the side walls, and the whole of the ceiling, are covered with Mosaic work, the ground of which is gold; the subjects represented on it are taken from passages in the New Testament. The whole has a solemn and grand appearance. The pavement also of Mosaic of a different kind is equally beautiful. The high altar is covered with silver richly embossed; and on gala days it is ornamented with several fine images of the same metal.

From thence we proceeded on a rugged road up the mountains, till we arrived at the monastery of St. Martino, which is a

---

been dedicated to the service of his country, and employed in the exercise of every amiable, every praiseworthy action. Captain Miller has left a widow and two young children, who have a pension from government of one hundred pounds a year.

large pile of building, fituated in a wild and defert country. The monks, who are of the order of St. Benedict, were gone to fee the fleet; but the lay brothers took us through the various apartments, which were handfome and convenient, particularly thofe of the prior. There is a good library, and a large mufeum of natural and artificial curiofities.

In defcending the mountains we were much pleafed with the extenfive profpect that opened to our view. Beneath us was the town of Monte Reale, from whence, by a gradual defcent, lay the road to Palermo. The fleet in the bay, the rich appearance of the furrounding country, and the high ftate of cultivation which appeared in the valley beneath, where the corn was already ripe, formed a combination of fo many ftriking objects as can rarely be met with.

On the 4th of June a royal falute was fired by the fleet, and another from the batteries on fhore; and his Sicilian Majefty gave a féte at the palace in honour of the birth-day of our beloved Sovereign; to which, with the ambaffador and his lady, and Lord Nelfon, the feveral captains of the fleet and their officers were invited. The ball-room was elegant, and filled with all the beauty and firft nobility of the kingdom. A large fuite of rooms was opened, and fruits, ices, and other refrefhments were liberally difpenfed. But the moft pleafing fight was the Queen of Naples furrounded by her daughters. Their elegant appearance, and filial attention to their royal parent, formed an interefting picture not often feen in that country; for the Italian females of rank feem to look upon maternal and filial duties as much beneath their notice. The King had formed a pharo bank, at which he was engaged the greater part of the evening. But as one bank was not fufficient for the numerous amateurs of that game, a detachment was ordered from it, at which a nobleman of the court prefided.

On the 5th I vifited an ancient caftle about a mile from Palermo, called Caftel Reale, which is fuppofed to have been the refidence of the Moorifh regent under the caliphs. There are fome good rooms in it, but an idea prevailing that it is haunted, no one has the courage to refide in it. There is a picture over a door in which are a number of figures fo difpofed that it is difficult to count them: three of us attempted it, and always differed in the number. This greatly encourages the fuppofition of its being under the dominion of evil fpirits. I had not time or leifure to develope the myftery, but fuppofe it arifes from the multiplicity of figures which, feen in different lights, appear more or lefs numerous.

The oxen of this country are not only remarkable for their fize and beauty, but for the uncommon length of their horns, which are frequently three feet long. A pair of them are preferved in the mufeum at St. Martino, which meafure nearly four feet.

In the meantime our fquadron was reinforced by four line of battle fhips, under the command of Rear-Admiral Duckworth, from Lord Keith. With concern we heard of the illnefs of the Earl of St. Vincent, who was then at Minorca. The fleet, confisting of twenty sail of the line, under Lord Keith, had sailed for Toulon to watch the motions of the French fleet; but as they had sailed from thence, he followed them to the Gulf of Genoa, where they were descried by some of his frigates. Lord Keith then returned to Minorca to acquaint the Earl of this circumstance, but first detached four sail under Rear-Admiral Duckworth to reinforce Lord Nelson's squadron, lest the enemy should proceed to the southward. Fortunately they did not; for though their fleet was greatly superior in every respect to that under Lord Nelson, yet his Lordship's known bravery would have induced him to engage them if they had come in his way; but this was an event, under the present circumstances, by no means to be wished.

On the 12th of June the fleet received troops on board for Naples: four officers and a hundred and thirty men were put on board the Swiftsure; and the following day the Prince Royal embarked on board the Admiral's ship. A royal salute was also fired on his Majesty coming on board the Foudroyant, in which ship Lord Nelson had now hoisted his flag.

The following day, the wind being unfavourable, the fleet worked out of the bay. In the afternoon the Bellerophon and Powerful joined, and spoke the Admiral, who immediately made the signal to tack, and stood towards the bay, in which we again anchored on the 15th, and disembarked the troops.

In the evening of the following day the fleet again got under weigh and ſtood towards the little iſland of Uſtica. On the 19th the Incendiary arrived from the Bay of Naples, and brought intelligence that Cardinal Ruffo, at the head of an army of Calabreſe, had arrived before Naples; and that a Ruſſian and Turkiſh reinforcement was on its march to join him. The Admiral returned to Palermo on the 21ſt, and the day after joined us, having on board Sir William and Lady Hamilton.

We now made ſail for the Bay of Naples, where we arrived on the 24th. As we paſſed Baia and Puzzoli the Admiral ſaluted the Neapolitan flag, which was flying at thoſe places; and on the 25th the fleet anchored in a line abreaſt of Portici.

Cardinal Ruffo with his Calabreſe, and the Ruſſian and Turkiſh auxiliaries, had poſſeſſed themſelves of Ponte Madelina, and the rebels were driven into the caſtles Nuovo and Ovo.[k] The French had ſhut themſelves up in the caſtle of St. Elmo, which is ſituated on an eminence that overlooks the city.

In this poſture of affairs the inſurgents, or, as they were generally termed, the Jacobins, offered to capitulate to the Cardinal on condition that they ſhould be allowed to march out with the honours of war, and be provided with veſſels to tranſport themſelves and families with their property to France.

---

[k] Caſtel Nuovo is in the heart of the city, and has a communication with the palace. Caſtel del Ovo is ſo called from its ſhape, being ſimilar to an egg; it runs out into the bay, and is joined to the land only by a narrow paſs and draw-bridge.

This had been agreed upon, and the convention figned by both parties. Captain Foote, who commanded the Britifh force at that time, alfo figned at the particular requeft of the enemy.

Lord Nelfon now arrived: it feems that, by order of his Sicilian Majefty, no terms were to be entered into with the rebels, but that their furrender was to be unconditional. They were accordingly brought into the fleet, and their arms were taken from them, and the principals were laid in irons.

The marines of the fleet were landed, and a party of them garrifoned the two caftles which had been vacated by the enemy.

On the 29th of June the trenches were opened before St. Elmo under the direction of Commodore Troubridge, who commanded the befieging army; and the place was fummoned to furrender: but the commandant determined to ftand a fiege. At firft Captain Ball was fecond in command, but his fervices being required at Malta, where already the Britifh navy had made good their landing, his place was fupplied by Captain Hallowell.[1]

---

[1] Captain Hallowell had in the courfe of this war ferved in fimilar fituations on fhore. At the taking of Baftia in Corfica, we find honourable mention of him by Lord Hood; he was in the batteries with Captain Sericold, and by his fide when that valuable officer fell. At Toulon Captain Hallowell particularly exerted himfelf in bringing off the troops at the evacuation of that place, and was the laft man on fhore at La Malgue. He was afterwards appointed to the Courageux, which fhip was unfortunately wrecked on the coaft of Barbary while he was on a court-martial in the Bay of Gibraltar. In the memorable action with the Spanifh fleet off Cape St. Vincent, he was a volunteer on board the Victory; and the Admiral was fo much pleafed with his fervices on that occafion, that he ftrongly recommended him to the Admiralty, and fent him home with the duplicates of the account of that action; in confequence he was immediately appointed to the Lively frigate, and fent out again to Lord St. Vincent, who foon afterwards appointed him to the command of the Swiftfure.

On the 3d of July a battery of three thirty-fix pounders and four mortars was erected about a hundred toifes from the walls of St. Elmo; alfo a battery of four thirty-fix pounders and four mortars was at the fame time conftructed at the oppofite angle by the Ruffians under the orders of Captain Baillie.[m] The Turks were employed in guarding particular depots; and, in the main, behaved very well.

It was the intention of the commander to ftorm the caftle in different places as foon as practicable breaches could be made. On the 5th another battery of two thirty-fix pounders was opened. In the meantime the three-gun battery being entirely deftroyed, the guns difmounted, and the breaft-work knocked down, the Commodore directed Captain Hallowell to conftruct another battery at the diftance of ninety toifes from the walls.[n] He was here ably fupported by a Swifs regiment commanded by Colonel Tchudy. An emigrant[o] of great merit and abilities likewife affifted.

[m] Who had entered into that fervice at the conclufion of the American war, and now commanded a Ruffian fhip of the line.

[n] This battery, which was admirably conftructed, and coft immenfe labour, was covered by fome trees which it was neceffary to cut down before it could be opened with effect on the caftle. This was a fervice of fuch danger, that none of the labourers could be induced to perform it. Commodore Troubridge and Captain Hallowell, with Colonel Tchudy and Mr. Monfrere, advanced before the works to cheer them by their example; being perceived by the enemy on the walls, a gun loaded with grape was levelled at them with fuch precifion as actually to cut the boughs and ftrike the ground between their legs, yet providentially not one of them was hurt.

[o] Mr. Monfrere, who had been an officer in the royal armies of France, had lately ferved on board the Seahorfe in the humble capacity of fchoolmafter; but Captain Foote foon difcovered the fuperior qualities of this gentleman, and recommended him to Commodore Troubridge, who gave fuch ample

The quick and well directed fire of this new battery, which was not perceived by the enemy till it opened upon them, aided by a smart cannonade from the rest of the batteries, induced them to surrender; and an officer appeared on the walls with a white flag, as a token of truce. The terms of capitulation were soon agreed on; and the French marched out and delivered up the castle to the British troops. They were then embarked on board of vessels in the bay, and sent to France.[p]

Commodore Troubridge next proceeded with the army to Capua. On the 21st of July he arrived at Caserta, where he rested his troops for that day; and the following morning encamped before Capua. The Swifs, commanded by Colonel Tchudy, took their station to the right of our troops, and the rest of the infantry, under General Bouchard and Colonel Gams, encamped on the left side of the Volturno. On the 22d a bridge of pontoons was thrown acrofs the river, to facilitate the communication between the different detachments of the army. The cavalry was commanded by General Acton. Batteries of guns and mortars were constructed at the distance of a hundred and fifty toises from the walls of the city; and on the 25th, some of them being completed, they opened and kept up an incessant fire upon the enemy, who returned it with equal

testimony of his good conduct to Lord Nelson, that by his Lordship's interest he was afterwards promoted to the rank of major in a Neapolitan regiment of infantry.

[p] No authentic accounts of the killed and wounded during this siege have reached me. I can therefore only state, that we lost one officer, Lieutenant Milbanke of artillery, who was killed by a musket shot while reconnoitering the castle. Two Neapolitan officers also fell in one of the mortar batteries by the same cannon ball.

spirit. On the 26th the trenches were advanced within a few yards of the glacis; and batteries were begun to be erected.

From the rapid approach of the besiegers the enemy were induced to capitulate without further opposition; and the terms they first sent to Commodore Troubridge being rejected, others were sent by him, to which they acceded.

On the 29th the French garrison marched out and grounded their arms on the glacis. They were then marched to Naples, under a guard of four hundred British marines and two squadrons of General Acton's cavalry, and were there embarked for France.[q]

Capua has always been confidered as the key to Naples; it is situated pleasantly on the river Volturno, on the road from

[q] Commodore Troubridge, in his official letter detailing the circumstances of the two sieges, speaks in the highest terms of the assistance he received from Captain Hallowell, as also from Captain Ofwald: he gives ample praise to Colonel Strickland and Major Crefwell, and the other officers and men of the marines; also to his two aid-de-camps, Lieutenants Lowcay and Davis, and Mr. Greig, an officer of the Russian navy who was serving with him on board the Culloden. The Russians under Colonel Baillie; the officers and men from the Portuguese men of war, also Colonel Tchudy and his brave Swifs, came in for their share of well merited eulogium; as did also Generals Acton and Bouchard, and Colonel Gams, and Count de Lucci, chief of the etat major. Monsieur Monfrere was also spoken of in peculiar terms of praise.

As the troops were on their return to Naples Serjeant Macknight, of marines, being lame from an accident, was riding on a baggage waggon, when he received a shot from an unknown hand, of which he soon afterwards died. He was much lamented, being as good a soldier as well as one of the handsomest men in our little army. Suspicions fell upon some of our allies, who had expressed great resentment, and had repeatedly vowed revenge, because they had been prevented plundering by the steady conduct of the British troops. A Neapolitan regiment, that relieved our marines at Capua, were no sooner within the town than they began to exercise that cruel and disgraceful custom. The colonel, who was at dinner with the commanders, was called out to quell the disturbance, and soon returned with an account that he was obliged to shoot two of his soldiers before they would desist from plundering a house in the adjoining street.

Rome, and contains fome handfome buildings. The furrounding country is perfectly level and highly cultivated. This city is celebrated by Silius Italicus for the luxury and debauchery that Hannibal and his army indulged in after the battle of Cannæ: it is about fifteen miles from Naples. The road to it lies through a rich and luxuriant country, where the hufbandman's toil is requited by a triple harveft. The tall poplars on each fide of the road were at this time loaded with vines that hung in feftoons between them; and the foil below was bearing at the fame time crops of corn, with melons and beans, and other vegetables in the intermediate fpaces, fo that not an inch of ground was unoccupied.

> [r] Illa tibi lætis intexet vitibus ulmos:
> Illa ferax oleo eft: illam experiere colendo
> Et facilem pecori, et patientem vomeris unci.
> Talem dives arat Capua. VIRG. GEORG. lib. 2.

During the five weeks in which thefe events were carried on, Captain Hood had an arduous tafk to fulfil at Naples, where he commanded a body of feamen who had taken poft in Caftel Nuovo. The Calabrefe, as well as Ruffians and Turks, had entertained hopes that Naples was to have been given up to plunder; and the Cardinal, through whofe means they had

---

[r] Round thy tall elms the joyous vines fhall weave,
And floods of lufcious oil thy olives give;
This, with due culture, thou fhalt furely find
Obedient to the plough, and to thy cattle kind.
Such fertile lands rich Capua's peafants till. WARTON's Tranf.

been thus marched from the furtheſt extremity of the Neapolitan dominions, had no power to curb their lawleſs acts, which broke out in various exceſſes. Captain Hood, by his firm and prudent conduct, at length ſucceeded in reſtoring good order; and it was remarked that Naples (ſo lately torn by inteſtine broils and revolutionary fury) never, in the moſt peaceable times, enjoyed a greater degree of tranquillity than under his government.

Previous to his taking this command divers atrocious acts of cruelty, and murders attended with circumſtances of the moſt ſavage nature, were perpetrated in the face of day. One of theſe, that I witneſſed, will be ſufficient to relate here in proof of this aſſertion. An unfortunate gentleman, ſuſpected of being a jacobin or rebel, was dragged wounded out of the houſe he had been concealed in, and in an inſtant was ſtripped and cut to pieces; his mangled limbs were drawn about the ſtreets, and his head roaſted before a fire kindled in them for that purpoſe. Some of our officers who were paſſing by, and obliged to witneſs the laſt ſcene of horror, of courſe expreſſed their concern and diſguſt at it, to the no ſmall aſtoniſhment of the mob.

During theſe tranſactions his Majeſty the King of Naples arrived in the Seahorſe from Palermo. He firſt went to Procida, but the day following came on board the Foudroyant, bearing the flag of Rear-Admiral Lord Nelſon; and his Majeſty was received with a royal ſalute from the whole fleet.

At this time feveral Neapolitan infurgents were tried, condemned, and executed; among the reft Admiral Carraccioli. He had formerly diftinguifhed himfelf by his zeal and courage when he commanded a Neapolitan fquadron, and fought under the command of a Britifh admiral. This unfortunate man had retired with his Sovereign to Sicily; perceiving that no fteps were likely to be taken by his court to oppofe the new order of things at Naples, he requefted and obtained leave to return thither for the purpofe of fecuring, if poffible, his large property in that quarter. His known courage and abilities then pointed him out, both to his countrymen and the French, as a proper man to head the marine whenever it fhould be formed; and he entered with zeal into the fervice. Perhaps he thought, as many others have thought, that the king's abdication of his throne, without making fo ftrenuous an oppofition as he might have done to the revolutionary fyftem, and his quitting his capital feveral weeks before any enemy approached it, might plead his excufe for joining thofe who were now refolved to erect a new government, fince they were abandoned by their old. Be that as it may, he was tried by a Neapolitan court-martial on board the Foudroyant, condemned, and executed the fame day on board a Neapolitan frigate then lying off the Mole.

While we were in the bay I amply indulged my curiofity in viewing the various objects that diftinguifh the capital and its environs. Among the reft, the town of Pompeii demanded a particular inveſtigation, and I viſited it, accompanied by a friend, before any one had yet ſeen it ſince the revolution. We found that ſeveral places had been opened, and new diſcoveries made by the French while they were maſters of the country. One houſe, that had been diſcovered, was in good preſervation. The pavement of the hall was of Moſaic work, having in the centre a ſmall fountain; and the paintings on the walls were perfect, and ſome of them well executed. In one room was a dining couch in the form of an horſe-ſhoe, on which the gueſts lay recumbent, and the viands were placed in the hollow of it. The couch being of ſtone, muſt, when uſed, have been covered with carpets or cuſhions.

In another place, which was only begun to be cleared away, there were many beautiful ornamental paintings on the walls. Whatever valuable ſtatues or coins (if any) were found, they had been removed by the diſcoverers.

It would require an abler pen to deſcribe the reſt of this curious place, or the other remains of antiquity which we viſited in the neighbourhood; I ſhall only obſerve, that they had in general ſuffered little injury.

The King had taken the precaution to remove the moſt valuable articles from his muſeum at Portici: but we were gratified by the ſight of ſome fine bronze and marble ſtatues there, which were found at Herculaneum; alſo the painted walls which had been removed from Pompeii, and curiouſly preſerved in their original ſtate; and a Moſaic pavement brought from thence and relaid at Portici. An equestrian statue, in the entrance of the palace, had been struck by a cannon ball, and the head knocked off; but, as I was informed it was the only modern part of it, the injury is not irreparable.

I visited the studio in Naples, and had the satisfaction of seeing the famous statue of the Farnesian Hercules, which, with several other fine pieces of sculpture, was in a state preparatory for removal, and had we not arrived they would soon have been conveyed to Paris; the boxes for the purpose were there, and gave proof of the ingenuity of the French, both as to the strength with which they were constructed, as well as the mode in which the figures were prepared to be safe from injury. The spaces between the legs and arms, and other extended parts of the statues, were filled with lime and plaister, so as to render the whole a solid mass.

On the 5th of August, accompanied by Mr. O'Bryen, I paid a second visit to Portici, from whence we proceeded on mules to the hermitage on the side of Mount Vesuvius, taking three mountaineers as guides. When we arrived at the hermitage, where formerly dwelt a friar who was the ciceroni of the mountain, and famous for his vintage of lachryma christi, a rich wine in great request, to our concern we found his cell had been broken open and rifled, as well as his small chapel adjoining. Our guides said that the jacobini had done it, and that the venerable man had been very ill used by them. We had reason afterwards to believe that these fellows were of the party, as they offered to procure us some of the wine above mentioned, which had been distributed among the neighbouring cottages.

The day was excessively hot, and the labour, after we were obliged to relinquish our mules, was very great. After crossing a plain of rocky lava, which proceeded from the chasm or valley that separates Somma from Vesuvius, we came to the crater from whence issued the torrent of liquid fire that overwhelmed Torre del Greco in 1794. The cinders a little way below the surface were still hot, and smoke issued from several places. From thence we proceeded to climb the great cone, which consisting of small pumice stones, we sunk at every step up to our ankles, and frequently, by its yielding to our weight, lost as much distance in a minute as we had gained in ten.

At length we arrived at the summit of the mountain, and seated ourselves on the brink of the crater, which appeared to be about a mile round. The inside was so steep that our guides assured us we should not be able to get out if we ventured to descend into it; and as smoke was issuing from several places with a rumbling noise, we desisted from the attempt. The surface of the bottom of the crater was nearly level and of a greenish hue; on firing a pistol into it the echo and reverberated sound continued for a considerable time.

From this place we had a noble view of the surrounding country. The plains before us were extended beyond the reach of the naked eye. Many of the neighbouring mountains, which we could now look down upon, plainly fpoke their volcanic origin from the crater or hollow on their fummits, fome of which had water in them, in others were thick groves of trees and fhrubs.

As we returned to Portici we obferved feveral half ftatues of a bifhop holding up his hand towards the mountain. Thefe we found to be the reprefentation of the tutelar faint of Naples, St. Januarius, who is placed in the attitude of forbidding the mountain to pour its fiery inundations on the grounds or palaces where he takes his ftand.

On the 6th of Auguft Lord Nelfon in the Foudroyant, having on board the King of Naples, and Sir William and Lady Hamilton, got under weigh for Palermo; the Prencipé Reale, bearing the flag of the Portuguefe admiral the Marquis Neyfa, accompanied them. The following day the Swiftfure failed from the Bay of Naples.

In the note page 207, Lieutenant Davis is mentioned as one of the aid-de-camps of Commodore Troubridge at the fieges of St. Elmo and Capua. It may be remembered that this officer was appointed by Admiral Nelfon to command the Fortune corvette, captured by the Swiftfure off the Bay of Aboukir. When Sir Sidney Smith took the command on the coaft of Egypt he retained the Fortune, which went with him to the memorable defence of Acre, where Lieutenant Davis was actively employed.

On the 4th May 1799, he failed under orders from Sir Sidney Smith to cruize for three weeks on the coaft of Syria, in order to cut off fupplies that might arrive from Alexandria for the French army before Acre, having under his direction the Dame de Graffe gun-boat. About three a. m. on the 8th, being at the diftance of four miles from the coaft near Jaffa, he fell in with a fquadron confifting of three frigates and two brigs. At day-break one of the brigs having a red enfign difplayed, came alongfide of him. Lieutenant Davis hailed her, and was anfwered with a broadfide and a volley of mufketry, when fhe hoifted French colours; he inftantly returned their falute, and a fevere, though unequal, conflict began. At fix a. m. all his cartridges, and the greater part of his fhot being expended, three of his guns difmounted, his mafts, yards, and rigging cut to pieces, and the enemy coming clofe upon his larboard quarter with intent to board, Lieutenant Davis was compelled to ſtrike his pendant, his colours having been ſhot away three times. At this time, too, the three frigates had got within gun-ſhot of the Fortune; further reſiſtance, therefore, would have been raſh and uſeleſs. The veſſel that engaged the Fortune proved to be the French brig Salamine, and carried 18 guns and 140 men. The Fortune had only 10 guns, four and three pounders, all in bad condition. Lieutenant Davis was badly wounded, and had loſt two men killed and four wounded out of a complement of 28 men, including himſelf and ſervant.

The frigates were the Junon, Alceſte, and Courageux, under the command of Admiral Perrè, who ordered the Fortune and gun-boat to be ſunk. After cruizing on the coaſt nine days longer, the ſquadron proceeded to the weſtward. On the 8th of June they fell in with Lord Keith's fleet, which captured the whole ſquadron when they had arrived within ſight of their deſtined port. Lieutenant Davis was thus enabled to rejoin his ſhip, the Swiftſure, in the Bay of Naples. The gallantry of his conduct in this affair needs no comment.

CHAPTER XII.

> .... Vallombrosa
> Cosi fu nominata una Badia
> Ricca, e bella, né men religiosa,
> E cortese a chiunque vi venia.   Ariosto. Can. xxii.

THE critical situation of the French in the Roman states, occasioned by the frequent defeats they had lately suffered in Lombardy, the Milanese, and at Mantua, induced Lord Nelson to send the Swiftsure to Civita Vecchia, the nearest sea-port to Rome, to see if any thing could be done to drive the enemy from thence, and aid the Austrians in their attack on the capital. The Swiftsure was proceeding thither, but an account arriving that the Seahorse frigate had been driven by a gale of wind on the rocks near Leghorn, it was judged expedient first to proceed thither to her assistance.

On the 10th of August we passed the mouth of the Tiber, and could plainly perceive the stately dome of the cathedral of St. Peter at Rome. In the evening we spoke the Balloon, Portuguese brig of war; and the day following worked to windward between Point Hercule and the island of Giglio.

On the 13th we anchored in the road of Leghorn, and had the satisfaction to find the Seahorse safe in the harbour, having got off from her perilous situation with trifling damage. The same evening the Minotaur arrived also.

The opportunity of seeing Leghorn, Florence, and even Rome, was now eagerly embraced by me, my kind friend and commander giving me permission to make that tour, and in the event of his success at Civita Vecchia, to join him there by the route of Rome.[s] Subsequent circumstances prevented this arrangement taking place, but it gave me an opportunity of enlarging my tour. A friend from the Minotaur was permitted to accompany me by the favour of Captain Louis, and we proceeded from Leghorn, bearing letters and dispatches for the British minister at Florence.

On the 15th we set off from Leghorn, proceeding through a level country, part of which was occupied by a forest of low

---

[s] I shall not particularize the circumstances that took place at Civita Vecchia, as I received only a concise account of them afterwards, which is here related.

When the Swiftsure appeared off that place a French officer of distinction came off with a flag of truce, but nothing was then decided. At another time when some Neapolitan vessels, (supposing the place was evacuated by the French), were making towards it, the French armed boats, and gun-boats of a large size, pushed out to bring them in. But the launch and large boats of the Swiftsure were sent to their assistance, and soon made the enemy retire, pursuing them with great spirit till under the guns of their own batteries, and nearly capturing them. Lieutenant Eylmer, in the launch, had a narrow escape; a shot from the enemy's battery, which killed a man who was in the act of taking aim, struck the powder-horn from his hand. Captain Hallowell had already entered into a negociation with the enemy, and paved the way for a surrender of the place, when he was recalled to attend the Admiral at Palermo. Afterwards Commodore Troubridge in the Culloden, and Captain Louis in the Minotaur, arrived on the station; and the French perceiving that all hopes of defending themselves against the united powers that attacked them on all sides were at an end, and thinking to obtain better terms from the English than the Austrians, consented to surrender. Captain Louis proceeded to Rome, and there received the submission of the enemy, who were marched from thence to Civita Vecchia and embarked in vessels that transported them to France.

oaks, and the fame day we arrived at Pifa. It being the feaft of the affumption of the bleffed Virgin, great preparations were making for the due folemnization of it. The evening was fpent by the higher orders at a grand ball at the theatre; from whence, at midnight, they fallied out to join the folemn proceffion to the cathedral, where high mafs was performed with all the pomp imaginable. The ftreets leading to the cathedral, as well as the pavement of the fame, were ftrewed with myrtle and laurels, which being trod on, fent forth a delightful odour. The fragrant fmoke of the cenfers, the blaze of torches and lamps which illumined the ftately fabric, and the folemn ftillnefs of the midnight hour, formed fuch a fcene of grandeur and delight as impreffed the mind with religious awe.

The next morning we went to view the fite of the late folemnities. The cathedral, which is a noble pile of Gothic building, is fituated in an area furrounded by thofe other celebrated ftructures, the baptiftry, the cemetery, and leaning tower. The brazen doors of the cathedral are defervedly admired. On them are reprefented paffages from the Old and New Teftament in baffo relievo, executed by Bonano Pifano, whofe buft is placed near one of the doors. There are alfo many fine paintings, and handfome monuments, and other fculpture in the aifles and chapels of the cathedral.

The baptiftry is a large circular building furmounted with a handfome cupola. It is built of marble, and is celebrated for a remarkable echo. The cemetery, or, as it is here called, il campo facro, or the holy ground,' is appropriated for the interment of the inhabitants of the city; its form is oblong, and round the area are cloyfters, the walls of which are decorated with paintings reprefenting various pieces of fcripture hiftory; the figures as large as life. Among the reft is one of the laft day; fome fatirical ftrokes at the monks in this picture would induce one to believe that it was meant to turn that body into ridicule, if we did not frequently meet with the fame in all Roman Catholic countries. In thefe cloyfters there are alfo many handfome monuments to the memory of celebrated warriors, ftatefmen, and others.

We next vifited the leaning tower, which is a handfome circular building of free-ftone. On the outfide it is divided into eight compartments, with galleries furrounded by pillars, gradually diminifhing in height toward the top, which give it a fingularly light appearance. But what moft characterifes this ftructure, is its being funk into the earth on one fide, and thereby thrown full five yards out of the perpendicular. Some people imagine it was the whim of the architect that caufed this inclination of the edifice; but that certainly is a vulgar error, for had he built it fo in order to fhew his ingenuity, he would have made it evident by erecting it on a pedeftal horizontal with the earth: but that having funk equally with the reft of the building, fhows it was a fault in laying the founda-

---

' So called from fome earth that was brought from Jerufalem by the crufaders and depofited here.

tion that caused it thus to lean. From the top of this building we had an extensive view of the surrounding country, which is highly cultivated and diversified by mountains, plains, and rivers, with a distant view of the sea beyond Leghorn. In the street leading from this venerable collection of sacred buildings we visited a foundling hospital, which reflects infinite honour on the founder and supporters of it. As there was a box to receive eleemosynary contributions, we with pleasure gave our mite in aid of so noble and meritorious an institution.

The city of Pisa is handsome, and adorned with many private and public buildings. The river Arno, which runs through it, adds greatly to its beauty, and might be highly beneficial to its commerce. But Pisa at present appears to have fallen from that opulence its stately buildings seem to promise, and is far from populous.

We next proceeded to the baths of Pisa, which are about three or four miles from the city. There are many spacious houses for the convenience of the fluctuating inhabitants. The hot baths are reckoned beneficial in gouty cases. The buildings appropriated for that purpose are commodious, and are also supplied with cold baths. Our journey from hence lay through a rich country at the foot of some high hills, and the groves of olives we passed through reminded us of the oil which is made in this district, and takes its name from the city of Lucca, at which place we arrived the same day. It is about fourteen miles from Pisa. The Austrians were in possession of this place, the French having very lately evacuated it.

As we had, in our haste to depart from Leghorn, forgotten to provide ourselves with proper passports, we were taken into custody by the guard, and carried before the Austrian commander. He addressed us in German, a language neither of us understood; but by the help of an interpreter we informed him of our country, and situation, and the object of our journey, which being corroborated by our letters addressed to Mr. Wyndham, we were civilly dismissed, and presented with Austrian passports. Having an introductory note to the Abbatè Christophani, we availed ourselves of it, and were politely received by that gentleman, and by him conducted to see a valuable collection of pictures belonging to the house of Bonvisi.[u] There is a good road either for carriages, or walkers, on the ramparts of the city, which are three miles round.

What, except the hope of plunder, occasioned the French to attack this unoffending little republic, I could never learn; but one use they made of it was to take possession of the armoury, which contained an ample store. The brass ordnance was of very curious workmanship, and highly embossed. Most of this had been removed and transported across the Appenines, as I shall hereafter mention.

Taking leave of the friendly Abbatè, we set off for Florence;

[u] This family seemed to be at Lucca what the family of the Medici was at Florence, though in a less eminent degree. The present Marquis Bonvisi is a minor.

and on the road paffed through the towns of Piftoia and Prato. At the former place we vifited a filk mill, in which is a fpinning machine of great ingenuity, feveral thoufand reels being fet in motion by one water wheel.

In the evening we entered the city of Florence, after a pleafant journey of about forty miles through a rich and cultivated country. And we could not but remark the difference between the inhabitants of Tufcany and the wretched people of Naples; the climate being the fame, it muft arife from the fuperiority of the government, which, though abfolute, is mild and equitable. We perceived a cheerful cleanlinefs that befpoke content in the perfons and countenances of the Tufcan peafantry, who are in general robuft and healthy, and the women are handfome, and neat in their perfons and habits.

At Florence we took up our refidence at the Grand Bretaigne, kept by Sneidroff, a German who fpeaks good Englifh, and is a very civil and obliging landlord, very different from the generality of hotel-keepers out of England.

After paying our refpects to Mr. Wyndham, the Britifh Ambaffador, by whom we were received with the greateft politenefs, and at whofe table we were at all times treated with the trueft hofpitality, we proceeded to examine the many fubjects of curiofity that are to be met with at Florence. The famous gallery demanded an early vifit, and we had the pleafure to find it had hitherto efcaped the defpoiling hand of the French; but their intention to remove the contents was vifible by the mark set on all the statues and pictures. Each piece was numbered, and " Pour la Republique François," was written on every one of them. The vast extent of this noble gallery, which forms two sides and the end of a small street, and is filled with chef d'œuvres of the arts, occupied a long morning to inspect in a cursory manner. And though we frequently repeated our visits, we always found new subjects of admiration.

From the centre of one of the galleries we entered an octagon room called the Tribune. In this cabinet is the finest collection of statues in the world. The Venus de Medicis, the Wrestlers, the Arrotino, the Dancing Faun, and Apollo; besides which, there are also some capital paintings of the first masters.

From hence we entered a suite of rooms in which are collected the best paintings by the artists of past and modern times, and a number of inimitable pieces of sculpture. The contents of one of the rooms attracted our attention in particular; it is entirely filled with the portraits of the most celebrated painters of the old school, and with some of later date, each done by the artist himself. In this assemblage of genius we had the pleasure to observe the portrait of our own countryman, Sir Joshua Reynolds. And the only piece of modern sculpture in the room, is the head of the Honourable Mrs. Damer, finely executed in white marble by herself. The portrait of Denner by himself, is finished in the usual stile of that master; each hair and vein is minutely expressed, yet the effect of the whole is good, which is seldom the case where such pains are taken in the detail. It would be an endless task to enumerate the contents of this far-famed gallery, nor will the scope of the present work permit it.

Adjoining the Palazzo Pitti is a museum which was founded by the Grand Duke about twelve years ago; yet, notwithstanding the shortness of the period, it already contains a very valuable assemblage of curiosities; and the arrangement of them is excellent. Among other things that particularly demanded our admiration is a complete series of anatomical preparations in wax; every part of the human frame is represented with the most exact nicety. There is also a series of the animal, vegetable, and mineral worlds following each other in regular order, classed and numbered with precision. Those productions that cannot be preserved in their natural state and colour, are so finely imitated in wax as almost to deceive the closest inspection.

The last thing we saw at the museum was so horribly fine, that at the time the ingenuity of the artist astonished us, the subject could not fail to fill our minds with horror. It is in three compartments; and represents the awful change which the human frame undergoes in the several stages of the plague. It is well worth the traveller's inspection, but will by no means suit a descriptive account.

To view the numerous subjects of this museum, in a slight way, occupied two mornings; it would require many weeks to examine them with the attention they deserve. The Abbaté Olmi, who had a share in arranging and preparing this invaluable collection, accompanied us, and explained the nature of it in a manner both highly entertaining and instructive.

Palazzo Pitti, the elegant residence of the Grand Duke, had met with sad usage from the French. This palace was built and decorated from the private coffers of the Grand Dukes, without any aid from the people; yet this circumstance does not appear to have raised any compunction in the breasts of these destroyers. The rich silk curtains which hung before the doors and windows, reaching from the lofty ceiling to the ground, had been wantonly hacked to pieces with their swords as far as they could extend them, and several of the most celebrated pictures had been stripped from their frames. The Madonna della Sedia of Raphael had been stolen by the wife of a commissary; but this being discovered by the commanding officer of the French army, it was restored, but again disappeared. Whether it has at length found its way to Paris is not known; the superb frame still remains where it hung. In this palace there are also some fine specimens of Mosaic work, and inlaid tables of the manufactory of Florence.

The gardens of this palace, called Boboli, are elegantly laid out, and adorned with fine statues and fountains. Near the city is a public ride much resorted to by the Florentine nobility. It belongs to a small palace, or rather farm, of the Grand Duke.

The river Arno runs through the centre of the city; in the summer it is very low, but when torrents from the mountains increase its waters, it has a very noble effect. Each side is faced with stone, and over it are several bridges of various architecture. One of these, called Pontè della Trinita, is remarkable for the peculiar form of the arches, which are uncommonly flat. In the summer evenings this bridge is a favourite promenade; and, to secure walkers from the interruption of carriages, the ends are at a certain hour secured with chains.

There are several theatres at Florence, but at this time only two were open; the Cocomero and the Pergola. At one of them we were presented with a very curious drama of *fifteen* acts; it lasted three nights.

The cathedral church is an elegant building entirely of black and white marble in compartments, and is surmounted with an octagon cupola. Near the cathedral is a stately square tower in which the bells are hung. It is composed of black, red, and white marble, in compartments. Near this building is the baptistery, also of marble, highly polished, the three brazen gates of which exceed in beauty those we saw at Pisa; the figures on them are highly finished in basso relievo. The celebrated Michael Angelo, speaking of these gates, said, they were fit to be the doors of Paradise.

The chapel of Medicis, adjoining the church of St. Lorenzo, would be the richeſt piece of architecture in the world if it were completed: it is compoſed of the moſt valuable ſtones, ſuch as lapis lazuli, jaſper, and oriental agate: the ceiling and altar are unfiniſhed.

There are many fine antique ſtatues which adorn the ſtreets and ſquares of Florence. On the outſide of one of the gates of the city is a modern triumphal arch, which is an handſome ornament to that approach.

It would far exceed the limits of this work, were I to enumerate all the curious exhibitions of ancient and modern ingenuity that are contained in this city. Suffice it to ſay, that whether the French have, or have not, robbed it in their laſt viſit of ſome of its moſt valuable works, there muſt ſtill remain ſufficient to claim the attention of travellers; and this city muſt always poſſeſs attractions to detain them within its walls for ſome time. The manners of the people, the climate, the various amuſements, and, above all, the ſecurity in which both perſons and property are held, would ever make it a moſt agreeable reſidence.[x]

Having heard much mention of a Benedictine convent on the Appenines, we ſet off for that place with Mr. Alloway (who had returned to Florence with Mr. Wyndham, whom he

---

[x] Aſſaſſination, ſo common in moſt other cities of Italy, is very unuſual here. Mr. Wyndham told me, that, for the ſix years he had reſided in this city till the French came, not one murder had been committed.

Cooper Wittyams del.t

I. C. Stadler sculp.t

Val Ombrosa, on the Apennines.

London Pub. by I. White, Fleet Street, 1801.

had accompanied in his late voyage to Sicily). Our road lay up a steep ascent, but having four horses to our carriage, we arrived in good time at a village about fourteen miles from Florence. The road now became impassable for wheels, and we proceeded on horseback through a romantic country, varied with steep ascents, barren heaths, or shady forests. By a narrow path winding round the side of a mountain we came to an ancient bridge, below which the torrents, swelled by late rains, came tumbling over the rugged rocks.

At length we entered a forest of pines, and by a winding road reached the venerable monastery of Vallombrosa, so called from the beautiful wooded vale in which it is situated, although nearly on the summit of the Appenines. The annexed view will give a faint idea of the picturesque scenery of the place, which deserved a far abler pencil.

We were received with hospitality and politeness by the monks: one, and sometimes two of them, attended us while the rest seemed entirely occupied by the duties of their profession. The monastery is a handsome pile of building, the rooms commodious and well furnished; the chapel is large and handsome, and quite free from that glitter of tinsel ornament that too often spoils the appearance of similar edifices in Roman catholic countries. One of the fathers conducted us through a wood, at the back of the house, to a small habitation on the brow of a rock. On our road thither we passed over a wooden bridge that led across a torrent formed by a waterfall of confiderable height. Soon afterwards our conductor fuddenly ftopped, and croffing himfelf, feemed to regard with particular marks of devotion a rock that was in a recefs overhung with ancient oaks and pines. On examining the object of his adoration, we perceived the rude impreffion of a man upon it: the worthy father told us it was a miracle that befel the founder of his houfe, who, while he was attending to the erection of the building above, fell from the height on the rock we faw, which foftened at his touch, and he efcaped unhurt. After this we expected to fee fomething worthy fuch a miracle in the ftructure he was employed upon when it happened, but found nothing more than a fmall houfe, in which were fome indifferent pictures; and in a little mufeum we were fhewn feveral fpecimens of a peculiar compofition like marble, reprefenting views of various places, which he faid was the invention of a Mr. Huggesford, an Englifhman, who had been a brother of their order.[y] The next morning we climbed to the top of the hills behind the houfe, and found ourfelves on a large plain on the fummit of the Appenines. From hence we had a view of the two feas on each fide the Ifthmus of Italy, the Adriatic and the Tufcan fea. After paffing two days much to our fatisfaction with thefe friendly monks, we defcended the mountain and returned to Florence.

[y] But Mr. Huggesford's tafte and induftry are alfo vifible in the grounds round the monaftery, which immediately ftruck us to have been the work of an Englifhman. The fcenery, in that part contiguous to the houfe, reminded us of the appearance of an Englifh park, where art is introduced to affift and not deftroy nature.

Cooper Williams del.

I. C. Stadler sculp

Crebillarico on the Appenines.

London, Pub. by J. White Fleet Street 1801.

Finding that the Arretines[z] advanced but flowly towards Rome, and that we might be long detained in their camp, fhould we follow our firft plan of going thither, we determined to fee thofe parts of Italy that had lately been wrefted from the French by the Auftrians and Ruffians. General Suwarrow had at this time been victorious in feveral hard-fought actions in the Milanefe, and was advancing towards Genoa.

We, therefore, after procuring proper paffports through the friendly affiftance of Mr. Wyndham, afcended the Appenines with a Vetturino,[a] who was to convey us to Bologna. The road, though fteep, was in general good. At Alle Mafchere we baited our cattle, and again fet forward. Climbing the mountain for thirty miles, we arrived in the afternoon at Cubillario; which is a lone inn on the higheft part of the road acrofs the Appenines. Here our muleteer advifed us to ftop; and we found our accommodations tolerably good.[b] While the fire was

[z] The Arretines are the country troops that rofe againft the French and helped to drive them from Florence; they were commanded by Colonel Mari. While the French remained at Florence, they had frequent fkirmifhes on the neighbouring mountains with thefe gallant patriots, who, without any affiftance from the higher nobility of the country, had rifen againft the invaders, and revenged, as far as lay in their power, the infults offered to their beloved Duke. In feveral actions they had compelled the French to retreat to Florence with great lofs. They were fometimes headed by Signora Mari, a beautiful and elegant woman, wife to the colonel. Like Clorinda fhe bravely led them, dreffed in a military habit, and well performed her part.

[a] The Vetturini are people who furnifh horfes or mules to convey travellers for a ftipulated fum; they alfo provide provifions on the road; but care muft be taken to enter into a written agreement before you fet off, and that the time they are to be on the road, and the places they are to ftop at, are fpecified. We took a carriage with us on the journey, and found the Vetturino fo flow in his motions, that we afterwards preferred the more expenfive, but pleafanter, method of taking poft-horfes.

[b] The plate gives an exact idea of an Italian inn. Under the arches the carriages are fecured from the weather; within them are the ftables, and the rooms above are appropriated for the guefts.

lighting above ſtairs (for the air was now exceedingly cold from the height of our ſituation, though it was in the middle of Auguſt) we went into the kitchen, and there found ſeveral of the country people warming themſelves and converſing on the events of the war, and the various changes they had lately witneſſed. One of them, to our ſurpriſe, declared, " that they might ſay what they would of the Ruſſians and Auſtrians, of Suwarrow or Prince Charles, yet the Engliſh Signior Pitt was the moving ſpring of all, for without him the French would never have been driven out of Italy." We were not a little pleaſed at this homage paid to our illuſtrious countryman in a place where we hardly expected that even the exiſtence of our iſland was known.

In the courſe of our journey up the mountains, we had paſſed ſeveral broken gun-carriages, and in ſome places perceived they had been tumbled over the precipices, broken pieces being diſ-covered in various directions; here a wheel, there a ſhaft or beam, and the gun in a third place. At Alle Maſchere we ſaw ſome Auſtrian ſoldiers who were employed in conducting theſe pieces of ordnance; and from them we learned that theſe were the guns which the French had taken from the arſenal at Lucca, and had abandoned on the road. They were now taking them to Bologna, from whence they were to be conveyed to Mantua. The ornaments on theſe guns, which were all of braſs, were exquiſitely finiſhed; the knobs at the breech repreſented the heads of various animals, or of men, curiouſly executed. The arms of the Republic, with suitable ornaments and inscriptions, were equally well done.

The following day we set forward before sun-rise. Just as we came to an opening of the mountains, from whence we had a magnificent extended view of Lombardy with numerous towns and villages on the plains below, the sun rose and tinged the mountain tops with the most brilliant colours. As we descended the winding road down the steep declivity we met several troops of Austrian cavalry on their march towards Rome. The romantic craigs of rocks that hung over our heads, the tall chesnuts, oaks, and pines, that seemed coeval with the soil, stone bridges decorated with crucifixes, the fertile fields that were in the vallies below, and the waters of the Adriatic, of which we occasionally had a glimpse at the extremity of the horizon, formed altogether a sublime picture.

At length we reached Pianoro, a small village at the foot of the Bolognese side of the Appenines; here we intended to breakfast, but the inn being already filled with the Austrian officers, part of the army having halted at this place, we were constrained to pass on above a mile to a wretched hovel, where however we contrived to make a hearty meal on an omelet; and from thence proceeded to Bologna. We now dismissed our veturino, intending to take post-horses; but experienced some difficulty in compassing this point, as all the horses were taken possession of by the military to transport the baggage and stores of the army. However, by making our case known to the commanding officer, we were allowed a pair of horses, to which our landlord contrived to add another pair by stealth, and we reached Tedo by nine o'clock.

This place is a lone house a little out of the high road, where we were informed Lord Bristol, the Bishop of Derry, had been confined by the French for some time. From hence we proceeded, the next day, through a level country to Ferrara. On our road we crossed a branch of the Po, called Rhino, the waters of which were not more than three feet deep.

At Ferrara we visited the Palazzo Parodiso, where is a most excellent library, consisting, as we were told, of eighty thousand books. Here we saw the original manuscript of the Orlando Furioso of Ariosto, also several original letters in the hand-writing of Tasso, Petrarch, and other celebrated poets. The chair and ink-stand of Ariosto are curiosities shewn with great marks of respect here. The tomb also of that poet is to be seen at the Benedictine convent; but the French, after turning the unfortunate monks out of their monastery, had converted it into an hospital. At this time it was shut up, as was also the chapel adjoining, where the tomb is deposited.

The fate of the Benedictine monks has been peculiarly hard: they are in general men of family, who have been used to the comforts of life; and, it is but justice to observe, they dispense the wealth they possess with a liberal hand. Thus rudely thrust out of their possessions into a world they had renounced, they were in danger of being starved, if the benevolence of their poorer brethren had not affifted them. The labouring poor in the neighbourhood of thefe monafteries have great reafon to lament the lofs of their employers and benefactors.

Ferrara once was a place of great opulence and confequence; but, fince it has fallen into the power of the Roman See, it has become quite the reverfe, and is now the dulleft place I faw in Italy.

From hence we next proceeded to Padua. Croffing the Po, we paffed through St. Madalena and Cofta, and changed horfes at the ancient town of Rovigo, and thence paffed through a diftrict which produces abundance of the largeft hemp; the country is marfhy and unpleafant, but highly cultivated.

We foon afterwards paffed the Adige, and from thence proceeded to Monfelicé, where we again changed horfes, and arrived at Padua in the evening. We were much ftruck with the pleafant appearance of this celebrated place. The cathedral, and other churches, the faloon or great hall, and the univerfity, are all interefting objects.

From Padua we followed the tract of the Brenta for fome miles, and were much pleafed with the handfome appearance of the villas that adorn its banks. That of Prince Pifani attracted our attention, and induced us to vifit it; and it well anfwered our expectations. The grand hall of this palace is truly magnificent, and the frefco paintings on the ceiling are admirably finifhed. Our attention was attracted by two oil paintings of the Tower of London, which were drawn to commemorate the landing of a prince of this family, who was formerly ambaffador from Venice to our court. One of the rooms of this palace is fitted up in the Turkifh ftyle.

Leaving this delightful manfion, we proceeded to Dolo, ten miles from Padua, and thence arrived at Fufina, nine miles further, where we left our carriage and embarked on the Lagune, or fhallows, in a gondola, and in an hour entered the city of Venice.

We took up our refidence at Pedrillo's hotel, the White Lion, on the grand canal, which, befides being a very comfortable houfe in all refpects, commands a pleafant view of the Rialto. The annexed fketch I made from the windows of our apartment.

Venice has been fo often defcribed, that I fhall only remark the alterations it has fuftained from the late vifit of the French, who deftroyed the ancient government, and did all the mifchief they could to the arfenal, and then gave it up to the Auftrians. The four brazen horfes that were brought from Conftantinople, faid to be the work of Lyfippus, and placed over the entrance of the cathedral of St. Mark, had been taken away by the French. We were informed that the removal of thefe celebrated horfes created much difturbance in the city, and would have been prevented by the populace, but their power was not equal to their wifhes.

The lions mouths at the top of the grand ftaircafe of the Doge's palace, into which anonymous accufations were thrown,

Grand Canal and the Rialto, Venice.

London, Pub. by J. White, Fleet Street, 1801

are deſtroyed, and the place cloſed up where they were fixed. The fine paintings in this magnificent palace remain as they were, being painted on the walls.

The cathedral of St. Mark is remarkable for the fine Moſaic work in the ceiling, as well as for the general beauty of the building.

We viſited many of the palaces of the noble Venetians, and ſaw the fineſt paintings of the Venetian ſchool, but could not help regretting the decayed appearance they have, which is not the caſe of paintings by the ſame maſters in other parts of Italy. I imagine it muſt be occaſioned by the ſaline humidity of the air.

The arſenal and dock-yard are admirably contrived: the ſhips, from the largeſt man of war to a galley, are all built under cover, ſo that they are not liable to be warped either by partial winds or the heat of the ſun. The French had exerciſed their ingenuity in deſtroying the ſhips that were on the ſtocks, but not in a ſtate to be taken away: they had built a ſtrong prop under the centre of the veſſel, and then, knocking away the piles that ſupported the ends, they were broken by their own weight. Several large gallies had been ſcuttled and ſunk; but theſe the Auſtrians had contrived to weigh and refit. In the foundry we ſaw the proceſs of caſting and boring braſs cannon. The armoury had been entirely ſtripped, and a uſeleſs piece of miſchief exerciſed; large cannon-balls had been rolled down the fine marble ſteps in order to break and disfigure them.

On Sunday evening we were much entertained at a concert of inftrumental and vocal mufic at the chapel of the Ofpedale della Pieta. All the performers are young women, who receive their education gratis at the hofpital. There are feveral other inftitutions of a fimilar kind.

We were told that in this city there were four theatres; at one of them we faw an opera in which they celebrated the conqueft of the Ruffians, Englifh, and Auftrians, over the French; but when the French flag was thrown down and deftroyed, it did not meet with that enthufiaftic applaufe that fimilar reprefentations receive at Florence.

That we might the better judge of the fize, as well as general appearance of this remarkable city, we afcended to the top of the great tower of St. Mark, which is three hundred feet high: from hence we had a noble view of the city; every ftreet of which is water, and the only carriages are gondolas and boats of traffic. There are, however, many narrow alleys that communicate with each other by bridges; of the latter there are faid to be more than five hundred. Round the city are a multitude of iflands of different forms, and appropriated to various ufes. Some are entirely laid out in beautiful gardens and handfome palaces, others have extenfive manufactories, or churches and convents. The gondolas have a very fombrous appearance, being univerfally black; but their convenience, and the fwiftnefs of their motion, render them the pleafanteft of carriages.

As our stay would not allow of a minute inspection of the various objects of curiosity that adorn this city, we were constrained to take only a cursory view of them. One day we proceeded in a gondola through the whole of the grand canal. The palaces, whose fronts are towards the canal, are mostly of the Grecian order, and boast the masterly hand of Palladio, Sansovino, and San Michelle; but, from the corrosive sea air, they have acquired a brown and dirty appearance. The floors of the houses here are of a composition of plaister highly polished, and of various colours, representing different kinds of marble. Though these floorings are common throughout Italy, they are much better finished and display greater taste here than elsewhere.

After passing four days in Venice, we returned to Fusina, and from thence measured back our steps to Padua. There are many handsome churches and other public edifices in this city; the church of St. Antonio is a noble Gothic building, founded so early as the year 1255; and is enriched with some capital paintings, particularly of the Venetian school. The botanic gardens are greatly admired by strangers for the convenient arrangement of the plants.

The great hall, or town house, is well worthy inspection: it appeared to us to be as large as Westminster Hall; round the upper part of the walls are paintings of the twelve signs of the Zodiac, and small circular windows are so disposed that the sun at a certain hour darts his rays on the sign that governs the month; so we were informed by our ciceroni, whether true or false, I shall not pretend to determine. In this hall Bonapartè gave a grand entertainment to the officers of his army, and the principal people of the place, but left the inhabitants to pay the expence of it.

Some cardinals had already arrived at Padua in order to form a conclave for the election of a Pope, in the room of the late unfortunate Pontiff, who had just fallen a sacrifice to French perfidy and ingratitude.

From hence we went to Vicenza; but the evening closed in before we reached the city: being circumscribed in point of time, we set off early the following morning; so that all I can say of the place is, that it appeared to us, on the morning of our departure, to be handsome and well built, and the situation remarkably pleasant. I can also vouch for the urbanity of the inhabitants; for, by mistake, we went into a conversationè of the nobility, where none but those who are properly introduced are permitted. But we were foreigners, and Englishmen; the rule therefore was politely dispensed with, and we were received with marks of attention and civility highly gratifying to us.

We have, however, to lament that we could not pay more attention to a place that gave birth to Palladio, and where some of the best specimens of his skill in architecture are to be found.

From Vicenza we passed through a fertile country to Monte Bello, and from thence to Caldiero, at each place changing horses, and by noon entered the celebrated city of Verona, and found there remnants of antiquity that fully juſtified all we had been told of it. The fine marble amphitheatre is in excellent preſervation, and gives a clear conception of the order and arrangement that was preſerved at thoſe public exhibitions, where ſuch multitudes of people were aſſembled. This amphitheatre is ſaid to be leſs than the Colyſæum at Rome, but much more perfect. It is capable of containing twenty-two thouſand and eighty-four ſpectators, all of whom could eaſily ſurvey the arena or ſpace where the gladiators engaged with each other, or with wild beaſts.

The river Adige runs through this city, over which are four handſome ſtone bridges. The ſtreets in general are narrow, but that called Il Corſo is long and ſpacious; in this ſtreet during the carnival are races for horſes and footmen. We alſo were ſhown two gateways, which our ciceroni aſſured us were ancient triumphal arches; one certainly was not, and I have reaſon, from ſubſequent information, to believe that the other has no claim to that title.

From the walls of the city we had an extenſive view of the ſurrounding country. The plain extending for three miles, and ſkirted by riſing ground, had lately been the ſcene of ſome gallant actions between the Auſtrians and French: the former with only ſixteen thouſand men engaged the latter ſtrongly poſted on the heights with forty-five thouſand men. The inhabitants on the walls anxiouſly beheld the combat. Towards the cloſe of the day a ceſſation of hoſtilities took place; the Veronese, fearing that their friends were in danger, could no longer be restrained, but insisted on being led to their assistance; the Governor complied with their wishes, and marched with them to the Austrian camp. When the day broke, and the French discovered the numerous reinforcement that appeared on the side of their enemy, they retreated with precipitation to the distance of seven or eight miles from the field of battle, imagining that the undisciplined troops would retreat to the city, which they did. But at this eventful moment a large body of Austrians troops from Vicenza and Venice arrived, and changing the face of affairs, the French were again beaten. They then attempted by a manœuvre to regain the city before the Austrians, but were once more foiled by them; for the Imperialists, being aware of their design, had loaded large and heavy barges with stones, and setting them adrift, they fell down the river with such rapidity, that striking the piles of a temporary bridge the French were obliged to pass, it gave way, and thus stopped their career. Many were drowned, and those who had already passed over were either taken or killed, and the rest of the army retreated.

In this city the celebrated Paul Veronese was born, and many of his fine paintings are to be seen in the churches and public buildings. Here also we were shewn some curious petrifactions of fish which are found at Monte Bosco: we bought several specimens which represent the fish in a very perfect state, even the bones and scales being visible; they are found in a soft white loamy stone. Besides these, crabs and oysters are also found in a similar state.

From Verona we journeyed for eleven miles through a rich and well cultivated country to the little town of Castel Nuovo, where there was nothing to arrest our attention.

The next place we came to was Peschiera, a strong fortress on the side of Lago di Garda; it commands a pass from the province of Brescia into the Veronese. When the Austrians were on their march from Brescia the French retreated from this fortress to Mantua, breaking down part of the bridge and destroying the road in their rear, which we found still in so bad a state as to be hardly passable.

From hence our road lay on the margin of the lake to Defenzano, a small town delightfully situated on the southern side of it. Being a fast-day we dined on a large trout just taken from the lake. From the windows of our dining-room we had a view of this beautiful sheet of water, which is thirty-five miles long and twelve broad. At the furthest extremity we beheld the majestic summits of the Alps rising as it were out of the bosom of the lake. Monte Baldo, a barren mountain, whose rugged sides overhang the eastern margin of the lake, opposed to the softer beauties of the western side, formed altogether an enchanting picture. In the evening we walked for about two miles along the shore through some delightful meadows. The weather was soft and pleasant, and a light breeze just served to ruffle the surface of the water, and fill the sails of the boats that were conveying merchandife from one town to another. Some tall poplars ornamented this quarter; and from hence I took the drawing which reprefents the narrow part of the lake towards Monte Baldo, with a fmall town or village at the foot of it. A promontory of land, that from this point of view had the appearance of an ifland, on which were fome buildings with a chapel and fortrefs, added much to the picturefque effect of the fcene.

We now retraced our fteps to Caftel Nuovo; from hence we paffed over a rugged and difagreeable by-road to Roverbello; and having croffed the Mincio,[e] early in the afternoon we reached Mantua. This city, fituated in the middle of a fwampy lake, has been the object of fevere contefts between the French and Auftrians in the courfe of this war. Bonapartè, after a fiege of many months, during which he loft a great number of men from ficknefs, took it by capitulation, the garrifon being reduced to the laft extremity by famine.

At the time of our vifit it had juft paffed into the hands of the Imperialifts, who in a few weeks retook it, advancing their works with aftonifhing rapidity to within feventy paces of the horn-work that defended the caufeway; from whence the

---

[e] When arrived at the banks of this river, Virgil's beautiful lines ftruck us as peculiarly defcriptive.
"Tardis ingens ubi flexibus errat
Mincius, et tenera prætexit arundine ripas."
VIRG. GEORG. lib. 3.

Where Mincio's ftream meand'ring flowly feeds
Around his ample fhores the tender reeds.

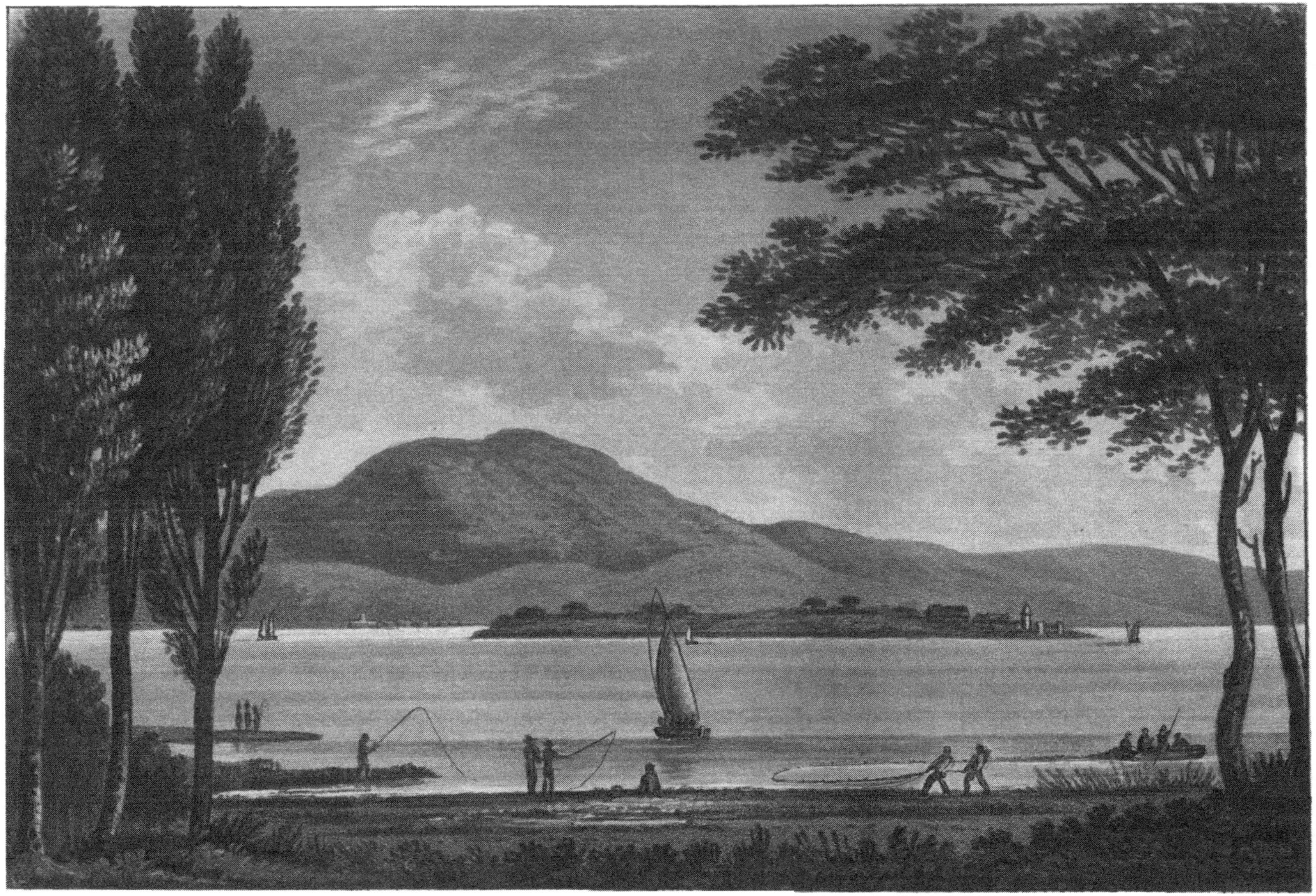

Cooper Willyams del.t J.C. Stadler sculp.t

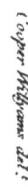

View on Lago di Guarda.

London: Pub.d by I. White, Fleet Street, 1801.

French were foon driven, and a breach being made in the walls of the town, and an efcalade refolved on, the befieged were induced to capitulate. As we paffed the caufeway the artificers of the army were bufily employed in filling up the ditches, and deftroying the works they had made in their late fiege, and alfo in rebuilding that part of the wall that had been battered down.

We put up at the Royal Auberge, which well deferves the name, as it has more the appearance of a palace than an inn. You did not enjoy the fumptuous apartments without paying well for them. We found it the moft extravagant inn we met with on this tour. The ftreets of Mantua are in general fpacious, ftraight, and adorned with handfome edifices. The cathedral, built by Giulio Romano,[d] is a fpacious building; many of the paintings in it are alfo by the fame mafter. The caftle, or ducal palace, has alfo fome capital pictures by Annibale Caracci, Palma, and one by Titian; the ceiling is by Giulio Romano. At the palace di Thé (named fo from its being formed like the letter T) we faw fome frefco paintings of Giulio Romano, who alfo gave the plan for this palace: the two moft remarkable are, the fall of Phaeton, and Jupiter's victory over the Titans; the figures of the latter being larger than life, have a terrific appearance. In the court-yard of this

[d] This celebrated painter and architect was interred in the church of St. Barnabas in Mantua; but by the alterations that have fince taken place in the edifice, the exact place where he lies is unknown. His houfe was oppofite to the church. It will be remembered by my readers, that honourable mention is made of him by our great dramatic poet Shakefpeare; fee Winter's Tale, act v.

palace we saw a large train of artillery, of various forms, and different kinds of compofition. We learned they were captured from the French, and confifted of a medley they had picked up in their various depredations. Some large pieces of ordnance attracted our attention, from the colour of the metal, and the fimplicity of their appearance, being turned quite plain, without any ornament. We found they were compofed of bell-metal, in which there feemed to be a large proportion of filver.

It is in the recollection of every one, that, at the commencement of the French revolution, the bells of all the churches in France were put in requifition, and melted down for the fervice of the Republic; and thefe were fome of them. I fhould imagine the noife they make when fired, muft be greater than thofe of brafs, which exceed iron guns in a fharp ringing found that follows the explofion. There were alfo fome beautiful pieces of more ancient ordnance from Lucca and other places.

In the evening we went to the theatre, which is handfome, and better lighted than is generally the cafe in Italy, and the performance was good.

From Mantua we proceeded through a fertile country till we arrived at the banks of the Po, which we croffed over in the fame manner as before in our road from Ferrara to Padua. The contrivance is ingenious, and peculiarly eafy and expeditious. Two large flat boats are faftened together, on which

Cooper Williams, del.t

I. C. Stadler sculp.

Flying Bridge on the Po
London, Pub. by I. White, Fleet Street, 1801.

a firm deck is laid; on the fore part is a beam erected on two poles, from whence a strong rope is extended into the centre of the river, and there fixed. Small canoes with short masts are placed at certain distances along the line to keep it clear of the water. When the passengers are all embarked the ferryman unhooks the side, and gives it a gentle motion with his pole, at the same time shifting the helm; the current of the river then contributes to aid its motion, and it swings over like a pendulum, with its head still to the stream, till it reaches the other side, where it is again fastened, and the passengers, horses, and carriages, are disembarked without any difficulty. When it returns the helm is again shifted, and the rope brought to the opposite side of the beam.

At the neat little town of Carpi we dined, and from thence passing through Modena, and by the fortress of Fort Urbino, we arrived once more at the St. Marco in Bologna, a house whose aspect is not so good as the entertainment, which is excellent.

The city of Bologna is remarkably striking in its appearance; almost all the public streets are accommodated with covered walks, with handsome though heavy corridores. The Asinelli tower, from its vast height, rising out of the centre of the city, gives a peculiar appearance to the city when seen from a distance. The buildings in general are not celebrated for beauty; but Bologna boasts of the finest collection of paintings of any city in Italy, Rome only excepted. The Caraccis have contributed by their excellent paintings, and thofe of their fcholars, to enrich the collections in this city.

From Bologna we retraced our fteps up the Appenines, and this time breakfafted and changed horfes at Pianoro, and were well pleafed with the civility of our hoft, and profited much by the advice he gave us concerning the impofitions of the people at the poft-houfes up the mountain, who frequently endeavoured to make us take more horfes, and even bullocks, to drag our light carriage, where there was no neceffity for it. On our journey we met part of the French army which had furrendered to the Auftrians, and were on their march under an efcort to Mantua.

At Pietra Mala we left our carriage, and, accompanied by a guide, walked over fome rough road for about a mile, to view the curious volcano, which, it is faid, has never increafed beyond its prefent bounds. The fpace it occupies, in the middle of a large open meadow, is about thirty paces in circumference; the ground within that circle has the appearance of burnt clay. From fmall chafms or cracks the flame rifes, but it never explodes or throws up lava like the volcanos of Ætna and Vefuvius. A remarkable circumftance attends this flame: in heavy rains it rifes to a great height, and blazes with redoubled fury; but a ftrong wind damps its ardour, and for a time it appears extinguifhed. The country people, as well as travellers, frequently roaft eggs or potatoes, and boil water by the flame; the ground near it appears to be hollow when ftruck with the foot, but it is not warm except at the fissures. Sometimes the chasms close, and new ones open, but never extend beyond the circumference abovementioned.

From hence we again set forward and reached our former lodgings at Cubillario. On the road this day a large mastiff jumped into the carriage, and seemed to caress us with singular marks of fondness. At Cubillario the servant informed us she remembered the same dog attending the French army on its march to Rome; probably it had lost its master, and was resolved to ingratiate itself with the first it met. We passed this night at Cubillario, where we met with some Austrian officers who seemed well pleased to enter into conversation with Englishmen.

From hence, at an early hour, we set off for Florence. In our descent down the mountain we were particularly struck with the appearance of that beautiful city; the river Arno winding and extending itself through a rich and well cultivated country, abounding with beautiful villas and romantic situations, and the plains covered with tall trees of various descriptions, and large groves of olives, whose deep green contrasted with the livelier tints of the vine, gave a peculiarly pleasing appearance to the landscape.

On re-entering Tuscany we could not avoid remarking the superior neatness and joyous countenances of the people contrasted with the inhabitants of the Ecclesiastic States. In the latter, beggary, idleness, and discontent, seemed to reign. One cause of this indeed might be attributed to the uncertain ſtate of their affairs, having as yet no regular government eſtabliſhed. The Auſtrians at preſent were maſters of it, but the event ſtill hung doubtful in the ſcale of fortune.

On our arrival at Florence we learned that Rome had not yet ſurrendered; we therefore paſſed another week very agreeably in viewing the curioſities of the town and neighbourhood, and in the ſociety of ſeveral agreeable people to whom we were introduced by the kindneſs of the ambaſſador. Among others we dined at a pleaſant villa belonging to Signor Donato Orſi, a rich and loyal banker of Florence. The villa is about two miles out of town, and, being on a riſing ground, commands an extenſive and beautiful view of the ſurrounding country: but what renders it moſt celebrated is, that it was once the property and favourite reſidence of the celebrated Machiavel.

Another time we paſſed the day at a Carthuſian monaſtery, a few miles out of the city. The manſion, which is ſpacious and commodious, is built on an eminence overlooking a ſmall and rapid river in which are found many rare ſtones and pebbles which, when cut, make excellent ſeals. An extenſive garden ſurrounds the building, and is guarded by a high wall beyond which the monks never go. Their habit is white, and their heads cloſe ſhaven: the rules of their houſe are very ſtrict; as, except on particular occaſions, they never converſe. The prior and a friar, who was brother to an abbate that accompanied us, received us with much hoſpitality; and appeared to enjoy the privilege of converſation, and amply made up for their general taciturnity. In our walks about the houfe and gardens we met feveral of the monks with their cowls drawn over their heads, and feemingly intent on their devotional meditations.

To examine the arts and manufactures of Florence demanded more time than we could afford; but among thofe we faw, the manufactory of inlaid marble demands fome notice. It was eftablifhed by the Grand Duke, and is carried on entirely at his expence. The marble is cut into thin pieces, and arranged in feparate compartments according to their colour and fhade; they are then cut into the fhape required, and curioufly fitted together on a table of flate. In this manner pictures are copied with the greateft exactnefs, and with confiderable effect. The mode of cutting it is by a copper wire ftrained on a bow, on which a little oil and emery is put, and with this it is continually moiftened.

The manufacture of alabafter, by Pifani, is well worth feeing. Here are copies of the moft celebrated ftatues, and vafes of different fizes clofely imitated, and finely executed: they are fold very reafonable.

The Studio, where youth are inftructed in drawing, fculpture, and architecture, owes its foundation to the munificence of the Grand Duke. We alfo vifited Signor Raphael Morghen, who is efteemed the firft engraver in Italy. He was at this time putting the finifhing ftroke to an engraving of the Laft Supper, from a painting by Raffaele, which has fince been publifhed.

The mountains furrounding Florence are in general quarries of the fineft marble, ufeful both for ftatues and architecture.

Being one evening attracted by the beautiful appearance of fome tranfparent vafes in a newly opened fhop in the ftreet Maggio, we entered it, and, while admiring the exquifite workmanfhip of the alabafter ftatues and vafes, our attention was called off by a tall venerable figure of a man with long grey locks flowing down his fhoulders, and wrapped in a loofe robe. On inquiry, we found he was a Swifs gentleman who lodged in the houfe. Our appearance alfo announced our being foreigners, and he imagined Englifhmen. He addreffed us in our own tongue with confiderable elegance, and faid he was too old to ftir out himfelf, but begged the favour of our coming to him; which in a few days after we did, and were much entertained by his converfation. He told us his name was Valltravers; that formerly when in the height of his fortune and health, he had vifited England for a confiderable time; that he had an eftate there, but by the fraud of his agent he could neither receive the income of it or fell it; that the troubles in Switzerland had driven him to take refuge at Florence, with the wreck of his fortune, attended by his niece. His age was eighty and upwards, and he faid he was a Fellow of the Royal Society. He prefented me with a tract he had written and publifhed in England in 1786 on the practicability of difcovering a northern paffage between the Pacific and Atlantic Oceans. This opinion indeed was so strong in the mind of the old gentleman that his discourse frequently turned on it.

The time now approached when we were obliged to take leave of a city where we had passed several weeks so much to our satisfaction. An account arrived that the Foudroyant had brought the King of Sardinia[e] to Leghorn; and thither we proceeded in order to join our respective ships. But, on our reaching that place, we had the mortification to learn that both the Minotaur and Swiftsure had sailed for Minorca. We were, however, introduced by Captain Sir Edward Berry to Captain Campbell of his Majesty's frigate Santa Teresa, who offered us a passage thither.

Leghorn is an open port, by which means its trade has flourished for a long time, and still continues to do so, notwithstanding the unsettled state of affairs in the neighbourhood, and the several changes of masters it has itself lately experienced.

It was confidently reported when we were there, that at the time it fell into the power of the French, the Jews were instrumental in producing that event. It is well known that the French had held out great immunities to them, and their grati-

[e] This unfortunate monarch had experienced the most cruel treatment from the French in requital for his making no opposition to them. When they compelled him to quit his kingdom and retreat to Sardinia, their malice still pursued him: no sooner had he sailed in a small unarmed vessel from Leghorn than some privateers immediately got under weigh to intercept him in his passage. Fortunately the Minotaur was on the station: Captain Louis, the moment he perceived their villanous intention, (of which too, it is said, he had received some private intimation,) resolved to convoy the unfortunate prince to his now last retreat; and he had the satisfaction of preserving him from the worst of misfortunes, by seeing him in safety to Sardinia.

tude has been proportionate. The hope of reaffembling as a nation, and perhaps replacing themfelves in the land of their forefathers, alfo ftimulates them to do all they can for thofe who have promifed to win the land of Judea for them.

The city is fortified, particularly on the land fide, which is well defended by ftrong ramparts and baftions; the ditches are broad, deep, and filled with water. The extent of the town is about two miles in circumference: canals communicate with the Arno, and convey merchandife through it from Pifa and Florence into the Mole.

The firft approach to Leghorn from the fea is particularly pleafing, from the picturefque appearance of the buildings. You firft enter the outer harbour, which is capable of holding frigates and large merchantmen; but there is not depth of water for fhips of the line. By a narrow paffage, defended on both fides by a caftle and pier-head, and a chain acrofs, you enter the inner mole, where galleys and fmaller veffels receive or deliver their goods. On landing the eye is ftruck with a magnificent marble ftatue of Ferdinand the firft duke of Florence, with four flaves in bronze, chained at his feet. At the time I am fpeaking of, the iron rails were under repair; the French having removed them, as they intended alfo to have taken away the ftatue.

The ftreets of Leghorn are ftraight and fpacious, and the houfes lofty and well built. A handfome piazza or fquare is in the centre of the town, which alfo ferves as a market-place.

The coral manufactory is worth seeing; it is exclusively in the hands of the Jews. The English factory, however, have the principal lead in commercial affairs.

Part of the city, through which the canal glides, reminded us of Venice; and we found that district to bear the name of Venezia Nuova.

The lazaretto is a large handsome building at some distance without the walls. About three leagues from the shore is a lighthouse built on a reef of rocks called the Malore, within which is the road where men of war anchored, but they are quite exposed to the fury of the winds, which sometimes blow strong gales on this coast. At Leghorn I met my old acquaintance Lieutenant Parker, who was bound for England with dispatches from Lord Nelson and the King of Sardinia. I mention this circumstance, as it was the last time I saw that gallant young man, who has since fallen gloriously in his country's service.

CHAPTER XIII.

Son già là dove il mar fra terra inonda,
Per via ch' esser d'Alcide opra si finse,
E forse è ver, ch' una continua sponda
Fosse, ch' alta ruina in due distinse.
Passovir a forga l'oceano, e l'onda
Abila quinci, e quindi calpe spinse.
Spanga, e Libia partio con foce angusta:
Tante mutar può lunga età vetusta.   TASSO, canto 15.

ON the 23d of September we embarked on board the Santa Teresa frigate, and soon after got under weigh for Minorca. On the 26th we passed a convoy from Leghorn under the care of the Mermaid, Captain Oliver. Mr. Erskine, commissary-general to the British army, was on board, having been to Tuscany to purchase cattle for the garrison at Minorca.

On Sunday the 29th we descried the island we were bound to, and in the evening worked into the harbour of Mahon, after a pleasant voyage, rendered more so by the friendly attention we met with from Captain Campbell. As we entered the harbour at night, we could not form any idea of its excellence, though, from the height of the land on each side, we were pretty well assured it must be a safe one when once entered.

As we paſſed the barracks at George Town, the lights in the windows made it appear cloſe to us; and on the other ſide the high white walls of the lazaretto ſeemed equally near. We learned the next morning that the Minotaur had returned to Palermo, and that the Swiftſure had ſailed for Gibraltar; my friend therefore re-embarked in another frigate for Sicily, and I remained to wait an opportunity of rejoining my ſhip.

In the mean time I took up my reſidence with my friend Brigadier-General Stuart, who introduced me the ſame day to the Lieutenant-Governor, Sir James Erſkine Sinclair.

The appearance of the town of Mahon is very remarkable; it is ſituated on an eminence at the further end of the harbour, and on the water's edge are a range of ſtorehouſes[f], by the ſide of which the merchants ſhips are anchored. Oppoſite to the town, on a low flat point of land, is the dock-yard. There is ſuch depth of water near the wharf that a ſhip of the line may be brought cloſe alongſide it, and be hove down without difficulty. There being little or no tide here, they have no dry dock. The town of Mahon is very irregularly built, and the ſtreets are uneven and ſteep. There are two large churches, and ſeveral ſmaller. The annexed view will give a pretty accurate idea of the principal ſquare, or grand place, where the guard is mounted: on the right is the cathedral, a plain unadorned ſtructure: in front, the building with corridors is

---

[f] The ſtorehouſes to the weſtward belong to the royal dock, in which are kept naval ſtores that can eaſily be tranſported acroſs the water to the dock-yard.

Grand Parade Chatham
London. Pub.d by I. White, Fleet Street, 1801

the town-houfe; on the left of which are a convent, the bifhop's palace, and the guard-houfe. This place is the general refort of the higher order of the inhabitants, and of the officers of the garrifon. The ftreets being pitched with fharp ftones, are very inconvenient to walkers; but the houfes are in general roomy and handfome. About two miles to the fouthward of Mahon is George Town, entirely inhabited by the military. Here is a handfome barrack, in which at this time the 28th and 90th regiments were quartered. About half a mile beyond, is Fort George, formerly Fort St. Philip, in which the 8th regiment and a party of artillery were now quartered under the command of Colonel Drummond. I was furprifed to find, inftead of the ftrong caftle I had heard of, nothing but a vaft heap of ruins; and the caufe of this only added to my furprife. When the Spaniards, with the help of the French, took this caftle the latter end of the laft war, being apprehenfive that, notwithftanding the ftrength of the place, it might be recaptured by us at a future day, they blew up the citadel and deftroyed the works. The fpacious bomb-proofs, capable of containing an army, were alfo involved in the general deftruction. A greater compliment could not be paid by an enemy than this action offered to the character of Britifh enterprife. However, during the fhort time it has been in our power, much has been done to render it again ferviceable; many of the bomb-proofs have been cleared of the rubbifh that had fallen into them; and though the caftle is no more, ftrong walls and batteries are erected, and the whole begins to offer a respectable appearance of defence. Some temporary barracks have been run up; but many of the officers at this time preferred remaining in their tents.

The roads in Minorca are rough and stony: the whole island indeed presents a barren prospect of rocks, covered in some places with a thin soil, which, by the industry of the inhabitants, produces tolerable corn. The gullies, or small valleys, where the soil is deeper, by the frequent accumulation washed into them by torrents of rain, are fertile, and bear excellent vegetables. They are also planted with fig-trees and vines.

The harbour of Mahon is perhaps the best in the world, being capable of holding a great number of ships, and having depth of water for the largest man of war to ride in perfect safety. It is landlocked on all sides with numerous coves, in which the merchantmen are brought close to the shore, while the rocky crags rising perpendicularly from the water's edge, are high enough to shelter them from the heaviest gales. In the centre of the harbour, on an elevated island, is the naval hospital, admirably calculated for the health and convenience of the invalids.

On the western side of the bay, not far from Fort Philipet, and nearly opposite to Fort George, is the lazaretto. It was built by the Spaniards since the last war at considerable expence. It is now made use of as a barrack, in which the regiment of De Rolle, and Brigadier-General Stuart's regiment of foreigners are quartered. The former regiment was at this time commanded by Lieutenant-Colonel Baron Durler, who was one of those unfortunate Swiss officers whose troops were barbarously murdered at the beginning of the French revolution in an ineffectual attempt to defend their sovereign from the attacks of a lawless mob. He, at that time, very narrowly escaped the general massacre, and as he was making towards the national assembly was twice in danger from the bayonets of the insurgents.

Brigadier-General Stuart's[g] regiment consisted of twelve hundred foreigners, most of them Germans; some of these were part of the Swiss regiment that served under the Spanish government when the island fell into our hands; many of them

---

[g] Brigadier-General John Lucey Stuart is descended from an ancient family in Scotland, a branch of which settled in America. At the breaking out of the unhappy war between the colonies and the mother country his family decidedly embraced the side of loyalty, and in consequence suffered severe hardships, and the loss of a large property. The subject of the present article entered at an early age into the army. In one of the actions fought during that war, he being then an ensign in the Guards, was shot through the thigh, of which wound he hardly recovered when he was again called into active service. At the commencement of the present war he accompanied the Duke of York into Holland, and was soon after raised to the rank of lieutenant-colonel, and then colonel in the army. Early in 1796 he accompanied General the Honourable Charles Stuart to Lisbon, with the rank of brigadier-general, and had the command of a brigade composed of foreign regiments, which, by his knowledge of the continental languages, he ably conducted. In 1798 he again served under the same general at the conquest of Minorca; and since that accompanied the ever to be regretted General Sir Ralph Abercromby to Egypt, where his conduct at the head of the foreign brigade is mentioned in terms of high approbation by General Hutchinson in his account of the severe action fought before Alexandria on the 21st of March 1801. His words are: " Brigadier-General Stuart and the foreign brigade supported the reserve with much promptness and spirit. Indeed it is but justice to this corps to say, that they have on all occasions endeavoured to emulate the zeal and spirit exhibited by the British troops, and have perfectly succeeded."

were men who had been taken by the French in Piedmont and Italy, and after undergoing severe confinement, and a variety of ill treatment, were induced to consent to be transferred to the Spaniards, by whom it is said they were bought from the French. In their passage they were taken by some of our cruizers and brought to Minorca, when they gladly accepted the offer of being inrolled in the British army: they were in a state of the utmost wretchedness when taken, naked, and almost starved. Being excellent soldiers, and in general remarkably well-shaped and strong men, they were at that time a great acquisition to our army. Their subsequent conduct in Egypt has fully justified the good opinion of them which I have often heard expressed by the brigadier-general.

In an evening the band of this regiment played under the walls of the lazaretto, on the margin of the bay. During the moon-light nights the effect was perfectly delightful; the evenings at this time were calm and serene, the water as smooth as glass; over its surface numerous small boats were constantly gliding along with considerable velocity. On the opposite shore was dimly seen the barrack at George Town; and in the coves the tall masts of the merchant ships just peeping above the land.

In the town of Mahon several regiments were stationed under the command of Brigadier-General Oakes; to whose acquaintance I had the honour of being introduced.[h] Having the

---

[h] In addition to the high military talents of this officer, his attainments and accomplished manners add a pleasing feature to the character of the gallant soldier. Being a proficient in music himself, he

pleasure also of being recognised by some officers of the 58th regiment who served in the West Indies while I was on the expedition under the Earl of St. Vincent, my stay in the island was rendered very pleasant; and in their society I made several excursions to different parts of the island.

The common mode of conveyance in Minorca is on mules and asses, though there are also many horses kept; but the former are generally more surefooted on the rocky roads. The ass, here called Boreco, is of a large kind, and rendered by good keep and care in its management very tractable, and is a much handsomer animal than those of England. The mule of Minorca is also very handsome, and often is found of an extraordinary size; I have seen a grey one that measured full sixteen hands high. The Honourable Colonel Paget of the 28th regiment had one of peculiar elegance in shape and colour, and of remarkable activity, but not of the largest size. There are plenty of partridges on the island, which afforded good sport to our officers. The heat during the summer is very oppressive, and frequently proves fatal to new comers. The troops lately encamped under the command of Brigadier-General Stuart, had lost many men by sickness. In the autumn and

---

arranged and directed the musical entertainments that were sometimes performed at this place. At his own house he held a weekly meeting, where the principal officers, and others, were hospitably entertained and amused with a concert of instrumental music.

In one of the hard fought battles on the shores of Egypt under the lamented Abercromby, General Oakes was severely wounded; and General Moore, who was near him, received a musket-ball at the same time: happily both these officers have recovered.

winter, the sudden transition from extreme heat to sharp cold weather is very prejudicial to Englishmen, who seldom take those precautions that almost all foreigners do, to vary their dress accordingly. The habit of the Minorquin women is very remarkable, and differs more from modern Europeans than any I had seen. At first landing I mistook the women for nuns of the mendicant order. They are long waisted, and wear a piece of muslin, and sometimes black crape, under their chins, which, rising up on each side the face, joins a handkerchief drawn tight across the forehead; over this they have a large piece of muslin, which extends from the top of the head downwards like a cloak. Some of them wear red mantles lappelled, and joined at the back with yellow ribband; below this, their hair, which is tied close to the head, is suffered to hang loose in form and quantity like a horse's tail.

Their petticoats reach but a little below the knee, of course they are remarkably attentive to the decorations of their legs and feet, which are universally, from the highest to the lowest, clothed in clean white stockings and neat round-toed shoes. The Minorquin ladies, it is said, wish much to adopt the more elegant dress of the English, but either from some jealous fancy, or a regard to the ancient costumè of their country, the men will not permit it. The men, indeed, have accommodated themselves to the more modern fashions, and have nothing very particular in their appearance, except the priests, whose immense flapped beavers overshadow them like an umbrella.

Inhabitants of Minorca.

London, Pub by I. White Fleet Street 1801.

The annexed drawing reprefents the mode of making butter in this country. The dairy woman is ftanding under a fhed, and holding by two pegs in the wall to fteady herfelf, while with one foot naked fhe ftamps in a tub of cream till it becomes butter. Two ladies and a prieft are on the right; a countryman, in the ufual drefs of the peafants of Minorca, is returning from work. The diftant view will give fome idea of the general afpect of the country. The fences are low ftone walls: at a diftance rifes Mount Toro, which is feen from every part of the ifland.

At Fort George I had an opportunity of obferving the method purfued by the natives to conftruct an arch. The procefs is fimple and curious. The workmen were employed in building a bomb-proof magazine, and at this time were forming the arched roof. Though the fpan of the arch could not be lefs than fifteen or fixteen feet, yet they had no wooden centre to work upon.

The ftones being accurately cut for the purpofe, one of them is placed on the wall from whence the arch is to fpring, and kept in that ftation by a prop; it is then carefully fitted and pointed with mortar. A fmall hole is left on the upper fide, into which a compofition called guifh (fomething fimilar to plaifter of Paris, but infinitely more cohefive) is poured, which penetrating into every vacant fpace, almoft inftantly hardens, and the ftone becomes fixed.

They then remove the prop and proceed to place the next

stone, and in like manner make it fast, till the arch is finished on each side, when the key-stone completes and secures the whole.

The stone used for building is very white and soft when first taken from the quarry, but soon hardens from exposure to the air. The guish is found in great plenty in pits, and is a kind of grey gypsum.

It may here be agreeable to the reader to learn some of the events that occurred at the capture of the island. The army, under the command of General the Honourable Charles Stuart, sailed from Gibraltar under convoy of the Leviathan having the broad pendant of Commodore Duckworth on board, and the Centaur, commanded by Captain Markham, with a few frigates and smaller vessels; and on the 7th of November 1798 they arrived off the Bay of Fournelles, on the northern side of the island. But the wind blowing strong out of that bay, the commanders of the expedition determined to attempt a landing at another place. The fleet accordingly stood towards Adaia. The entrance of the harbour is narrow and difficult: it was defended by a four-gun battery, which fired one shot as the Argo frigate led in. The enemy, intimidated at the boldness of the attempt, instantly fled, previously blowing up the magazine. The troops then landed: the 28th regiment, under Colonel Paget, first gained the heights, and attacked the enemy. They seemed irresolute in their conduct, and, on his pushing forward, retreated with expedition across a valley, and halted on a hill on the other side. The enemy now made their appearance from another quarter in great force; and one division marched towards the fort above mentioned, but were compelled to retreat by a heavy cannonade from the men of war covering the landing. By six in the evening all the troops were landed, and immediately marched in pursuit of the enemy, who, by their knowledge of the roads, retreated faster than they could be followed. Some seamen being landed, under the command of Lieutenant Buchanan, to drag the cannon, performed their work in a dark night, and through the worst of roads, in a manner that excited the surprise of the army, and gained them the greatest credit. The Commodore in the mean time had taken possession of the Bay of Fournelles, and with the marines of the fleet had garrisoned two of the forts at the entrance, which the enemy had evacuated.

The army proceeding along a broken and hazardous road, which led round the hill of Mount Toro, at length arrived at Mercadal. The obstacles they had to overcome were such as must reflect much dishonour on the enemy who permitted them to proceed; but British intrepidity was not to be daunted by difficulties, and the army pushed on through a most rugged country, till they came in sight of Ciudadella,[1] into which city

---

[1] Ciudadella was formerly the capital of Minorca; but the English, when it fell into their hands, for the convenience of the harbour, removed the seat of government and of commerce to Mahon, where it has remained ever since. Ciudadella is surrounded with an ancient high wall, and some modern bastions and fortifications have been added to it.

the Spaniards had concentred all their strength in expectation of receiving reinforcements from Majorca.

In the mean time, on the 14th, Commodore Duckworth having received intelligence from General Stuart that four ships of the line were seen between the islands of Majorca and Minorca, put to sea immediately with two ships of the line, a forty-four gun ship, and three armed transports, and stood towards Ciudadella. Great part of the crews were at this time on duty on shore. Early the following morning, being off Ciudadella, the enemy's fleet, consisting of five sail, were seen from the mast-head steering for that place. The Commodore made the signal for a general chace, the enemy at the same time hauling his wind for Majorca. At noon the ships were made out by our squadron to be four large frigates and a sloop of war. The Argo was dispatched after the latter, which kept her wind.[k] The Commodore not choosing to leave the coast

---

[k] It is disagreeable to be obliged to bear testimony so often even against an enemy. But truth demands it. When it has been the misfortune of our seamen to fall into the hands of their enemies, whether French or Spaniards, they have met with the severest ill treatment, almost without an exception. The officers indeed, in some few instances, have been treated tolerably, but the men have been given up to plunder and ill usage. Admiral Duckworth received an additional proof of this in a letter from Captain Bowen of the Argo, who had been dispatched after the Spanish brig as above related. Captain Bowen stated that the brig proved to be the Peterell, captured the day before by four Spanish frigates. She was now commanded by Don Antonio Franco Grandada, second captain of the Spanish frigate Flora. He further informed the Admiral that the Spaniards behaved very ill both to the officers and crew of the Peterell, having robbed and plundered them of every thing. One of the poor fellows, who had saved forty guineas, resisted the Spaniards who attempted to take them from him, for which he was murdered by them and thrown overboard. I have often witnessed the very different conduct observed when the fate of war has put the enemy into our hands. Their private property has always been reserved for them, and if any of the crew have been detected in stealing or appropriating to himself the smallest part of it, he has instantly been punished with severity, and the cause of it has been explained to the

unprotected on which the troops were landed, and finding there was no immediate prospect of coming up with the enemy, steered towards Ciudadella, leaving the Centaur in pursuit of them. On the Commodore arriving off the coast he dispatched Lieutenant Jones with a proposal to the General to cannonade Ciudadella with the ships, but found that the enemy had already entered into articles of capitulation. The Swiss regiment in the service of Spain had intimated to the besieging army their determination not to attack them, and as soon as the surrender of the place was concluded, they joyfully entered into our service. The Centaur at this period returned from pursuing the enemy, who had evaded him and reached Majorca. A detachment of the army under Colonel Paget had marched from Mercadal on the 9th to Alaior, and from thence to Mahon, which place made no resistance. Colonel Paget then proceeded to Fort St. Philip, and summoned the garrison, which also surrendered, and he took possession of the place.

The captors did not find much of value on the island. In the arsenal were a few stores, fourteen boats, and a small brig of war on the stocks. There were three merchantmen in the port, one only of any value.

The possession of this island in time of war is of the highest importance to our navy; that part of it, at least, that is stationed in the Mediterranean.

prisoners, to encourage them, and convince them that by applying for redress to the British officers they would always receive it.

At the period of the action of the Nile we had not a port that we could freely enter; and had the event of that day been different from what it was, we might have beat about, from one end of the Mediterranean to the other, without finding a friendly port to receive us. Malta[1] or Minorca, for the harbours of each are in some respects similar, are and ever will be of the first consequence to the British navy.

The round towers that have been constructed since the island fell into our hands, deserve particular mention from their great utility and small expence. They are built of stone, and have but one entrance, which is by a ladder that can be easily taken in. On the top is one gun, generally a twenty-four pounder, which traverses round with great ease. One I visited, called Musquito tower, was commanded by a lieutenant of artillery and twenty men, who were all comfortably accommodated. On the ground floor were the stores, below which was a reservoir of water. The rotundity of the object makes these towers peculiarly adapted to check the landing of an enemy on the coast; few

---

[1] Malta was at this time closely blockaded by a squadron of British ships. Captain Alexander Ball, who so gallantly commanded his Majesty's ship the Alexander in the battle of the Nile, had landed on that island with a party of seamen and marines, and conducted the blockade on the land side with great ability. His conciliating manners had brought all the natives of the island to join his standard, and induced them to hope that whenever the fort and town of Valette surrendered, they should be continued under the protection of Great Britain.

Afterwards a detachment of troops arrived commanded by General Pigott, and the French garrison being so closely besieged on all sides that they could receive no supplies, at length capitulated.

General Pigott being appointed military governor, Captain Ball rejoined the fleet, carrying with him the esteem and love of the islanders. For his eminent services he has since been created a baronet; and the Lords of the Admiralty have lately appointed him to be the naval commissioner at Gibraltar, in the place of J. N. Inglefield, Esq. who had been promoted to the same situation at Halifax.

Cooper Willyams del.t

The Bay of Fournelles.

London, Pub. by I. White, Fleet Street 1801.

I. C. Stadler sculp.

men are wanted to work the gun, and they are very little expofed. At Corfica one of thefe towers did great damage to a feventy-four gun fhip of ours, and at length obliged her to retire; nor would it have been taken at laft, but that fome of our troops got upon a height that commanded it, and with their mufketry compelled them to furrender.

Such towers as thefe might be of infinite fervice along our own coaft, particularly in thofe quarters where an enemy is moft likely to make an attempt. One upon Berry Head would command the entrance of Torbay, and the materials are at hand. The expence of conftructing thefe towers is fmall. One piece of ordnance alone is required; few men are neceffary; and they are almoft completely fecured from any danger, and might with eafe check an enemy attempting to land. Accompanied by my friend Major Crougee of the 58th regiment, I rode to Adaia to fee the fcene of the debarkation of our troops. The ground they had to attack was ftrong; and the enemy, had they been fo inclined, might have done them a confiderable deal of mifchief.

At another time I accompanied Captain Flamingham of the artillery to Fournelles, of which he was governor. The entrance of the bay is defended by two forts; and on an ifland in the centre of it is a block-houfe and open battery. This bay has the appearance of being an inland lake, as the entrance is very narrow, and from fome points hardly difcernible.

The annexed view I took from the village of Fournelles.

The block-house island, and Mount Toro rising out of the horizon, are the principal objects. The following day Governor Flamingham accompanied me to Mount Toro. We first took boat and visited the island. The upper part of the block-house is of wood, built very strong, having guns which are mounted and worked as on board of men of war, and loopholes for musketry. We again took boat from thence, and landed on the southern side of the bay, where we found our mules. We proceeded through rugged roads and narrow defiles till we arrived at the foot of Mount Toro.

This was the road through which General Sir Charles Stuart had marched his army, and the seamen had dragged cannon. The first must have been difficult; and nothing but the veracity of the officer who related it could have made me credit the latter. In some places the road was so narrow as not to admit the passage of a cannon, and the seamen were obliged to drag it through still more uneven paths before they could proceed. The darkness of the night also rendered these difficulties greater.

Our road up Mount Toro was peculiarly pleasing. As we ascended, the prospect extended to our view, till at length arrived at the summit, the whole island lay displayed before us; and in the misty horizon the island of Majorca was just visible.

Mount Toro, situated nearly in the centre of the island, is by some supposed to derive its name from a bull, on account of some marvellous feats performed there by that animal in former times: but it more probably owes the appellation to the Moors, who called it El Tor, or the Mountain, by way of eminence, being the higheſt land on the iſland. Its ſummit is crowned with a monaſtery of Auſtin friars: the building, like moſt of the monaſtic houſes, is ſpacious and convenient; and it has a neat and well built chapel.

Mount Agatha, ſomething leſs than Mount Toro, riſes about five miles to the north-weſt of that mount. On its top is a chapel dedicated to St. Agatha.

Beſides Mahon and Ciudadella, there are three other towns on the iſland: Mercadal, which is at the foot of Mount Toro; Fererias, between that place and Ciudadella; and Alaior. The two firſt are poor mean places; the laſt is tolerable, and is eſteemed a good quarter for our ſoldiers. It is ſituate about half a mile out of the high road, and ſeven miles from Mahon.

This high road was formed by a Britiſh governor of the name of Kane, who appears to have exerted himſelf in the moſt patriotic manner for the good of the people over whom he preſided. The roads before his time were ſcarcely paſſable. He formed the grand plan of a direct communication between the two principal places of the iſland; and with incredible labour ſucceeded in making a road from Mahon to Ciudadella, in as ſtraight a direction as the natural inequality of the country would allow.

The iſland of Minorca was firſt taken by the Engliſh under Major-General Stanhope, for the King of Spain. At the peace of Utrecht it was given up to the Britiſh government. The inhabitants, bigotted to their ancient cuftoms, ftipulated that they fhould ftill continue to be governed by their old laws, which, with the free exercife of their religion, was granted to them.

In 1782 the united powers of France and Spain made a vigorous attack upon this ifland with an army of fourteen thoufand men. The garrifon in Fort St. Philip's being weakened by a dreadful ficknefs, and greatly reduced in numbers and ftrength, was at length obliged to capitulate. Nine hundred and twenty foldiers, failors, and artillery, with about forty-five natives, Jews, and Turks, were all that marched out of the fort. Since that time it has remained in the hands of the Spaniards, till taken by Sir Charles Stuart in 1798.

I now paffed my time very pleafantly with my friends at Mahon. Balls and concerts were frequently given. At the former the Minorquin ladies, in the habits I have before defcribed, formed a ftriking contraft to the more elegant and becoming appearance of the Britifh ladies: at the latter a brother of the celebrated Kelly, who is in the humble capacity of a drummer in the 8th regiment, was permitted by his colonel to exhibit his vocal powers. Though he is very inferior to his brother both in voice and knowledge of mufic, yet he is far above mediocrity, and gave great fatisfaction to his auditors.

On the 12th the Foudroyant, bearing the flag of Lord Nelfon, with fome other fhips of the line and frigates, arrived in the Bay of Mahon. On paying my refpects to the noble admiral I was very kindly received, and a method pointed out by which I might fpeedily rejoin the Swiftfure. Sir Edward Berry, who had rejoined Lord Nelfon, now commanded the Foudroyant; and Captain Hardy (who, for his exertions in the Mutine, when the Britifh fleet was in purfuit of that of France, as alfo at the action on the 1ft of Auguft, had been made poft into the Foudroyant) was appointed to the command of the Princefs Royal frigate. The admiral foon after failed again for Sicily. Lord Keith now commanded in the Mediterranean.

On the 26th the Culloden, Commodore Sir Thomas Troubridge,[m] anchored in the harbour; and a few days after the Leviathan, bearing the flag of Rear-Admiral Duckworth, arrived.

On the 31ft the man of war brig that was found on the ftocks when the ifland was captured, was launched. Captain Buchanan, who was appointed to command her, gave an elegant entertainment on the occafion. Immenfe crowds were affembled to fee the launch, and the arfenal exhibited a gay fcene of all the principal officers and ladies of the ifland. The brig was named the Port Mahon, in honour of the place.

The Peterell floop, commanded by Captain Auftin, arrived about this time. In a daring attempt to bring off fome veffels near Toulon, fhe had met with a very warm reception. The

---

[m] Commodore Troubridge had been recently created a baronet for his able fervices, particularly at Naples, in the reduction of St. Elmo and Capua.

first lieutenant, Mr. Brenton, who commanded in the boats of the brig, was unfortunately shot through the breast, and was brought to the hospital here, but died of his wounds in a few days. He was a gallant and accomplished young man, and fell lamented and respected by all who knew him."

Being introduced by Sir Thomas Troubridge and Brigadier-General Stuart to Admiral Duckworth, I was invited by the admiral to take my passage in the Leviathan for Gibraltar; and accordingly, after parting with my hospitable friends at Minorca with regret, I embarked on board the Leviathan on the 12th of November, and the next morning we sailed from the harbour of Mahon.

The weather was fine and the wind favourable. In nine days we came in sight of the coasts of Spain and Africa; and on the 21st anchored in Rosia Bay, Gibraltar. The day following the Leviathan, with the Vanguard and Bellerophon, got under weigh and sailed for Cadiz; off which port we arrived on the 23d. Nothing occurred of moment till the 28th, when we fell in with the Powerful of 74 guns, Captain Drury, who was confined to his bed by illness. The following day we were joined by the Swiftsure. Captain Hallowell coming on board the Leviathan to wait on the admiral, with him I returned on board the Swiftsure to my very great satisfaction, after an absence of fifteen weeks.

" He was a younger brother of Captain J. Brenton, who now commands the Cæsar (the flag ship of Sir James Saumarez) and the second son of Rear-Admiral Brenton, lately deceased.

On the 30th we anchored in the Tagus, not far from the castle of Belem, in company with the Leviathan, Powerful, Vanguard, and Bellerophon.

Lisbon is a place so well known and so often described, that I shall not say more of it, than that the heaps of ruins which salute the eye at every turn, remind the stranger of the dreadful calamity that overwhelmed this city in the year 1755 by a fearful earthquake, which shook the firmest buildings to their foundations, involving castles, stately palaces, and the mansions of poverty, in one undistinguished ruin. But that these sad memorials should have remained for so long a period unremoved, raises in the stranger's mind no very favourable opinion of the government, or of the industry of the inhabitants.[b]

On the 6th of December we again got under weigh, and sailed with the rest of the fleet for a cruize on the coast of Spain. We were now constantly assailed by gales of wind with rain, accompanied by a heavy swell, which did not however prevent our giving chace to several ships. The stormy weather continuing, caused the Powerful to spring a leak, and soon after

[b] At the hospitable mansion of William Stephens, Esq. a merchant of the first eminence both for property and respectability in the place, the navy were at all times generously entertained; and I, having an additional claim to the same in an introduction from an esteemed and respected friend in England, was received by him and his family with every mark of attention and friendship. Mr. Stephens has established a manufacture of glass in Portugal, of which he has the exclusive sale; but this monopoly of the article, so far from being an injury to the public, is the reverse, for no where is glass cheaper or better. I much regret that the shortness of my stay at Lisbon prevented my having the pleasure of accompanying him, as was settled, to his elegant mansion, called Marenhia Grande, where the manufactory is established. It is about forty miles from Lisbon.

the Vanguard alſo received ſuch damage that the admiral directed thoſe ſhips by ſignal to part company; and on the 21ſt they ſailed for England.

On the 23d we gave chace to a Spaniſh brig, which we took, and ſent under convoy of the Minerve frigate to Liſbon. She proved to be the Volcano, bound from Corunna for South America.

On Chriſtmas-day we gave chace to a fleet, which we found to be the Arethuſa frigate and a convoy.

On the 30th we captured another Spaniſh brig, La Belle Defiada, which was alſo ſent to Liſbon: during the chace the Bellerophon parted company, and did not rejoin the fleet till thirteen days after. On the 1ſt of January 1800, being off Cape Finiſterre, the Leviathan loſt her main-top-gallant-maſt in a gale of wind; the ſea running mountains high, attended with heavy ſqualls of rain. After which we had two days of calm, accompanied with thick miſty weather, and then a freſh breeze from the northward. On the 7th gave chace to a lugger. After firing many ſhots at her ſhe brought to, and proved to be a Guernſey privateer, which reported ſhe had captured on the 2d inſtant a valuable Spaniſh ſhip bound to Lima. The gales again aſſailed us, and we ſuffered from our ſails being ſplit and the old leaks of the ſhip breaking out afreſh, ſo that the chain-pumps were continually kept going.

On the 10th the Flora frigate joined us with orders from Lord Keith. Our attention was now kept up in the hope of meeting with the Spanish galleons, which were at this time expected from the Spanish settlements in America, as also an outward-bound fleet, which was hourly expected to sail from Cadiz to Lima. On the 12th the Bellerophon rejoined the fleet. During the night of the 17th we parted company from the fleet in a gale of wind, which continued with unabated violence all the following day, but subsided towards the evening.

On the 23d we saw a strange sail, but a squall of wind carried away our fore-top-mast, which in the fall brought down with it the main-top-gallant-mast, and we were obliged to give over chasing in order to clear away the wreck and replace the masts that were lost. Providentially only two men were hurt by this accident, and they not dangerously. The following day one of the seamen, named Hamlyn, was thrown from the cap of the main-mast into the sea by the rolling of the ship; a boat was instantly lowered down to his assistance, but in vain, for he was drowned.

On the 26th a brig was descried, with Portuguese colours displayed, seemingly in great distress, but it being a calm we could not approach her. The following day we were rather nearer, and a boat was sent to her. The officer on his return reported that she was deserted by her crew; a monkey and a dog were the only living animals on board, and they would not quit the vessel: she had only a small cargo of salt; her pumps being choked, and her masts gone by the board, she was left to her fate.

On the 29th we again anchored in the Tagus. At this time I went to the opera at Lisbon. The performance and the singing were good, but the female characters being represented by men, had a very disgusting effect, the Queen of Portugal having prohibited the appearance of women on the stage.

The Prince of Brazil had however revoked the order since the illness of the Queen, but as yet only two female singers were engaged.

On our entering the Tagus we perceived the wreck of a ship thrown up on the beach near Belem castle, and were informed that it was the remains of the Weymouth. She was on her passage to Gibraltar with the Cambrian fencible regiment, commanded by the Honourable Colonel Edwards.[p] Having put into the Tagus, by some mistake she anchored on the shoals, and was lost. Admiral Duckworth, without delay, made an arrangement to transport the regiment to its destination; and the officers and soldiers, with their wives and families, and the few stores they had saved, were distributed on board the fleet.

On the 3d of February we all got under weigh from the Tagus, and after a pleasant voyage of eight days, anchored in the Bay of Gibraltar.

As the Swiftsure had suffered a great deal in the late gales, it was thought necessary to caulk and repair her, and she was taken into the Mole for that purpose. I therefore took this

---

[p] Now Lord Kensington, an Irish peer, but whose seat and property are in Pembrokeshire.

opportunity of accepting the invitation of a friend, at whofe houfe I took up my abode, and was by thofe means enabled to make further inveftigations into the natural as well as artificial curiofities of the rock: the refult of which I fhall now detail. My friend, who is an officer of engineers, and gifted with extraordinary talents for drawing, lent me his aid in the bufinefs, and in his company I found both an inftructor in the art I was fond of and affiftance in inveftigating the features of a place that has long been the object of admiration, and has defervedly excited applaufe for the many gallant defences it has made againft numerous hofts of foes.

Gibraltar is an infulated rock of about feven miles circumference. On one fide it is joined to the province of Andalufia in Spain, by a low flat fandy plain; the reft of it is furrounded by the fea. The diftance from the fandy plain, now called the Neutral Ground, to Europa Point, which is the extreme fouthern part of the rock looking towards Africa, is three miles. Gibraltar, the Mons Calpe, and Apes Hill, on the African coaft, the Mons Abyla of the ancients, alfo bore the appellation of the Pillars of Hercules; as that hero was fuppofed here to have terminated his labours, and having penetrated thus far, and feeing the vaft profundity of the Atlantic Ocean, which appeared to have no bounds, he declared that beyond this there was no proceeding. It was in thofe days efteemed to be the weftern boundary of the earth.

The name of Gibraltar is derived from the Moors, Gibel

Tarif, or the Mountain of Tarif. Tarif was a Moorish general, who made a settlement here about the year of Christ 725, at which time the Moorish castle on the northern side of the rock, great part of which exists at this day, was erected by him, to secure a communication with the shores of Africa.

After having alternately changed masters, sometimes falling under the dominion of the Spaniards, at others under that of the Moors, it finally was attached to the Spanish dominions in the year 1462. From that time it remained in their possession till 1704, when the English, under Sir George Rooke, made themselves masters of it.

The Spaniards suffered inconceivable mortification at the loss of this fortress, which was justly esteemed the key of the Mediterranean; they sought various ineffectual means of redeeming it, and an army was immediately assembled under the command of the Marquis de Villadarias, a grandee of Spain. Finding his attempts to reduce the garrison by force frustrated by the vigilance of the besieged, and the intrepidity of the British fleet under Admiral Sir John Leake, he formed the desperate plan of attempting it by stratagem. Accordingly five hundred volunteers took the sacrament never to return till they had made themselves masters of the place. They effected their purpose so far as to gain the highest part of the rock, and lodged themselves in St. Michael's Cave. The following night they scaled Charles the Fifth's wall, surprised the guard at Middle Hill, whom they put to death, and by the aid of ropes and ladders got up several hundreds of their army, a detachment of which was stationed at the back of the rock to succour them. At this moment they were discovered by the British garrison, and a strong detachment of grenadiers was instantly marched from the town against them. In the onset the Spaniards were worsted, many of them slain, and many precipitated themselves from the summit of the rock, and were dashed to pieces. A colonel, thirty officers, and the rest of the troops, were taken prisoners.

Thwarted in all their attempts to reduce the garrison, the siege was at length turned into a blockade on the land side, after the loss of ten thousand men on the part of the enemy, including those who died of disease, while the garrison lost about four hundred.

In 1720 the Spaniards, under pretence of preparing an armament to assist the garrison of Ceuta, which was at that time besieged by the Moors, made an insidious attempt on Gibraltar, but were again foiled by the activity of Colonel Kane, governor of Minorca, who arrived in time to prevent their designs.

At the end of the year 1726 the garrison was once more attacked by a formidable army, and was equally fortunate in repelling it.

But the most memorable siege that perhaps ever happened, is that which was sustained by this garrison under the command of General Elliot, which commenced in 1779, and continued without intermission till February 1783, a period of three years, seven months, and twelve days, when the combined armies of France and Spain were compelled to retreat from the effects of British valour.

Since that time every possible addition has been made to render the place invulnerable. The galleries, which were begun under General Elliot, have received vast additions under the government of General O'Hara, who has been indefatigable in rendering the rock impervious to future attempts from the enemy.

The town of Gibraltar is built at the base of the north-western side of the rock; it is bounded on the north by the land-port grand battery and the Moorish castle, and on the south by the Moorish wall. This wall extends from the summit of the rock, and terminates in the south bastion near the landing place called Ragged Staff.

The town is about a mile long, and has a narrow irregular street through the centre from north to south. In this street is the governor's house, formerly a religious building, and it still retains the name of the convent. Between this and the grand parade is the Spanish church: what remains of the ancient edifice is Gothic, and probably owed its origin to the Moors when they were in possession of the place. The drawing here given represents the entrance to it, or gateway, which, though a good deal decayed, and sadly disfigured by modern additions, is a good specimen of that ornamental style of building. General O'Hara, the governor, is at present adding much to the conve-

Entrance to the Spanish Church, Gibraltar

London Pub by I. White, Fleet Street, 1801

nience and elegance of the town by paving the main street; and it is to be lamented, that in case of another siege (should the Spaniards be mad enough to commence one) it must be again destroyed.

There are many good houses in the town; among the rest the residence of the chief engineer Colonel Fyers, bears a conspicuous appearance. It is pleasantly situated on a rising ground towards the north end of the town, and commands an extensive view of the bay.

The convent is well adapted for the residence of the governor, being a spacious building of four sides, with cloisters round the quadrangle. The present governor[q] has greatly improved it by adding a large saloon, in which during the winter a weekly ball is given to the garrison.

Towards the bay a strong line of fortifications extends from Water Port to the New Mole, with several noble bastions and works of superior construction. The King's Battery, erected in the year 1773, when the Honourable Lieutenant-General Cornwallis was governor, is of prodigious strength; in proof of which I need only state, that it resisted the main attack of the floating batteries and men of war on the 13th of September 1782, that

---

[q] Just as this page is printing an account of the death of the gallant general is announced in the public prints. I shall not therefore be accused of flattery in giving the following testimony to his character.

General O'Hara must be sincerely regretted at the rock, where he was long deservedly accounted the father and protector of suffering merit. His purse was ever open to the calls of humanity; and many an instance of his generous benevolence has been related to me by those who have received benefit from his munificence.

celebrated day on which General Elliot and his brave garrifon gained fuch immortal honour in repelling the fevereft attack ever made on a place of equal fize. Of this battery Major-General Boyd, the lieutenant-governor, who at that time commanded the garrifon, laid the firft ftone in 1773, when he made the following remarkable fpeech: " This (faid the general) is the firft ftone of a work which I name the King's Baftion; may it be as gallantly defended as I know it will be ably executed, *and may I live to fee it refift the united efforts of France and Spain.*"[1]

Above the town on the fide of the rock feveral fmall houfes have fince been erected, chiefly inhabited by the officers of the garrifon; many of them have little gardens, which, from the warmth of the climate, produce oranges and vines. On the northern fide many ftrong batteries are erected on the points of the rock, commanding the whole of the neutral ground and the Spanifh lines: they are all of confiderable height above the level of the ifthmus; the loweft of them being not lefs than four hundred feet above the level of the neutral ground.

But the moft extraordinary work of art are the galleries, which are excavated from the folid rock, having at certain diftances port-holes that overlook the Spanifh lines.

The annexed view of a part of the grand gallery leading to

---

[1] This wifh was amply gratified at the memorable defenfive victory gained over the combined powers of France and Spain on the 13th of September 1782. The governor, General Elliot, took his ftation during the hotteft period of the attack on the king's baftion; and General Boyd commanded at the fouth baftion, from whence he had a full view of the glory obtained by the work of which he had the honour of being the founder. Vide Colonel Drinkwater's Hiftory of the Siege of Gibraltar.

Inside of a Gallery, Gibraltar
London, Pub.d by I.White, Fleet Street, 1801

St. George's Hall will give some idea of them. St. George's Hall is also an excavation of a similar nature. It is a cave of a circular form, in a projecting part of the rock, and is of great dimensions and considerable height.

I should imagine, that in case of a heavy cannonade from these galleries, the concussion of the air in them would render the noise insupportable and endanger the falling in of the roof; but of this I do not pretend to be a competent judge.

The isthmus that separates the rock of Gibraltar from the Spanish dominions, is a low flat sand, from whence the ingenious historian of the siege of Gibraltar concludes, that Mons Calpe must formerly have been surrounded by the sea; but the strong current that now runs between the coasts of Africa and Europe, which would in all probability have passed with equal rapidity to the northward of the rock had there been a passage for it, would have continued to keep that passage open. From this circumstance, I should think it has never been other than what it now is, especially as the sandy plain is not known to have increased or diminished since it has been noticed by historians.

This plain, commonly called the Neutral Ground, is about half a mile across at the narrowest place, and increases in width towards the main land. On the Spanish side, at the distance of a mile from the rock, a strong line of fortifications is carried across this plain, in length about seventeen hundred yards, reaching from the shore of the bay to that of the Mediterranean.

At each end of this line is a strong fort. That on the east side is called Fort St. Barbara; the other, which commands the anchorage at the Old Mole, is named fort St. Philip.

The extreme height of the rock is thirteen hundred feet perpendicular above the level of the sea. On the summit, a sharp ridge running from north to south, divides it into two unequal parts. That facing the west is a gradual slope to the water's edge, interspersed with rocks; on this side the town is situated. The eastern side, which faces the Mediterranean, is almost perpendicular from the sea, and presents a barren rocky appearance, on which are found a multitude of wild apes, which are said to be peculiar to this rock, and of a different species from those found in Spain, but similar to those that inhabit Mons Abyla, or Apes Hill, on the opposite coast of Africa. The rock of Gibraltar has several caverns of great depth and extent; one of them, called Pocoroca, is near the summit of the hill, directly over the centre of the town, and under Middle Hill battery.

The annexed view represents the entrance of this cavern from within, with the curious pillars that seem to support the roof. These pillars, as well as the pendent rocks from the roof, are formed by the constant dripping of water, which petrifies in its descent, taking the most fantastic shapes. Several of these pillars have been cut down in order to be made into tables and slabs, as they are capable of receiving a high polish.

Interior of Poa Poa Cave

Cooper Williams delt. I.C. Stadler sculpt.

London. Pub'd by I.White, Fleet Street, 1801

This cave, during the laſt ſiege, was intended for the reſidence of the governor, and partly fitted up for that purpoſe; but the deſign was dropped, and it ſerved as a powder magazine for the batteries on the heights. A road leads from this cave to the old Mooriſh wall, which I before obſerved reaches from the top of the rock to the land-port gate of the town. On it is a foot-path, accommodated with ſtone ſteps at certain diſtances, for the more eaſy aſcent or deſcent of paſſengers. Above this wall is a round tower, uſed as a ſignal-houſe. It commands a view up the Mediterranean and of the entrance of the bay from the eaſt and weſt.

A curious incident is mentioned in the hiſtory of the late ſiege, of an eagle which perched on the ſignal-ſtaff at the moment the combined fleets of France and Spain entered the bay. The garriſon believed at firſt that it was a ſignal for another fleet, and immediately concluded that the Britiſh admiral was in the rear of the enemy. Elated with the hope, a general huzza took place along the lines; in a ſhort time however the miſtake was diſcovered, but the omen was looked upon as favourable for the Britiſh arms, and ſo it proved.

The preſent governor, General O'Hara, has cauſed another ſignal tower to be erected on the ſouthern point of the rock, which, beſides being the higheſt part of it, commands a more extenſive view of the Straits to the weſtward, and, when completed, it will be both an ornament, and highly beneficial in conveying much earlier information to the garriſon below.

From the opening in the Moors Wall, a road leads to another opening in Charles the Fifth's Wall; which alfo extends, from the fummit, in a parallel direction with the former. From hence two roads branch off; the one leads to the Sugar Loaf Point above mentioned, the other downwards towards Europa. Near this latter road is the entrance to St. Michael's cave, the largeft and moft extraordinary cavern on the rock.

Being anxious to inveftigate this wonderful cave, I proceeded thither in company with Captain Brenton of the navy, and Captain Whitmore of the royal engineers: having provided ourfelves with torches to enable us to take drawings of the interior. The entrance is narrow, not more than eight or nine feet; from thence we defcended by a fteep flope of wet earth that rendered our footfteps very infecure. At the bottom of this declivity the cave widens confiderably in all directions; and we difcovered, by the help of our torches, the entrance of feveral other fmaller caverns. This veftibule, or hall (if I may fo call it) of the cavern, is fupported in the centre by a vaft column of petrified water, ribbed in a curious manner; and the arched roof is ornamented with numerous icicles of the fame matter.

Proceeding eaftward by a rugged path, we at length entered a fecond chamber, fupported on all fides by pillars of petrifactions of various colours and fhapes: fome bore the refemblance of organ-pipes, others of Gothic flutings; feveral of them feemed to be fifty or fixty feet high. Here, on a rifing

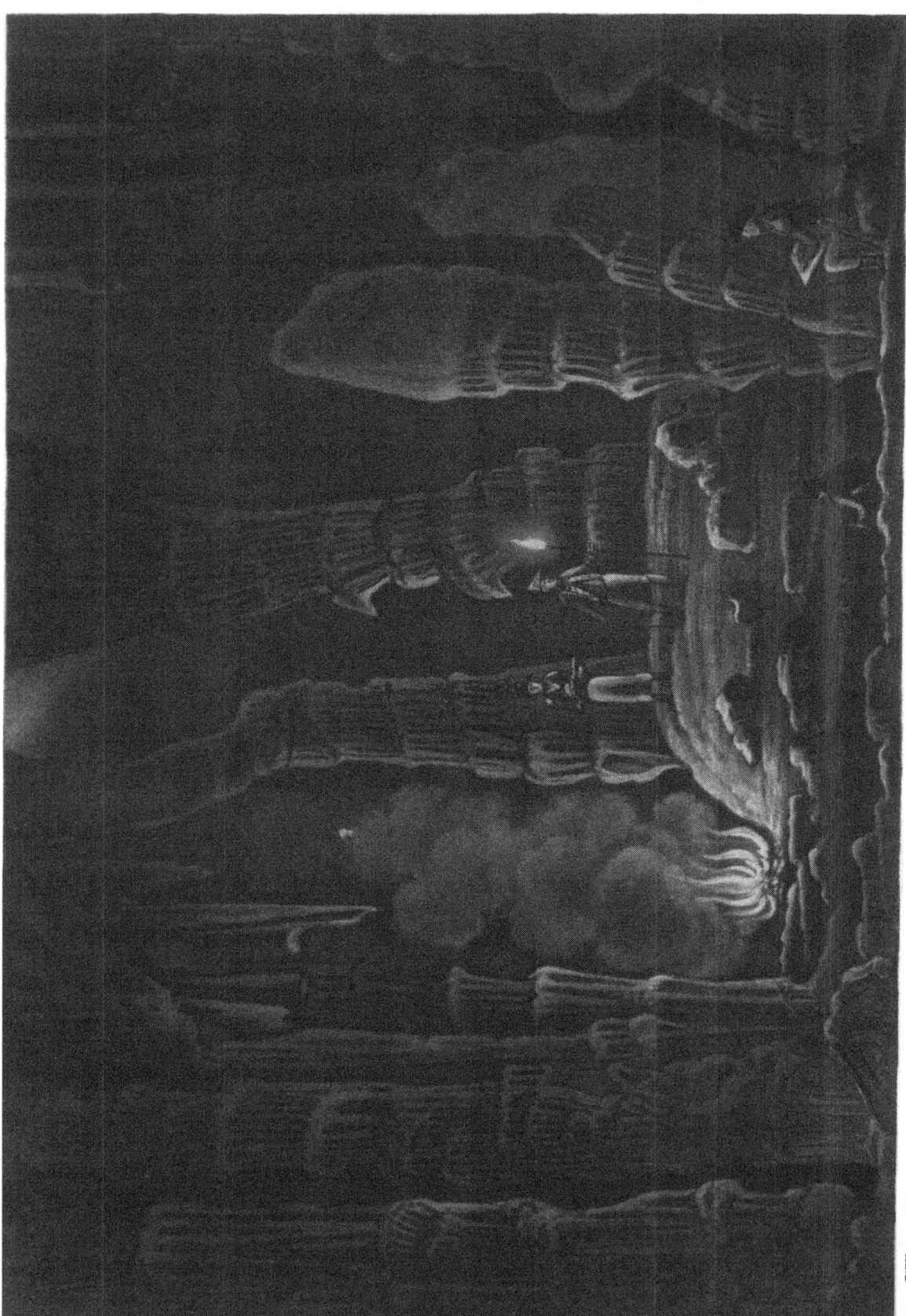

S.t Michael's Cave Gibraltar

London Pub by I White Fleet Street 1801

ground like an altar, we lighted a fire; and having placed several torches on the projecting points of the rocks, besides those held by our attendants, we took several sketches of the wonders of the cave. The annexed view represents the sketch I took, but neither pen nor pencil can give an adequate idea of the sublime and terrific appearance of this work of nature.

The roof of this chamber represents the pointed arch of a Gothic cathedral; the petrified stalactites in some places hang in the form of curtains; in others vast pillars, curiously embossed and fluted, reach from the top to the bottom. At the upper part, between the two opposite columns, is seen a dim ray of light issuing from a fissure in the rock above. On all sides are deep caverns that penetrate downwards into the bowels of the earth.

Some people, I was informed, had endeavoured to penetrate the abyss below, but had always been obliged to give over the attempt before they could reach the bottom, on account of the grossness of the atmosphere, which not only rendered their breathing difficult, but denied them the use of their torches, and hazarded their being deprived of light in an abyss surrounded with dangers.

Colonel James, in his History of the Herculean Straits, gives the following curious account of his adventures in this cave. " Towards the south end of this cave there are passages between the pillars that lead into other apartments; all are supported by pillars, some standing single, others three or four in a clufter; and the roofs of thefe apartments have the above petrified rays, which refemble the glories of fome Roman-Catholic altar. In the centre of one of thefe chapels is a large deep pit, down which fome Englifhmen having loft their way and flipped, were, by the affiftance of ropes and men (let down) happily faved, though much bruifed. Down this abyfs I defcended with others, till at length I arrived at a fmall hole of eighteen inches diameter, when finding the air too grofs, we thought it more advifable not to defcend any further, having fufficiently fatisfied our curiofity: however, before we returned (notwithftanding our torches burned dim, and we fetched our breath much fhorter than in the open air) we let down a rope with a weight at the end, through the above hole, fifty feet before it lodged; whether that was the bottom of the pit I cannot pretend to fay. Our defcent to this fmall hole was four hundred and eighty feet: as we let ourfelves down we found little apartments on either fide to reft ourfelves in; likewife jettees, on which thofe that fell were ftopped from falling lower. This long gallery (if I may fo call it) flopes in fome places, on which you put your feet when you lower yourfelf by the rope, and then you hang perpendicular for a hundred feet before you can touch the rocks, which are nothing but petrified water, as is likewife the bottom where we ftood, which once was open; and, in time, the hole of eighteen inches will be entirely clofed. I was very much furprifed, as was every one, at the entrance of the abyfs, occafioned by the man who went firſt down ſtriking his heels againſt a ſheet of petrified water which hung hollow from the rock; the ſound was like a deep-toned bell, but to thoſe above it was ſo confuſed that they knew not well what to make of it. I muſt obſerve, that on every jettee, likewiſe in every apartment or reſting place, a man was placed with a torch, which being in a ſtraight line to the entrance of the pit, formed a romantic and horrible ſcene."

There are various ſoils on the peninſula of Gibraltar. Towards the ſummit are rough and craggy rocks, with ſmall quantities of black mould in the interſtices, from which grow the palmeto and ſeveral other kinds of ſhrub; but the intenſe heat of the ſummer generally burns them up, and the whole mountain then bears a brown and deſert appearance. The town ſtands on a red ſand, which extends as far to the ſouthward as the New Mole, where it becomes rocky; and towards Europa Point there are ſtrata of marble and good free-ſtone.

On the weſtern ſide the rocky precipices are here and there ſeparated by ſand banks, which ſlope from the water's edge half-way up its ſides; but whether caſt up by the ſea, or conſtantly crumbling from the apertures of the rock above, I could never learn; each idea has its difficulties. It riſes too great a height above the level of the ſea to have been thrown up by the violence of the waves; and it ſeems ſtill leſs probable that ſuch vaſt accumulations of fine ſand ſhould have been emitted from the hard rocks.

Near Catalan Bay, at the back of the rock as it is called, or the eaſtern ſide, is a vaſt heap of this ſand, which reaches more than two-thirds up the precipice.

Catalan Bay is a romantic ſpot to which the Spaniſh ſmugglers reſort and depoſit their contraband goods, which are afterwards conveyed in ſmall quantities round to the town. There is a cavern in the bottom of this bay that has been inhabited by an ancient Spaniard for more than forty years. He and his ſon and daughter have made a little garden near it, where they produce plenty of vegetables, which they carry to market at Gibraltar; and they alſo poſſeſs an herd of goats, whoſe milk they alſo turn to a good account.

In your road to this bay you paſs the Devil's Tower, which is ſituated at the baſe of the rock at the north-eaſtern extremity. In the map I have given a draught of this building. It is ſituate on a ſingle rock, and has no door-way; which I ſuppoſe has cauſed it to have the name it bears: it appears to have been a work of the Moors.

I have alſo added another ſmall drawing on the map, of the northern face of the rock, which I took from the neutral ground near the Spaniſh lines; and another of Ceuta Point, on the coaſt of Africa, where the Spaniards have a garriſon. They have repeatedly baffled the attempts of the Moors to regain this place, who are as anxious to poſſeſs it as the Spaniards are to make themſelves maſters of Gibraltar. There are ſeveral gardens on the rock; the governor has an handſome one at the convent, in which are ſeveral fine palms, and other natives of the more fouthern climes. Mount Pleafant, the refidence of Commiffioner Inglefield, is by far the moft picturefque place on the rock. The gardens are laid out with great tafte; the trees, which confift of the various productions of warm climates, have reached a height that could hardly have been expected from the fcanty foil. The orange and lemon trees, the ftately cyprefs and the locuft trees, form a delightful retreat from the extreme heat which prevails during the greater part of the year. The houfe, though fmall, commands an extenfive view of the bay and of the town of Algeziras, which is on the oppofite fide of the bay; to the left of it is feen Cabritta Point, over which a fignal tower gives intelligence to the Spanifh gun-boats at Algeziras of the approach of our fhips, when they generally row out to a fandy bay near the point. As the ftrange fhips approach the bay and haul round the point they are frequently becalmed, and the current fets them in towards the Spanifh coaft. The gun-boats then fecurely attack them, taking their ftations with every advantage; and as they carry very heavy guns, they are enabled to batter the fhips from a diftance, which renders them fo fmall a mark that they feldom receive any damage in return.

Infignificant as thefe gun-boats may appear, they have frequently done much mifchief, even to our line of battle fhips when becalmed, which they have attacked with confiderable advantage, lying under their fterns, and raking them, without being in much danger themfelves.

Lately a fleet of thefe gun-boats, of which ten carried each a twenty-four pounder, and two were fchooners carrying two twenty-four pounders each, with a French xebec privateer of eight guns, attacked the Speedy brig of war, commanded by Captain Brenton, who had two veffels under convoy bound for Gibraltar. The conteft, though fo unequal, (for the Speedy had only fixteen fmall guns) terminated moft unfavourably for the Spaniards, who at firft attempted to take the merchant fhip, but Captain Brenton paffing between them enabled her to get to her anchorage in fafety. They then united their efforts to carry the brig, which had got to the eaftward of Europa; but the Speedy boldly bore down to her refcue, and cutting through the line of the enemy, obliged them in a fhort time to relinquifh that defign alfo. The Spaniards then made hafte to get under the protection of the guns of Fort St. Barbara, and from thence proceeded to Malaga, leaving the trade for feveral weeks unmolefted.

The Spaniards loft feveral men in this action, and were otherwife much damaged. The Speedy was alfo a good deal fhattered, and was nearly funk by feveral fhot below the watermark, which prevented her carrying fail on the larboard tack: fhe was obliged to bear away for Tetuan Bay, to ftop her leaks. The gallantry of this action was beheld by the garrifon at Gibraltar with the greateft admiration. So near were the combatants at one time, that an officer hailed Captain Brenton from the batteries on Europa Point; but an order of the governor that no guns should be fired without his orders, to prevent unnecessary alarms, prevented his receiving any assistance for a long time, though so near a friendly battery. At length a gun was fired from it, but the business had already been ably executed by the gallant little brig, in which two British seamen were killed and one wounded.[s]

On the 24th of February Admiral Duckworth in the Leviathan, with the Incendiary, Captain Dunn, sailed from Gibraltar to the eastward, and on the 25th the Swiftsure followed them. The wind being strong from the N.N.W. we could not get through the Straits to resume our station off Cadiz; and hazy weather coming on, we lost sight of our consorts.

On the 1st of March we anchored in Tetuan Bay, where we found the Thalia, Captain Nesbit. It blew hard for two days, and owing to the plague we could have no communication with the shore.

---

[s] Captain Brenton has since been rewarded for his gallantry, by being promoted to the rank of post captain and the command of the Cæsar, the flag ship of Rear-Admiral Sir James Saumarez, K. B. And the Bay of Algeziras has again witnessed his exertions on that memorable day when the intrepidity of British valour was so unhappily thwarted by calms and currents, which drove them under the fire of formidable batteries in their attempt to cut off a French squadron. But nothing daunted by the failure of his first attempt, the gallant admiral, with astonishing celerity, refitted his shattered fleet, and pursued the vainglorious enemy, who, compelled to seek for shelter in flight, at last reached Cadiz, but not without the loss of two of their first-rates that were burnt in the action. Sir James Saumarez, in his official letter, gives very unqualified praise to the able exertions of Captain Brenton in getting his ship ready for service after the damage sustained in the first attack. As a proof of the good order and loyal spirit of the Cæsar's crew, I need only mention that several of them who had been wounded in the first action, as soon as they heard that the ship was getting under weigh to follow the enemy, escaped from the hospital, got on board a boat in the Mole, and rowed alongside the ship, requesting to be taken on board; which they were, and they immediately went to their quarters.

On the 3d we again got under weigh, and ftood towards the Straits of Gibraltar, and the fame day fpoke the Phœnix frigate, Captain Halfted. The next day we fell in with the Leviathan, and the day after anchored in Rofia Bay. We ftaid only three days at anchor, and again got under weigh. But the wefterly winds prevailing, we could not beat through the Gut againft the ftrong current which conftantly runs into the Mediterranean. On the 10th, however, a light breeze from the eaftward fprung up, and we got through without farther difficulty.

On the 13th, being in the latitude of Cadiz, we received intelligence that a fleet of men of war and merchantmen, bound from thence to Lima, were ready to fail; we therefore cleared for action. On the 14th we fpoke two Portuguefe men of war, the St. Sebaftian and Principe Reale; the latter bearing the flag of the Marquis de Neyfa: they were on their paffage from Palermo to Lifbon. On the 29th we fell in with the Balloon, Portuguefe brig, commanded by an emigrant, the Count de Blofville, with an Algerine corfair of 22 guns in company, which he had lately captured. On the 31ft a fail was fuppofed to be defcried by the man at the maft head; but as the haze cleared up it proved to be a whale fpouting up water.

On the 3d of April we gave chace to a fchooner under American colours, which at length got under the guns of the caftle of Larache, a Moorifh port on the weftern coaft of Africa, when fhe fired a gun and hoifted Spanifh colours. On the 5th, however, we had the good fortune to fall in with the long expected Spanish squadron which had sailed a few days before from Cadiz for the Spanish settlements on the coast of South America. Two of the fleet were captured the next morning, but the admiral making our signal, we were obliged to proceed to the southward, and in four days after took the schooner that had lately sheltered herself under the guns of Larache. She proved to be a Spanish merchant vessel bound from Malaga to Vera Cruz. In the evening of the same day we spoke an American, who gave us the pleasing intelligence that she had seen Admiral Duckworth, in company with the Emerald and Incendiary, with a Spanish squadron of two frigates, and several merchant ships.

The object of our pursuit being accomplished, we shaped our course for Gibraltar; and on our arrival there, on the 19th, had the satisfaction to find the admiral had anchored with the prizes, consisting of two frigates and seven merchantmen; but at the same time learned that the Sabina, a fine frigate richly laden, and four merchantmen, had escaped to Cadiz. Had we not unfortunately been ordered to chace to the southward, in all probability not one of them would have escaped. Captain Dunn, in the Incendiary, had captured two of the same squadron. The frigates had a cargo of quicksilver on board, to the amount of a hundred and forty tons, which was intended to work the mines of Peru and Mexico.

While we were at anchor in Rosia Bay an accident befel the

Swiftsure that had nearly proved her destruction. We were lying at single anchor, a heavy squall came on from the westward, which at length increased to a strong gale, blowing directly into the Bay. The cable snapped close to the ring of the anchor, and we were driving broadside on the rocks, whose rugged sides offered a dismal prospect of certain destruction. The stream anchor was instantly let go, which fortunately brought her up, and she rode out the remainder of the gale in safety. To add to the uncomfortableness of our situation, the wreck of the Medusa was seen just astern of us: she was lost in the same Bay in 1798.

On the 2nd of May we once more sailed on a cruise on the Spanish coast; the Leviathan, Emerald, and the Netly schooner in company; and the next day looked into Cadiz harbour. As we stood in near the batteries the Spaniards fired several shot, but none of them took effect.

On the 4th we fell in with the Inflexible, with a squadron of transports having six thousand troops' on board, under command of General Pigot. They were bound for the Mediterranean.

On the 31st we stood into Lagos Bay. A curious circumstance took place when we were near shore. We experienced two opposite currents of air; the lofty sails were taken aback, while the lower sails were filled. By taking in the former we soon gained our anchorage off the town of Lagos.

† They formed a part of that gallant army that has since gained such never-fading honour on the plains of Egypt.

This Bay received the British fleet, under the Earl of St. Vincent, after his glorious victory over the Spaniards.

The town of Lagos is small, and has not much to boast. There are several convents and churches.

On the 4th of June we sailed from Lagos Bay, and the following day fell in with two frigates, the Seahorse and another; on board of the former were Rear Admiral Sir Richard Bickerton, Bart. Sir Ralph Abercromby, General Moore, and several other officers of rank, bound for the Mediterranean. In the evening they parted company.

On the 8th we also spoke the Pegasus frigate, Captain Pengelly, with troops for Minorca; Major Doyle was a passenger in her. The following day a large spermaceti whale passed near the ship.

After again looking into Cadiz Bay we returned to Gibraltar, and took up our old station in Rosia Bay.[u] The fleet of transports, &c. with troops, had sailed in the morning for Minorca.

Rear Admiral Duckworth being appointed to command at the Leeward Islands, Rear Admiral Sir Richard Bickerton took the command on this station, and hoisted his flag on board the Swiftsure. On the 16th we again got under weigh, with a fleet of merchant ships under convoy of the Sheerness, Sensible,

[u] Lieutenant O'Brien, first lieutenant of the Swiftsure, received his appointment of commander of the Transfer brig of war, at that time on the coast of Egypt, and in a few days sailed for that station. Lieutenant J. Laws Waters became first lieutenant of the Swiftsure in his place. Captain O'Brien has since been promoted, for his services on the coast of Egypt, to the rank of post captain, and the command of the Kent, the flag ship of Rear Admiral Sir Richard Bickerton.

and Resource. Generals Grinfield and Martin were on board this fleet on their passage for England, with several ladies from Gibraltar, whose husbands were embarked on the expedition to Egypt.

On the 19th the convoy parted company, and we took our station off Cadiz. On the 23d his Majesty's ships Dragon, Captain Campbell, and Kent, Captain William Hope, joined from England.

After cruising for a fortnight without any occurrence worthy of notice, on the 7th of July we were joined by the Hector, Captain Elphinstone, also from England. At this time were detained many Americans and Swedes, that would endeavour to enter Cadiz notwithstanding the blockade.

On the 11th a sloop privateer was seen by the fleet; it being calm, Captain Campbell sent an unarmed boat to her, which was fired upon with musketry by the privateer's crew. On this insult some more boats, manned and armed, were sent from the Swiftsure and Dragon; these, after a smart action, in which, however, none were killed or wounded, boarded her and brought her into the fleet. She proved to be La Mouche with an English letter of marque. The captain of her, in excuse for his conduct in firing upon a man of war's boat, said that his crew had forced him below; but as he could not prove this, he and his vessel were sent to Gibraltar. Had any of our seamen or officers lost their lives in this business, it could have been deemed no less than murder. The crew of the privateer confifted of a motley affemblage of vagabonds from all nations, and one of them was proved to be a deferter from the Sirius. Nothing but the policy of annoying the trade of the powers we are at war with, can juftify the permiffion given to thefe privateers, who not unfrequently have letters of fervice from both nations; fo that whatever comes to hand is with them a prize.

Circumftances of a private nature now rendered my return to England neceffary, and having received permiffion to that effect from Sir Richard Bickerton, to whofe polite and friendly attention while under his command, I feel greatly indebted, I embraced the opportunity of returning to Gibraltar in the Kent, Captain Hope having kindly offered me a paffage with him. But juft as we entered the Straits the Anfon frigate hove in fight; and Captain Durham obligingly gave me a paffage to England. I had the pleafure to find my friend Captain Brenton was alfo a paffenger.

On the following day, being the 1ft of Auguft, we fell in with the Swiftfure; and I accompanied Captains Durham and Brenton to pay our refpects to the admiral. After again undergoing the pain of parting with friends with whom I had lived on the moft pleafant terms for near three years, I returned on board the Anfon.

Having a fleet under convoy to guard, our voyage was neceffarily protracted; but on Tuefday the 2d of September 1800, I had the happinefs once more of beholding the coafts of my happy native land. We were detained in quarantine at Plymouth till the 7th, when an order arrived for the Anson to proceed to Spithead, where we arrived the following day, and were not released from the thraldom of the yellow flag till the 10th, when I, with the rest of the passengers, debarked at Portsmouth.

Having thus concluded the narrative of what came under my own observation, or was acted on the station during the time I was on it, I must beg leave to add a few lines to the memory of the gallant ship which for several years had been my abode.

As her track, while she bore the British flag, was marked with many a trait of glory, so was the concluding act of the illfated vessel distinguished by such firm heroic resistance, as left the enemy a mere wreck, and little to boast of in the capture.

The Swiftsure had been reported to be in a very leaky condition for a long time, as I have had occasion to mention in the preceding pages, yet she was obliged to retrace her steps to the shores of Egypt without receiving the repairs she stood so much in need of. At length Lord Keith sent her with a convoy of cartels and light transports from the Bay of Aboukir to Malta. Captain Hallowell on the passage received intelligence of a strong squadron of the enemy being in those seas. Prompted by a laudable zeal for the service, and considering the comparative infignificance of the convoy, he formed the refolution to quit it, and make the beft of his way to reinforce the fquadron of Sir John Borlafe Warren. Unhappily on his paffage he fell in with the hoftile fquadron on the 24th of June 1801. Perceiving the very fuperior force of the enemy, he refolved for once to endeavour to efcape from them; but the leaky and foul condition of the Swiftfure was ill matched with the faft-failing Frenchmen. Captain Hallowell finding there was no profpect of getting away from them by keeping on a wind, determined to bear down and engage the fhips to leeward, confifting of two line of battle and a frigate, in hopes that if he crippled them he might get away from the others; but in this he was difappointed. The Indivifible of 80 guns, bearing the flag of Rear-Admiral Gantheaume, and the Dix Aout of 74 guns, being in clofe order, and within half-gun-fhot of the Swiftfure, opened their fire: this was inftantly anfwered, and a fevere action took place, which lafted, notwithftanding the great difproportion of force, for an hour and fix minutes.

During the action Captain Hallowell made feveral efforts to get to leeward of the enemy, but their fuperior failing baffled every attempt.

The other two line of battle fhips now ranging up alongfide the Swiftfure ready to pour in a deftructive fire, the Indivifible and Dix Aout being almoft aboard of her, and her mafts, and yards, and rigging cut to pieces, the decks lumbered up with the wreck, all hopes of escape cut off, and no prospect of succour presenting itself, Captain Hallowell, to save further useless effusion of blood, determined to surrender to superior numbers. With pain, as he truly expressed it, he ordered his Majesty's colours, which he could no longer defend, to be taken down. The following extract from Captain Hallowell's letter to the admiral on this melancholy event will, I doubt not, prove acceptable to my readers.

"Most sincerely, my lord, do I lament our having been opposed to so very superior a force, as, from the steady and gallant conduct of the officers and men I had the honour to command on this occasion, and with whom I had been acting nearly four years on various services, I have not a doubt of what would have been the issue of the contest on more equal terms."

The loss in killed and wounded was not so great as might have been expected; but the masts, sails, yards, and rigging, were cut to pieces, and the whole ship received so much damage that the enemy were six days repairing her, that she might be able to proceed with them to Toulon. When Lord Keith dispatched the Swiftsure for Malta he took out many of the best men, by which means she was eighty-six men short of complement, besides having fifty-nine sick on board from a bad fever brought off by those who had acted with the army before Alexandria.

Lieutenant Davis, who had been wounded before when captured in the Fortune, and afterwards when serving with the army in Egypt, was this time also the only officer who was hurt, but not dangerously.

It is but justice to observe, that in this instance the French treated their unfortunate prisoners with great humanity: but Admiral Gantheaume is as well known for his honourable conduct as for his courage, and his name will ever bear the respect due to humanity and bravery.

Captain Hallowell having obtained permission to return to Minorca on his parole, a court-martial was assembled on the 18th of August 1801, on board the Genereux, at Mahon, to try him for quitting the convoy, and for the loss of his ship; who, after a minute investigation of all the circumstances, delivered the following sentence.

" The court is of opinion, and it appears to them from the narrative of Captain Hallowell, supported by the best possible evidence to be obtained, that the convoy under Captain Hallowell's charge was of very little importance in any point of view; that his determination to leave the said convoy and join Sir John Warren, was dictated by sound judgment and zeal for the service of his king and country. And the court is further of opinion, that the loss of his Majesty's late ship Swiftsure was unavoidable; and that the conduct of Captain Hallowell, his officers, and ship's company, in defence of the Swiftsure, was highly meritorious; and that Captain Hallowell displayed great judgment in the mode he adopted to avoid so superior a force, and equal gallantry in the execution of the plan so formed. They do therefore adjudge that they be honourably acquitted; and they are honourably acquitted accordingly.

Signed by the court."

As a counterpoise however to this misfortune, I am enabled to state, that though the Swiftsure is the only British ship that was in the action of the Nile, which is now in the possession of the enemy, a complete destruction has been made of every one of the French fleet opposed to us on that memorable day. Le Genereux and Le Guilleaume Tell, the only two ships of the line that escaped from Aboukir, were taken in 1800 by some of the squadron under the immediate orders of Lord Nelson. The former on the 18th of February, the latter on the 30th of March; and one of the frigates also, La Diane, that escaped with those ships, was taken on the 24th of August following. The other frigate, La Justice, was captured at the surrender of Alexandria. So that, on the whole, the victory by Rear-Admiral Nelson achieved on the 1st of August 1798, may, in all its confequences, be fairly reckoned as complete and decifive as was ever obtained by the Britifh flag.[x]

[x] I forgot to mention, in its proper place, a circumftance fo peculiarly charaƐteriftic as muft render it interefting to my readers. In the fixth chapter the Swiftfure is defcribed as bufily employed after the aƐtion in getting up pieces of the wreck of l'Orient. Among the reft a large part of the main-top-maft was brought on board. Captain Hallowell caufed a coffin to be made of the wood and iron from this maft, with an infcription on the lid. This he prefented to Lord Nelfon, who received it as a moft valuable acquifition, and intends when his career of terreftrial glory is terminated, that his remains fhall be enclofed in it.

www.ingramcontent.com/pod-product-compliance
Lightning Source LLC
Chambersburg PA
CBHW080857230426

43663CB00013B/2563